Hounds and Hunting in Ancient Greece

HOUNDS AND HUNTING
IN ANCIENT GREECE

BY DENISON BINGHAM HULL

Decorations by Virgil Burnett

THE UNIVERSITY OF CHICAGO PRESS

CHICAGO AND LONDON

THE UNIVERSITY OF CHICAGO PRESS, CHICAGO & LONDON
THE UNIVERSITY OF TORONTO PRESS, TORONTO 5, CANADA

LIBRARY OF CONGRESS CATALOG CARD NUMBER: 64-23424

MANUFACTURED IN THE UNITED STATES OF AMERICA

To Dolly, with Love

CONTENTS

PLATES AND FIGURES

Preface

A few years ago I was invited to speak at a dinner at the Rose Tree Fox Hunting Club not far from Philadelphia. The title of my speech was "Hunting by the Book," and its substance was that because I had started hunting late in life, I had found that the way to speed up my education in the sport was to read every book on horses, hounds, and hunting that I could lay hands on, not excluding the Greek.

After the dinner, Wilbur Ross Hubbard, a friend of mine and one of the most experienced and competent masters of hounds in the United States, who like myself was a guest, approached me and said:

"You know, Hull, I was most interested in what you said, because I learned in exactly the opposite way."

He was not scornful of the idea of learning by reading; he was just amazed that I had learned as much as I had that way, for it is true that most fox-hunters get their knowledge of the sport from experience alone, just as he did. Books play little part in their sporting education. This, I think, is an unfortunate fact, not because I do not believe in practical experience as the best teacher of all, but because the result has been that there are not enough books on hunting by people who know exactly what they are talking about and none at all on ancient Greek hunting by anyone who has ever had experience of a similar nature.

The truth is that there have been few things written on that subject by anyone at all. The first book was Otto Manns' *Über die Jagd bei den Griechen*, published in Cassel in 1888 and 1889. Otto Manns was, unfortunately, not a hunting man; he was a German schoolmaster who certainly had never hunted and probably had never even seen a hunt. The next was *Sport in Classic Times*, by A. J. Butler, published in 1930, a breezy volume intended to show that the Greeks and the Romans were not just stuffy textbook figures but real people of flesh and blood who enjoyed sports just as much as we do. The author, although a classical scholar of sorts, evidently had had some experience in hunting; but his book covers so many other sports that he cannot go into detail, and, excepting large parts which are simply translations and paraphrases of classical authors welded together into a continuous narrative, is superficial and lacking in accuracy. The third and best book is *Essai sur les chasses romaines*, by Jacques Aymard, published in 1961. It contains a great deal of useful information about Greek hunting, but it is, of course, primarily about Roman hunting in the grand manner. Aymard is a classical scholar, but evidently not a hunting man; and although he tells us many interesting things, he makes no attempt to solve any of the technical puzzles left us by Xenophon and the other classical Greek writers.

Reference books are always useful. Pauly-Wissowa's *Realenkyklopädia* has an excellent article under the heading "Jagd" and another under "Hund." Neither was written by a person with hunting experience. The *Oxford Classical Dictionary* is very brief but to the point on hunting: it refers us to Xenophon, Oppian, Grattius, and Nemesianus. This is the best advice of all.

Scholars who have produced critical editions of these four authors have, of course, given much useful information in their introductions and footnotes. A. W. Mair, for instance, did a marvelous piece of research for the Loeb edition of Oppian. E. C. Marchant made some excellent comments in the Loeb edition of Xenophon's *Scripta minora*. He admitted that he knew nothing about horses, and his admission could be applied equally well to hunting. Almost every editor has contributed to our knowledge of ancient Greek hunting, but it is obvious that not one of them has ever hunted. Furthermore, when they run into some puzzling passage, they almost invariably (and quite understandably) run for help to other classical authors for a solution and rarely appeal to modern knowledge. This kind of research is, of course, not to be scorned, for it increases our knowledge of what the classical authors had to say on the subject, but it does not always tell us what they meant. And on the occasions when editors do consult modern authorities, the latter are now sometimes out of date. I have in mind Otto Keller's *Die antike Tierwelt*, published in 1901, a very valuable and informative work, although inadequately annotated, which is badly in need of revision in the light of present-day knowledge of zoology and of natural history.

Lack of familiarity with hunting, however, is not confined to modern scholars. It can be seen in ancient works of art representing scenes connected with the chase. In the Metropolitan Museum in New York there is a sarcophagus from Cyprus with a scene representing a hunt that runs the length of one side. Every man in this scene is wearing full armor. From unimpeachable sources we know they wore no such thing, and anyway the armor was much too heavy for the occasion.

Excellent artists as the Greeks were, they were not all hunting men and certainly not all hound men. We could say the same thing about our own artists. There are, of course, notable exceptions: the marble hound in the Acropolis Museum, for instance, shows real understanding of the characteristics of the Laconian hound which it so beautifully portrays. On the other hand, the marble hound in the Art Museum in Basel shows very little understanding of hound proportions, despite the fact that the artist had real feeling for his subject and portrayed the tension of the hound's muscles with great skill. But the statue can hardly be identified with any breed, past or present. It is difficult to agree with the identification given it by Professor Schefold, that of a "true Molossian of the second class," an identification taken from Otto Keller's system of classification of ancient dogs. In this particular beast there are no characteristics that could be derived from any Molossian or even a half-bred related to that breed. It is, however, a marvelous nightmare dog, a hideous creature that could only have existed in mythology or the religion of the chthonian gods, and if Professor Schefold's contention is true, and I think it is, that the artist intended to represent a demon-dog from the underworld, then he has succeeded admirably—and what more could we expect of any artist?

The same difficulty in identifying breeds can be found in the vase paintings: some show obvious breed characteristics, so there can be no question about them, but others are so vague and indefinite that we have no idea what kind of dog they were intended to represent.

Of course thorough familiarity with modern hounds and with every detail of modern hunting will still not prevent our having difficulty understanding the ancient sport because of Greek terminology. It is different, so it is not always easy to be sure just what it means. If English has its hunting jargon, so does Greek, although it is far less developed in its obscurity. If English is sometimes ambiguous, so is Greek, even though it is a far more precise language. One of the smaller problems we encounter, for instance, is the proper way to translate the Greek word *kynegetes*. According to its etymology, it should mean "dog-leader," and so a man who hunts with dogs. And there is another Greek word, *kynagogos*, with etymology that is almost identical. But the contexts in which these two words appear make it evident that the first, *kynegetes*, means no more than a man who hunts, whether with or without hounds, while *kynagogos* means the man who has the actual physical management of the hounds. How shall we translate these two words?

In English we have three possible words to use. One of these is "hunter," which in colloquial American usage means a man who hunts. In English hunting jargon, however, it means a horse used for riding to hounds. We can, of course, say "hunting man" for a man who hunts, but we should not say "huntsman" unless we mean the man who handles the hounds in the field.

Xenophon makes it clear that when he says *kynegetes* he means the man who handles the hounds. But the same man appears to be the man who owns them also. So when translating Xenophon, it seems best to translate this word as "master of hounds" or "huntsman," meaning an amateur huntsman, but never simply as "hunter."

Arrian, however, makes it clear that although the *kynegetes* is the owner of the hounds, he does not take out more than one or two at a time. He is hardly the official who is called "huntsman" in English hunting jargon—but we cannot be absolutely sure. Ordinarily *kynegetes* seems to mean no more than "hunting man," or perhaps just "hunter," and never "master of hounds." At times, however, the word seems to imply care of the hounds, so it might even mean "huntsman." At any rate, it is impossible to be absolutely consistent in the use of English terms to translate the Greek simply because the duties and functions in the two systems of hunting do not correspond exactly.

The differences come to light very quickly when one reads the Greek. In the first place, Greek hunting was a relatively modest sport, resembling rabbit hunting as practiced in the United States, more than organized fox hunting as practiced in the British Isles, in spite of the fact that the Greeks used packs of hounds. No one can say with any certainty how many of Xenophon's friends and neighbors went out hunting with him as Scillus, but it is as good a guess as any to say that the number of participants in any Greek hunt was not over six, not counting the hunt servants. Frequently it was less. The social and economic background of the Greek hunting man did not make huge hunts in the Persian fashion possible. The Greeks knew about them, of course: Xenophon had seen them in Asia Minor when he was with Cyrus and the Ten Thousand; but they were not adopted until the time of Alexander the Great, for they were oriental and autocratic in nature and did not suit the Greek temperament. The Roman emperors, of course, loved this sort of thing. Athenaeus describes a procession in which hunt servants led twenty-four hundred hounds through the streets. We can imagine the big battues in which beaters went ahead and drove the game out of covert into the mouths of the hounds. Hundreds of horsemen followed, striking down whatever had escaped the hounds. The slaughter must have been sickening. The countryside where such a hunt had been held would have remained bare of wildlife for years afterward.

The Greeks not only could not afford this sort of thing but did not like it. They preferred the individual character of the small hunt; and the game they preferred was not something exotic that nobody had seen before but something they could bring home and put in the pot or something dangerous enough to give them a chance to display physical courage. They could hunt almost anywhere at almost any time they pleased. Only a few sacred spots were barred to them, such as the island of Delos, sacred to Apollo. It was possible for a man to hunt not only over uncultivated land but over crops, too, all without so much as asking by your leave; the only exception made was in the case of professional hunters who made a living by selling game on the market. They had to keep far enough away from the city to give young men a chance to learn the sport. Not until Roman times was there any restriction: then the Emperor Theodosius restricted the hunting of lions to royalty, a restriction that could hardly have been felt. As for closed seasons, there were none. Naturally one did not hunt on days when there were religious festivals, but that was not because of any desire to conserve game but for religious reasons, and there were other things one could not do, anyway.

Such is the background of hunting in ancient Greece. I found out about it almost by accident. As I explained to the members of the Rose Tree Fox Hunting Club, I read Xenophon's *Cynegeticus* out of curiosity. I wanted to see if there was anything in it useful to me. Then I read Arrian's *Cynegeticus*. Next, thinking that someone else might be interested, I wrote out translations of both and added some flippant drawings. Finally, at a meeting in Boston, I mentioned to Eric Havelock what I had done; he is now Stirling Professor of Greek and Chairman of the Department of the Classics at Yale; at that time he was Chairman of the Department of the Classics at Harvard.

"Which author do you think knew the most about hunting, Xenophon or Arrian?" he asked. I told him.

"Did you say why in your Introduction?" I had not written one.

"Why not?" Well, I had not thought anybody would be interested.

"I would," he said.

Right then I decided to write it. It did not take long; and it did not take long to realize that a translation, unless there is something special about it, is not a book, no matter what sort of Introduction you put in front of it; and that even two translations with a doubly long Introduction are no better than two non-books. Something original has to be added so that the translation becomes a useful tool, an explanation of the exposition you have made. Besides, as I struggled with my Introduction and polished up my ragged translations, I realized that I did not know anything about Greek hunting anyhow.

So I decided I had better find out. I read all the classical authorities first and did not bother to try to find out what other people had to say about Greek hunting until I ran out of books in Greek or Latin. Then, assuming that other people had found Greek books that I did not know about, I read Manns, Butler, Aymard, and the appropriate entries in Pauly-Wissowa. Surprisingly enough, each of these referred me right back to the very books I had just read. I was much encouraged. If I had read everything the Greeks had written about how they hunted, I must know all the facts that anyone else knew—unless I had not understood what I had read or unless there was something to be found in the world of art and archeology. It did not take long to discover that there were no hunting artifacts left and that most of the useful information was to be found in illustrations of the classical myths: the story of the Calydonian boar hunt, Actaeon, the labors of Heracles, and such stories. Anyway I knew that I had already found out enough to write that Introduction and that I had one big advantage over anyone who had already tackled the subject: I had had hounds of my own, and from my own experience I could fill in gaps that others would be compelled to leave blank.

So I began to write down what I had learned, referring from time to time to the five-by-seven cards on which I had written quotations from my sources. I discovered that the better I understood the sport, the more intelligible and enjoyable the quotations became, until I wished it were possible to share this discovery with everyone. Obviously, of course, my book could not consist only of fragments or it would be intolerably dull and completely incomprehensible. Still, there was no reason why I should not include a few of the longer and better sources, not just because they confirmed my own conclusions (a thing they do to the point of seeming to duplicate what I have written), but because the Greek authors are far more interesting when properly understood and it is entertaining to hear them tell about hunting themselves.

So at the end of the book I have included a translation of Xenophon's *Cynegeticus*, the best of the ancient authorities on the sport; excerpts from the *Onomasticon* of Julius Pollux, which amplifies Xenophon's remarks; and Arrian's *Cynegeticus*, which describes a somewhat different form of sport.

Here then is my Introduction. Perhaps that is the title I should have given it, for there is no question about the fact that the subject has barely been touched. I have tried hard not to make mistakes, but no book has ever been wholly free from them, and so I earnestly hope that my mistakes will stimulate someone to take the trouble to correct them.

D. B. H.

ACKNOWLEDGMENTS

It would have been impossible to write this book without the help and advice of a great many people, and I want to thank them for everything they have done for me. It was Eric Havelock who got me started, and I want to thank him for the education he gave me in the process; it has been enormously rewarding.

There are many others also to whom I owe thanks for their help: Sterling Dow, professor of archaeology at Harvard; Herman H. Fussler, director of the University Library at the University of Chicago; Eric Hamp, associate professor of linguistics at the University of Chicago; George M. A. Hanfmann, professor of classical archaeology at the Fogg Museum of Art, Harvard, and field director of the Sardis Excavation; Barbara Lawrence, curator of mammals at the Museum of Comparative Zoology, Harvard; Francis P. Magoun, Jr., professor of English, emeritus, Harvard; Professor Ernst Mayr, director of the Museum of Comparative Zoology, Harvard; Wallace E. McLeod, of Victoria College, Toronto; Maxine Neidinger, librarian of languages and fine arts at the University of Chicago; Clifford Pope, curator of reptiles, emeritus, at the Chicago Museum of Natural History; Ruth Schoneman, librarian of the Ryerson and Burnham Libraries at the Art Institute of Chicago; Hadley C. Stephenson, D.V.M., consultant to the Center for Research in the Diseases of Dogs, at Cornell University; E. Leland Webber, director of the Chicago Natural History Museum. Thanks are due also to Kimon Friar, editor, and Christopher G. Janus, publisher, of *Greek Heritage;* and to Jeffrey R. Short, Jr., for helping me to get illustrations.

*"Wot a many things are wantin' to 'unt a country plisantly—
Things that would never enter the 'ead of a sailor!"*
John Jorrocks, in R. S. Surtees' Handley Cross

I Equipment for Hunting

CLOTHING

To the modern youth who is just about to begin riding in the traditional English fashion, the question of what to wear, particularly if he has not been brought up in a fox-hunting family, can present embarrassing possibilities. He has heard of riders who have been sent home for wearing the wrong kind of hat, scolded for pinning the stock the wrong way, ridiculed for wearing breeches of the wrong cut or color, and ostracized for wearing a coat with a belt in the back. Although the stories he has heard have often been exaggerated in the telling (for no good sportsman would think of scorning another for trivial reasons, particularly reasons connected with the purse), it is nevertheless true that English fox-hunters are very conservative, stick closely to what tradition demands they wear, and expect others to dress as they do.

1

But to the young Greek of the classical period, who was "just changing from childhood to manhood," the problem of dress was nowhere nearly as difficult. In the first place, the Greeks wore very little at any time and stripped completely for athletic contests—women were not permitted to attend, although their presence would have made little difference anyhow—so that the only problem the young Greek had was to choose clothes that would make him inconspicuous to the game he hunted and would give him freedom of action.[1] His choice was easy, for there were only two garments available, which all Greeks, men and women alike, used.[2] These were the tunic, or undergarment, and the cloak, or outer garment. Our young hunting man always wore the tunic and sometimes the cloak.

The tunic was called the *chiton*, and there were two principal types, the Doric and the Ionic.[3] The Doric chiton was made of wool and was extremely simple; the Ionic was often made of linen and in later ages even of silk. Sometimes it was very elaborate, particularly for women's wear. The garment worn for hunting was never the Ionic but always the very simplest form of Doric chiton. We shall therefore confine our description to that.

A rectangle of woolen cloth was first woven to the exact size—the chiton was never cut from a larger piece—and for a full-length garment was roughly six feet square, the exact size varying, of course, with the size of the wearer and with the length of garment he wished to have. He held this rectangle before him, folded the top edge over for a depth of about eighteen inches, and then folded it along a vertical line so that it would go around his body, with the top edge folded over on the outside. Next he pinned the top together with two big pins that came right over his shoulders, leaving a space between the pins for his head and a space at the side next the fold for one arm. After this, he usually tied a belt around his waist, in order to hold the garment in place. Sometimes he pinned the open side together; sometimes he had it sewed together beforehand; and sometimes he simply let it hang open. The open chiton was common in Sparta and symbolized the Spartan way of life.

2

The length of the chiton varied. Women almost always wore it full-length so that the edge touched the ground. Men, on the other hand, usually wore it about knee-length, although occasionally longer. For hunting or for any other active occupation, they wore it hanging only to the middle of the thigh. Workmen—who were usually slaves in the ancient world—left their chitons unpinned at the right shoulder in order to give maximum freedom to their right arms. Sometimes, in order to hold the fabric closely in place, men as well as women put a ribbon around the back of their necks, pulled the ends down in front over their shoulders, passed them back, and tied the ends together in back. The statue of the Charioteer of Delphi has such a ribbon; his chiton, by the way, is a full-length Ionic model, sewed together along the top edge, and so full that it falls part way down the upper arms, thus giving an appearance of sleeves.

The cloak, or outer garment, was a rectangular piece of cloth, usually woolen, which went under a number of different names, although all cloaks are essentially the same garment. The commonest and best known was the *himation*, a voluminous sheet of wool. The wearer tucked one corner under his left arm from in front, flung the whole thing over his left shoulder and around his back, brought it over his right shoulder—or under, if he preferred—then across the front of the body, and tucked the end under his left arm again. He was then so completely enveloped by his himation that he didn't need to wear anything under it—and often didn't.

Other cloaks were the *chlaina*, the *tribon* ("threadbare cloak"), the *pharos*, and the *sisyra* ("goat's hair cloak"), which were worn in various manners. Sometimes men wore them in the way a football player wears his blanket; sometimes they wore them like shawls; and sometimes they actually used them for coverlets or blankets. But for hunting or other active occupations, the most useful cloak of all was the *chlamys*, the Thessalian or Macedonian military cloak. It was perhaps the smallest of all and was simply draped over the left shoulder, brought around the back, and then pinned together over the right shoulder. It was not held by the arms, and its normal position left the right arm completely free so that, if necessary, the wearer could slip it around in back, leaving his left arm free also; the cloak would then hang down behind him, suspended from his neck. Also, if the occasion arose, he could take it off and wrap it around one arm so that he could take it with him while he ran.

In addition to his tunic and his cloak, the ancient Greek had footwear and headgear. Indoors he normally wore nothing on his feet, but when outdoors he sometimes wore sandals. The ordinary sandal was no more than a sole bound to the ankle with thongs; and so for hunting, when greater protection for the feet and ankles might be needed, the young Greek hunting man wore "hollow sandals," that is, boots fastened by thongs around the lower leg. Only when he was stalking game did he discard these and go barefoot.[4]

Usually the Greek wore no hat, but he had a choice of two kinds if he needed one for hunting. The first was the *petasos*, a Thessalian felt hat with a low crown and a broad brim, usually worn by farmers who had to work under the hot sun; it can be seen in representations of the god Hermes, whose petasos, like his sandals, was equipped with wings. The other was the *cyne*, or dogskin cap; it could be worn alone as a leather helmet or under a bronze helmet as a liner. For hunting lions or wild boars, it might very well have been used, but we have little evidence that it was. Perhaps the Greeks considered safety measures effeminate.

The usual costume for hunting, therefore, was a very short chiton of inconspicuous color, a chlamys of similar hue, boots, and perhaps a broad-brimmed felt hat. This costume was not a uniform in any sense, for it was a costume very likely to be worn by anyone who was active. Indeed, the chlamys and the petasos were habitually worn by the *ephebi*, youths of eighteen years of age who were serving their one or two years of military duty and were undoubtedly participants in many hunts.[5]

WEAPONS

Sticks and clubs, spears and javelins, bows and arrows, were the weapons used by the Greeks for hunting. The exact type of weapon depended on the quarry to be hunted.

4

For hunting the hare, they needed nothing more than a club or harestick—perhaps it was the same weapon under a different name.[6] This club was carried by the huntsman or the master and was used either to dispatch the hare after she was caught or to knock her down by throwing it at her from a distance, in the modern manner.[7] In later ages we hear of huntsmen carrying barbed hunting spears, tridents, or three-pronged spears.[8] These three weapons may also, for all we know, have been one and the same.

But for hunting big game such as the lion, the tiger, the bear, or the wild boar, bigger weapons were needed and were used, and the information we have about them is more complete. To begin with, the Greek warrior was a spearman. He preferred the spear to all other weapons for combat, and it was therefore natural for him to use the spear for hunting the more dangerous animals. The hunting spear was essentially the same as that used for war. It was about nine feet long and had a shaft of dogwood, a head of iron, and a spike at the butt end.[9] The head was about fifteen inches long and was made up of three parts, all forged in one. The first was the flute, or socket; the second was the spit, a solid extension forward from the flute, with wings, or blades, on each side; and the third was the tongue, or point, formed by tapering the wings down to a single sharp point. For hunting wild boars a variation of the usual hunting spear was used: it had teeth attached to the socket behind the wings. These teeth, sharp as a razor, projected out and forward slightly so that the boar could not run up the shaft of the spear from the impetus of its charge.[10]

In the Homeric age the spear was usually thrown overhand on all occasions. In the fifth and fourth centuries before Christ, it was thrown overhand when hunting or when engaged in individual combat; but it was held at hip level, like the medieval pike, when used in the phalanx, and was therefore used much less for throwing. As military spears became used more and more for thrusting, they became longer and longer, until finally they reached an extreme length in the Macedonian pike, which was seventeen feet long. The length of the hunting spear, however, probably remained unchanged.

The manner of throwing the spear overhand is described by Pollux as follows:

Advancing the left foot and keeping the right foot back so that the measure of the stride is as great as in battle, let the man keep his advancing side at an angle corresponding with his foot, stretch his hand over backwards, grasping the middle of the boar-spear, and hold it out firmly with the right hand turned back. And with his left hand let him aim the iron for the mortal blow, and let the right hand thrust the boar-spear with all its strength.[11]

A lighter weapon than the spear was the javelin; the hunting man carried two.[12] Like the spear, the javelin had a head of iron, with edges as sharp as a razor, and a shaft of ash, beech, or dogwood. In the middle it had a loop of leather which was given a turn or two around the shaft. The fingers were then inserted in the loop; the javelin was held out backwards with one hand only (for it was very much lighter in weight than the spear) and was then thrown overhand with a turn of the body. As the hand let go, the thong twisted around the butt unwound and gave it a spin like that of a rifle bullet.[13]

The hunting man was also advised to carry a sword. The Greeks had two kinds, both made of iron, both used for cutting as well as for thrusting, both with a guard for the hand consisting only of a crossbar; neither was more than eighteen inches in length, so they were really no bigger than daggers.[14] One was the *machaira*, curved like a scimitar and sharpened on one edge only. Xenophon had encountered a similar weapon in the hands of the barbarians during the expedition of the Ten Thousand and had recommended its use by the cavalry, but it is nowhere mentioned in connection with hunting. The other, the one recommended for hunting, was the *xiphos*, a double-edged straight sword with a blade that usually swelled in width near the middle so that it was leaf-shaped. But oddly enough, although the hunting man was advised to carry a xiphos, he was not expected to use it except in dire emergency, when he could use it for self-defense against some unexpected attack by lion, wild boar, or other big beast.

To us today it would seem that the bow would be the logical weapon for people to use for hunting when they had not yet acquired firearms. To some extent the Greeks did use it, but not as much as we might expect. It was not a native weapon: it was acquired; and it was used most on the periphery of the Greek world wherever contact with barbarian bowmen made it necessary.[15] The Greeks almost never used it on each other. It is true, of course, that the bow is frequently seen in vase paintings and that Homer mentions Teucer, the skillful archer; gives a detailed description of the bow of Pandaros; and repeatedly refers to Apollo as "the god of the silver bow."[16] But these references are all to events at the time of the Trojan War; by the classical age the use of the bow had been given up by many of the Greeks, although the Cretans still used it and were universally acknowledged as the best archers.[17] Yet even the Cretan archers with the Ten Thousand had difficulty contending with the barbarian bowmen until they had captured some of the bows and arrows used by the enemy.[18] And for hunting the red deer, the one animal which we should think most suited to hunting with bows and arrows, Xenophon does not even suggest the possibility. It was not until Hellenistic or Roman times that bows were regularly used for deer hunting. For some reason the Greeks had little confidence in the bow. They always preferred to come to close quarters.

But the bows the Greeks did use were excellent weapons. There were two principal types: The first was the self bow, made out of a single homogeneous material, usually wood; this type was the Cretan weapon. The second was the composite bow, made of a combination of materials laminated together; the Homeric bow was of this type and so was the Scythian bow, which had the characteristic double curve we know as "Cupid's bow." It was acquired from the Scythians when the Greeks first encountered them, about 600 B.C., for it does not appear in vase paintings before that time very often. It was a little less than three feet long and was made like a sandwich with a wooden core. Strips of horn were cemented on the belly side of this core (the side toward the bowman), and molded sinew on the other side.[19] In spite of its shortness, it was a powerful weapon, capable of shooting an arrow as far as any bow made since. The barbarian bows encountered by the Ten Thousand in Asia Minor were nearly four feet eight inches long, and it is probable that after that time Greek bows were made nearly the same length.

The arrows of these same barbarians, according to Xenophon, were more than thirty-six inches long; those of the Greeks must therefore have been a little shorter.[20] The shafts may have been of wood or perhaps of reed, depending on the materials available. The arrowheads were of many kinds so that it is impossible to point out any one that could be called typical. Mycenaean arrowheads were sometimes merely flat plates of bronze with a point and two barbs, but the arrowheads of the classical period were more usually made with two or three blades attached to a socket, with barbs or spurs forming part of the blades; the types varied greatly, and none can be called characteristically Greek. The butt end of the shaft had a nock and feathers. The "three-pointed" arrows mentioned by Homer must have been the Mycenaean type.[21]

The bowman, when shooting, occasionally knelt, but usually he took much the same stance as the modern archer; that is, he stood with his left shoulder toward his target with his legs apart, held the bow in his left hand in a vertical plane, fully extended his arm— one need only try drawing a bow with bent arm to discover the reason—and drew the string (of twisted gut, sinew, or perhaps hide) to his chest, neck, or ear, depending on how much power he intended to give his shot. The barbarian, says Xenophon, held his bow below the center and leaned forward as he shot, as if to give the arrow an extra shove on its way.[22] The Greek drew the string with the thumb, with forefinger resting on it; or with the forefinger, with thumb resting on it; or with his three middle fingers. All three methods were used by every bowman so that he might keep his fingers from becoming too tired to permit accurate shooting.[23]

Although Vergil refers to the use of the sling for hunting, the Greeks used it very little, perhaps because this weapon was considered suitable only for slaves.[24]

8

HOUND TACKLE

For his hounds the huntsman had collars, leashes, belts, and aprons.[25] These were all made of leather. The collars were soft and broad and were sometimes lined with sheepskin so that they would not chafe the hounds' necks. The belts also were made of broad straps, extended crosswise from the shoulder around the sides, covered the back behind the points of the shoulder blades and the flanks, and even extended to the pubic regions. There were spikes sewed to them in order to protect a bitch from being served when in heat. The leashes were made with a loop at one end so that the servants who led the hounds could hold them better. Sometimes the collar was made all in one piece with the leash, but Xenophon comments that those who have leashes made this way "do not watch out for the hounds well."

His statement is not clear at first glance. But on second thought we remember that the Greeks had no buckles such as we have[26] and that their hound collars were fastened on with thongs. If the collars were made in one piece with the leashes, every time a hound was slipped the collar had to be untied; and every time the hound was tied up again, the collar had to be tied again. If the collars and leashes were made separately, the collars could be left on the hounds when they were slipped. It is true, of course, that the leashes would still have to be tied and again untied, so that there would still be the same number of operations to perform. But tying a leash to a collar is infinitely easier than tying a collar around the neck of a struggling hound, as everyone who has ever tried it, even with modern buckles, can testify. The difficulty is to get the collar tight enough so that the hound will not slip it over his head but not so tight that it will choke him to death. So if the Greek hunt servants put on collars made in one piece with the leashes, they would sometimes make the collars too loose, and a hound or two would get away. Then the master would certainly say that the servant did not "watch out for the hounds well." And if a hound were choked to death, we can be sure the master would say something worse!

NETS

For the actual catching of their quarry, the Greeks often used nets into which their hounds drove the game. It was certainly a lot safer to catch a lion in a net than to have to kill him with only a nine-foot spear; and if one were going to cook and eat a hare, it was better to catch her in a net than to have to pull her out of the mouths of the hounds, half-eaten already.

Hunting nets were intended as traps, rather than as mere barriers, and were therefore very ingeniously designed. They had to be strong, large, and light, for they must not break when the quarry hit them, must be big enough to catch him, and must be light enough to be carried easily, for they were carried to the covert every time hounds went out and were carried home again at the end of the hunt.[27] In addition, the man who placed the nets needed to be thoroughly familiar with the country and with the habits of the quarry he hunted. Indiscriminate placing of nets was not only wasteful but even likely to alarm the quarry and so to drive it away. And when the nets were set up, they must be set up so they would operate as intended, otherwise the whole day's effort would be wasted.

The nets were of several kinds. There are at least six words in Greek which mean net, and each means a different kind; these six do not include any of the large number used for fishing. These six are the *seine*, the *panagron*, the *insert*, the *road-net*, the *long-net*, and the *purse-net*, of which there were two kinds, one for hare and the other for wild boar.[28] We do not know much about the seine and the panagron, but by analogy with the fishing nets of the same names, we can guess that they were drag-nets or sweep-nets used to draw across fields in order to haul in the very smallest game. They cannot have been very effective. The insert was a net of unknown size and shape used to fill up the gaps between the larger nets.

But the two kinds of purse-net, the road-net and the long-net, are described in considerable detail by both Xenophon and Pollux, so by careful attention to the meaning of the words found in their descriptions, to the methods used in other times and other places when nets were made by hand, and to the practical requirements of hunting, we can make a reconstruction that is at least consistent and probably very much like the nets actually used by Xenophon. Other men may have used other nets, however, so we cannot say that this reconstruction is the only one possible.

At any rate the material from which all four of Xenophon's nets were made was linen thread. The best flax for making this thread came from Phasis (modern Poti), a city situated in Colchis at the eastern end of the Black Sea. Another source of excellent flax was Carthage. As the Carthaginians were primarily traders, it is possible that the Carthaginian flax really came from Sardinia, for good flax was known to have come from there as well as from Egypt, from Sardes (Croesus' capital), and, according to Pausanias, from Elis.

But wherever it came from, the flax was first spun into exceptionally fine threads; these threads then twisted together to form strands; and the strands, in turn, then twisted to form the twine from which the fabric of the nets was tied. The number of threads in each strand and the number of strands in the twine varied with the strength required. The strength required varied not only with the size of the quarry hunted but also with the size of the net, for a big net, if stretched tight, would require stronger twine than a small or a slack one.

We do not know the exact size of the thread used, but we can get an idea of it by comparing the biggest net used by the Greeks with the biggest net used by modern poachers in the nineteenth century. The biggest poacher's net is three hundred and sixty feet long by about five feet wide.[29] It is made of either silk or hemp and is so light that it can be wound around the body of a man and carried concealed beneath an overcoat. The biggest Greek net was one hundred and eighty feet long by ten feet wide—half as long and twice as wide as the modern net—and therefore contained the same number of square feet of netting. The Greeks, of course, had no need to wind their nets around their bodies and conceal them, but they did have to roll them up and put them in leather bags in order to carry them to and from the coverts. So even the longest

Greek net must have been made of unusually fine material, and the smaller ones must have been incredibly fine.

We can do no more than guess the fineness. The threads may have been as fine as those in a modern cambric handkerchief—the Greeks could spin thread as fine as that, for the Egyptians before them had spun it even finer.[30] For making the purse-nets for hare, three such threads were twisted together to form a strand, and then three such strands were twisted together to form the twine from which the netting was tied. Now we do not know exactly how the Greeks made their nets, but for lack of any other better information we can assume that they were made the same way as modern hand-made nets. Hand-made nets are made today with two tools, the *shuttle* (sometimes called the needle) and the *mesh-pin* (sometimes called the spool). The shuttle is used to carry the ball of twine while the net-maker moves it back and forth, tying the knots with which the net is fastened together; the mesh-pin is used to form the meshes of the net and keep them all the same size.

To begin a net, the net-maker first winds the twine around the mesh-pin, tying it each time to a slightly heavier piece of twine which he holds so that it runs lengthwise to the mesh-pin. This piece of twine is called the *margin*. After finishing the first row, the net-maker pulls out the mesh-pin and starts the next row. He gives the twine a turn around the mesh-pin and ties it to the first loop of the first row, using a knot known as a *sheet bend*. Then he takes another turn around the mesh-pin and ties the twine to the next loop and continues in this fashion until he has finished the row. Thus he makes row after row until he has completed the net. He can, of course, make the first row without a margin by using an extra mesh-pin to hold the twine in place until he has been able to tie it to the next row. It is usual, however, to make the net with a margin and often to add another margin at the other edge.

The method of tying the sheet bend, which is also known as the *fisherman's knot* or *Becket bend*, is more easily demonstrated than described, although a diagram will perhaps make it clear. It is the simplest knot that can be devised for the purpose. It must not slip, and there is almost no other way of making a simple knot that will not slip.[31] It is very likely therefore that the Greeks used it from the earliest times.

The meshes made in this way are diamond-shaped rather than square; that is, the twine runs on the diagonal of the net rather than parallel to the sides or ends. The diamond shape is the traditional shape for the mesh of nets, and it is only recently that anyone has even imagined a net with meshes that are square, like those of a tennis net. Evidence of the antiquity of the diamond shape is ample: all modern hand-made nets are formed that way, and so were medieval nets like those illustrated in Gaston de Foix's *Livre de chasse*,[32] written in about 1387. In addition, Julius Pollux, writing in the time of the Emperor Commodus, says, "The mesh is the continuous four-sided interval in the nets, formed by four knots, which become rhomboidal when the net is stretched." The rhomboid, or diamond shape, is also shown in relief on a gold cup of about 1500 B.C. found in the tholos tomb in Vaphio in Laconia, now in the National Museum in Athens.[33]

To make the purse-net for hares, the net-maker first made his netting in the form of a cylinder about fifty-five inches long and forty inches in diameter, with no margin on either the top or the bottom edge. The meshes were six inches on a side. Through the last meshes at the bottom of the cylinder he ran a line called a *cod-line* (we shall use the terms used by modern net-makers wherever they fit), and then drew the meshes together and tied them, thus forming the *cod-end* of the net, a bag which Pollux says resembles a woman's hair net. Through the meshes around the upper end of the cylinder, the open mouth of the bag, he threaded a line called the *skirting-line;* and after running the skirting-line through, he perhaps tied a loop at one end of it and then threaded the other end through this loop, thus forming a noose, so that a pull on one end of the skirting-line would draw the mouth of the bag together. Or, alternatively, he might have threaded a second line through the last meshes and thus have provided the arrangement described by Pollux when the bag was set on its side.

The huntsman or the net-watcher set up the purse-net by first turning it up on one side, facing the mouth in the direction from which the hare might come, and then propping it open with forked sticks, about thirty inches in length. These sticks were also used to keep the cod-end of the net up so that there would be room for the hare to enter when she ran through the mouth. After this the skirting-line was tied to a big stone so that just as soon as the hare hit the net it would fall off the sticks, the hare would struggle to get out, and the resulting action would close the mouth of the net as it pulled away from the stone.

The road-net, on the other hand, was made in an entirely different way. It was a rectangular sheet of netting a little over ten feet in height and was made in four different lengths: twelve, eighteen, twenty-four, and thirty feet. The meshes, of course, were diamond-shaped, just as the meshes of the purse-nets were; and they were the same size, that is, six inches from knot to knot. But because the road-nets were bigger than the purse-nets, their twine was made heavier: it was of twelve threads instead of nine, twisted either in four strands of three threads or three strands of four threads each—Xenophon does not say. The twine was tied to a slightly heavier cord which was permanently fixed to the top and bottom edges of the netting, although not across the ends. These, of course, were the *margins* and were an indispensable part of the net, because a big net, like any flexible material made in diamond-shaped units, would pull out like a pantograph and completely lose its shape unless held on opposite sides. The row of half-meshes between the netting and the margin is today called the *lever* but had no known name in antiquity. On the other hand, the row of full meshes at the ends had a name in ancient Greece, even though it has none today. This name is literally "end-elbows" but might better be translated *end-meshes*. Across the top of the road-nets was a skirting-line, but this, instead of simply being threaded through the upper row of meshes as it was in the purse-net, was attached to the margin by *bands*. A similar skirting-line was attached to the bottom margin in the same way. The two skirting-lines were sometimes distinguished by calling the upper one the *head-line* and the lower one the *foot-line*.

In each end-mesh there was something which the Greeks called

14

a "breast." From the description and uses of the "breast," it seems apparent that it was what is now called a *clinch*, made out of a cuckold's neck or loop which was seized and lined with twine so that it formed a grommet to reinforce the clinch. The clinches of one net could be tied to the clinches of another, probably by small pieces of twine, but perhaps by means of the skirting-line, although the latter method seems unlikely because the skirting-lines were needed for tying the net to the ground.

The road-nets were held in position by *forked sticks* inserted between the upper and lower margins; it was neither necessary nor desirable that the bottoms of the sticks be stuck deeply into the ground, because the whole apparatus must fall over and trap the quarry quickly. The skirting-lines were then attached to the ground, perhaps by means of pegs, but perhaps by means of stones, just as the purse-nets were.

The forked sticks were about five feet long, and the netting about ten feet wide. The apparent discrepancy between these two dimensions has caused editors a great deal of unnecessary difficulty. The dimensions are clearly stated, but because of the editors' assumption that the nets stood up like tennis nets or fences, they have been convinced that there was either some error in the manuscripts or some obscure method of counting the knots. Otto Manns, by counting knots by threes—that is, by counting meshes—makes the road-nets and the long-nets come out approximately the same height as the forked sticks, particularly if the sticks were pushed down into the ground just the right amount.[34] But his system will not work for the purse-net for wild boars; in fact, it will not work unless the number of knots, counting from top to bottom, is divisible by three. Surely, if we were intended to count by meshes, Xenophon would have said so.

The explanation of the apparent discrepancy between stakes and nets is very simple and should have been clear from Xenophon's description of the purse-net for wild boar. Because the netting was much wider than the sticks were long, the excess was draped out back, that is, in the direction away from where the hare was coming. This excess material formed a fold or *bosom*. When the hare hit the netting, she would already have run across part of it lying on the ground. When the net pulled off the sticks, the whole thing would collapse on her so that she would be imprisoned between the upper and lower meshes of the bosom. This is precisely the way a modern poacher's net works, even though the discrepancy in dimensions is less today than it was in ancient Greece.

The long-nets were similar in design and operation to the road-nets, but the dimensions were different. The long-nets were sixty, one hundred and twenty, and one hundred and eighty feet in length, but all the same height, for the meshes were the same size and there were the same number of knots. Like the road-nets, the long-nets had margins at top and bottom and skirting-lines attached by bands. The material of which they were made, however, was heavier; in this case the twine was made of sixteen threads, probably twisted from four strands of four threads each. And again, because they were bigger, the means of joining them, net to net, was stronger. In the clinches, instead of grommets of twine, were eyelets of metal.

The long-nets were set up in the same way as the road-nets; but the props were shorter, for they were only forty-five inches long instead of sixty, so the bosom in the net was bigger. The reason for this difference, together with the sameness of height of the nets, is hard to discover. Perhaps it is because the Greeks were more afraid that the hare would jump over the top of a net set up in the road than one set up in a field but at the same time wished to keep the netting the same height so that the two different types of net could be joined together neatly: the netting of both would flow from end to end of the line of nets in one continuous sheet, rising where the sticks were longer and falling where the sticks were shorter.

The remaining type of net which has been described for us is the purse-net for wild boar.[35] In general form, it was exactly the same as the purse-net for hare, but the materials were, of course, very much heavier and the dimensions greater. The twine for this type of net was made of forty-five threads, each consisting of three strands, each strand twisted from fifteen threads. The meshes were fifteen inches on a side, much bigger than the meshes for the hare, and the depth of the bag was about nine and a quarter feet. The diameter was between four and five feet, probably nearer the latter figure, for the exact size depended on how much the net was stretched, and it had to be stretched to hold it in place.

Here again there has been confusion about dimensions. The depth is no problem, if we will be patient enough to count knots by ones. The circumference is the problem, but it need not be, if we are willing to accept the reading of the very manuscript which E. C. Marchant says is the best: this is the one known as Vindobonensis IV 37. In it, the last line of chapter x, section 2, of Xenophon's *Cynegeticus* reads, *hikanoi de pentekaideka*, "Fifteen are enough." Fifteen what? The reference should be clear, for the previous word is *daktylion*, "rings." Both *hikanoi* and *daktylion* are masculine plural, so that the former must refer to the latter. The sentence therefore reads, "Fifteen rings are enough."

Sauppe left it that way, but Marchant did not. For some unknown reason he changed *hikanoi* to *hikana*, which is neuter plural and refers to nothing; it is only an adverb. When he revised his text for the Loeb edition, Marchant evidently was bothered by the *iota* at the end of the word and so changed it to *hikanai*, which is feminine plural and must therefore refer back to *arkyon*, "nets," which is also feminine plural and occurs earlier in the paragraph. The sentence now reads, "Fifteen nets are enough." Grammatically this makes sense, but practically it is utter nonsense, for we know that the nets were set up after the boar had been tracked to his lair by the hounds and not before. Once the position of the boar had been established it would be risky to waste the time needed to set up so many nets. Furthermore, rings are needed around the mouth of the net in order to make the skirting-line run easily when such a heavy beast as a wild boar was caught; if it were simply threaded through the last meshes, it would surely bind. And, finally, fifteen rings give us the circumference and, therefore, the diameter, the one dimension Xenophon is supposed to have forgotten to mention. The diameter is between four and five feet, adequate for a beast usually about twenty-four inches high at the shoulder and seldom known to have exceeded thirty-eight. Such a net is big enough.

SNARES AND TRAPS

For catching deer and wild boar a footsnare was sometimes used.[36] It consisted of three parts, the *crown*, the *rope*, and the *clog*. The crown was a ring woven of yew without bark; through the center of this ring, nails of both iron and wood were driven so that they pointed toward the center, like spokes of a wheel without a hub. The rope was tied in a noose at one end and attached to the clog at the other. The clog was a piece of ilex or oak three inches in diameter and twenty-two inches long.

To set up the footsnare, the hunters dug a hole in the ground the same diameter as the crown, as deep as it was wide, and tapering toward a smaller diameter at the bottom. Next they laid the crown over the top of the hole and put the noose over the crown. Then they put the rope and clog in shallow grooves to one side. After that they concealed the whole thing by covering it up; first, they used small twigs to serve as beams over the hole, then leaves, next dirt from the hole, and finally dirt taken from a distance so that the boar or deer would be as little suspicious as possible that something had been prepared for it.

When the deer or boar stepped on the place where the footsnare had been set, the wooden nails gave way, and the iron nails sprang down sufficiently to let the animal's foot through. When the beast lifted its foot, the iron nails held the crown from falling off, and the crown in turn prevented the noose from dropping off. Then, when the animal began to run, the clog dragged along behind, both hindering its escape and leaving a telltale mark in the earth that was easy to follow.

Another type of trap was used for catching lions, tigers, or other big game. The hunters dug a deep trench in a big circle, leaving an island in the middle. There they tethered a live goat and then built up a fence of brush around the outside of the trench. When the goat bleated in the night, the lion or tiger which came to investigate

18

could not see the goat and ran around the fence, looking for a way through. When it discovered no way through, it jumped over the fence and landed in the ditch, which was too deep for it to escape.[37]

Another device often mentioned by Latin writers, which the later Greeks used too, was the *formido*, or scare, a long line of cord into which brightly colored feathers had been strung at intervals. The feathers fluttered in the breeze and frightened the game toward the nets so that the hunters were able to shoot, spear, or catch it with nets.[38]

OTHER EQUIPMENT

In order to cut away the underbrush around the site where nets were to be set up, the huntsman carried a large knife which probably resembled a modern machete. Hunt servants also brought axes for cutting heavier growth.

To carry nets and forked sticks to and from the coverts, the hunt servants also carried a large calfskin bag,[39] resembling, perhaps, an oversize golf bag. To bring the quarry home, they used poles or sticks, probably cut in the field, and carried the game home tied by the feet to the poles which rested on the shoulders of a couple of servants.

Mastiff, greyhound, mongrel grim,
Hound or spaniel, brach or lym,
Or bobtail tyke or trundle-tail. . . .
        Shakespeare, King Lear, *III. vi*

II The Breeds of Hounds

THE HOUNDS OF ANTIQUITY

How many breeds of dog has Shakespeare named in the three lines
from *King Lear* quoted above? Most people would say three: the
mastiff, the greyhound, and the spaniel. Then they would add that
there are several kinds of spaniel and which did Shakespeare mean,
the cocker, the clumber, the springer, the King Charles, or perhaps
the field spaniel? Obviously the bobtail tyke and the trundle-tail
were never breed names; the word "hound" means any one of
several different breeds—except when used derisively or humorous-
ly—and who ever heard of a brach or a lym?

A little research will soon show us the surprising fact that in the Middle Ages "mastiff" meant a mongrel. It will also tell us that "brach" and "lym" meant hounds that hunt by scent, tracking hounds. The brach ran free, like the modern foxhound or beagle; and the lym was taken out on a leash and used for tracking in the same way the modern bloodhound is. Shakespeare, therefore, has named perhaps only two breeds. We must do more research if we want to find out more.

If we want to find out about the ancient breeds of hounds used in Greece, we have a somewhat more difficult job than looking up brach and lym, and we are in for some surprises, too. It is not hard to discover at least sixty-five names in Greek and Latin literature that may represent breeds, but we soon discover that some are merely synonyms and others are only indications of the places the hounds came from or of the man who first bred and raised them. A few others are plainly not hounds or hunting dogs at all: the little Melitaean, or Maltese, was only a ladies' lap dog.

Another thing we soon discover is that the ancient Greek hounds did not look anything like the flop-eared, sad-eyed creatures we call hounds today; indeed, nothing of the sort can be found in either Greek or Roman art. We can quickly avoid the mistake that Shakespeare made when he described Theseus' hounds in *Midsummer Night's Dream:*

> My hounds are bred out of the Spartan kind,
> So flew'd, so sanded; and their heads are hung
> With ears that sweep away the morning dew;
> Crook-kneed, and dew-lapp'd like Thessalian bulls;
> Slow in pursuit, but matched in mouth like bells,
> Each under each. A cry more tuneable
> Was never holla'd to, nor cheered with horn,
> In Crete, in Sparta, nor in Thessaly.

This is magnificant poetry and shows a real understanding of hunting—but not of hunting in ancient Greece. Theseus himself, the Theseus of mythology, would not have recognized these hounds, for Shakespeare was describing the southern hounds of the England of his own day.

So it is tempting to abandon the use of the word "hound" and use instead the words "hunting dog." For that matter, it is tempting to give up the very word "breed," on the ground that the Greeks kept no studbooks and had no systematic way of recording pedigrees.

But words carry implications as well as primary meanings. "Hunting dog" implies a dog used for shooting game, particularly birds; "hound" implies a dog that follows his quarry by scent. The best word for our purpose is "hound," and we can hardly give up the word "breed" in the face of the evidence that the Greeks took a great many pains to keep their bloodstock purebred: Oppian, in discussing possible crosses between different breeds, recommends keeping the breeds pure;[1] and Xenophon goes to some length to explain that puppies should be fed by their own mothers rather than by foster mothers because the milk of mongrels, the only dogs usually available for foster mothers, is not good for the purebred.[2] Besides, the Greeks paid enough attention to their own genealogies to show that they had a very high opinion of good breeding, and, as they treasured good hounds, they naturally took pains about the breeding of them. Witness, as an example of their interest in breeding, the genealogy of Patreus, the hero for whom the city of Patras was named. Pausanias gives it, and it is ten generations long.[3] It is, of course, largely fictitious, and there may never have been anyone by the name of Patreus, but the very fact that such a genealogy was invented to satisfy the people of Patras shows that the people of Patras believed such things were important; and if they did, then it is probable that the people of every city in Greece, most of which had eponymous heroes, had exactly the same feeling. Hound-breeders who insisted on the importance of pure bloodlines paid attention to the breeding of their hounds with every bit as much care as the modern hound-breeder.

Patreus' genealogy tells us something else, for it is confined entirely to the male line, a thing that seems natural to us today because we have inherited the same system from the Greeks but that might puzzle and confuse other races accustomed to tracing ancestry through the female line. What it tells us is that in breeding the sire was considered more important than the dam, a theory that most breeders held very strongly until the modern science of genetics revealed the actual workings of inheritance; indeed, many breeders still believe it. We know now that the reason the sire seems to have more influence than the dam is that one doghound can sire a hundred puppies in one season while a bitch can have only six or eight. From the practical point of view of the breeder, the sire really is more important than the dam; it's his capacity for quantity production that makes him so.

We can be sure, therefore, that Greek hounds were carefully bred, even if we do not yet know what breeds they were. We can be sure, also, that not all breeds were native to Greece, for the Greeks were a maritime people whose country was almost more the Aegean Sea than the Greek peninsula itself, and consequently they were well acquainted not only with every harbor and inlet of their own sea, but the whole of the Mediterranean and the Black Sea, too. Later, during the days of the Roman Empire, they traveled to places as far separated as Tibet and the British Isles, where they learned about breeds of hounds they had never encountered during the fifth and fourth centuries before Christ.

So we shall take a quick journey through the known world of the Greeks, traveling in a wide swing from west to north, from north to east, thence south, west, and finally back to Greece itself; and in this journey we shall list the names of hound breeds that we encounter, putting down whatever there is to know about them as we go.

EUROPEAN BREEDS

In the Spanish peninsula, where we begin, the first breed we meet is the *Iberian*, mentioned by both Pollux and Oppian.[4] It is possible, of course, that this breed was not found in this place at all, because there was an Iberia in the Caucasus; but it is more likely, because of the dates of both Pollux and Oppian, that these hounds came from modern Spain and Portugal. Unfortunately we know nothing about them except their names and can't even guess what they were like.

Next are the Italian breeds, not more than four in number. The first of these, the *Ausonian*, may be nothing but a generic term for all Italian dogs, for it is the name of the tribe that inhabited Campania when the Greeks first settled in the neighborhood of Naples.[5] The second, the *Sallentine*, is no more than a name to us.[6] The third, the *Tuscan*, was covered with shaggy hair and would actually point to where the hare lay hidden.[7] Perhaps this breed was one of the progenitors of the modern setter, but tempting as the idea may be, the evidence is wholly inadequate and might even fit the wolf, for wolves have been known to point game just the way the setter does. The fourth, the *Umbrian*, would not stand up to the game it ran down, a fact—if it is a fact—that tells us nothing.[8]

But although so far we have found nothing of importance, our next names are really helpful. There were two Celtic breeds described by Flavius Arrianus in the second century after Christ,[9] the *Segusiae* (at times misspelled *Egusiae*) and the *Vertragi*. These two breeds have sometimes been lumped together,[10] as if they were two names for one breed, because Arrian calls them both "Celtic hounds," but they were actually very different. The Segusiae were named for the Segusiavi, a Celtic tribe that lived in the province of Gallia Lugdunensis, a province that includes modern Lyons. These hounds had excellent noses and good cry; their speed was as good as that of any tracking hound; but their one fault was that they were inclined to dwell and would not drive on after the quarry, for they gave tongue on the trail (the cold line of the hare going to her form) just as readily as on the hot scent of a running hare. That they hunted by scent rather than by sight is made very clear by Arrian, for he explains that they hunted in the same way as the Cretan and the Carian hounds and therefore showed nothing new in their way of working. So, he said, there was no point in telling anything about them beyond mentioning the fact that they were wild and wretched-looking and that their cry was so mournful that people likened them to roadside beggars. Although Arrian had little use for them, they are important to us, for it is quite possible that they were the earliest ancestors of whom we have record of all the true modern hound breeds—the bloodhound, the basset, the beagle, the harrier, and the foxhound.[11]

The other Celtic breed, the Vertragi, were certainly greyhounds. Not only are there dozens of representations of greyhounds on ancient coins of dates which make it certain that the greyhound is the animal represented, but the very name of this breed tells us what they were. *Vertragus*[12] is a perfectly good Celtic word composed of two parts, *ver*, an intensive, and *trag*, which means "foot"; so that taken as a whole the word means a creature with "lots of foot," as modern horsemen say. The same word appears again later in Old French as *veltre*, which means greyhound.[13] It is true that Arrian brought their name into his text abruptly after discussing the Segusiae, but he did so by using the adversative particle *de*, thus contrasting the slow and pokey tracking hounds with the swift and graceful gazehounds. The tracking hounds were wretched-looking too, and so could not have been the gazehounds that were pleasing to the eye of the hunting man because of the sheen of their coats.

Whether Xenophon ever saw a greyhound or not is open to debate. Arrian is sure that he had not, but Xenophon had seen gazehounds while he was in Asia Minor with the Ten Thousand.[14] What they were is not certain; they might have been ancestors of the modern saluki. At any rate Xenophon's ideal is a tracker, while Arrian's is a greyhound, long from head to stern and sturdy and symmetrical, with a light and well-knit head and a muzzle that came to a point and was not cut off square. With heads like this, hounds should have necks that were long and willowy, so that they would bend when the hounds strained at their leashes. Heavy heads were bad, Arrian said, but he did not seem to object if they were swine-chopped. The ears were big and soft and appeared to be broken because of their softness, although if they stood upright it was not a serious fault unless they were little and stiff. An ear such as Arrian describes is known today as a "tulip ear," an upright ear that has begun to fold over at the tip, and is characteristic of the greyhound. Broad breasts were preferred to narrow, the one requirement that sounds unlike the greyhound, although how broad is not specified. The shoulder blades must stand apart a little. Legs should be round, straight, and compact; loins, strong;

belly, slack; flanks, pliant; the hind legs, longer than the front; the coat, rough (unlike the modern greyhound, but like his cousin the Cà Eivissenc, or Ibizan dog), soft, and pliant; and the tip of the stern, a bit shaggy. Any color was satisfactory, nor was it bad if the color was solid. Arrian had no objection, either, to light-colored eyes, providing they were bright, a detail in which he differs with practically all modern breeders. There was little difference in conformation between doghounds and bitches.

Apart from the broad breasts and the character of the coat, Arrian's description fits the modern greyhound very well, and certainly fits the Cà Eivissenc even better—and who knows but what the Balearic Islands, where the breed hunts rabbits today, may not have been a stopping-off point on the greyhound's journey from Egypt to Gaul. Although the Celtic greyhound was not used by Greeks or Romans much before the Augustan age, it was not a new breed but only a variety of one of the oldest in existence.

Another European breed was the *Agasseus*,[15] or Agassaean dog, a British breed, described as small, like the little table-dog (we call them lap dogs today), but exceedingly ugly, shaggy of hair and dull of eye, with sharp claws and venomous tusks. This breed sounds like some variety of terrier, perhaps resembling the modern border terrier, although the dullness of eye is certainly not a characteristic of that breed. In addition to the Agassaean, the British bred other dogs for hunting, which were imported into Gaul by the Celts and used alongside their own home-bred dogs not only for hunting but for war.[16] It has been suggested that these were ancestors of the bulldog, but there is no evidence either for or against the idea.

Across the North Sea, near the Rhine, were hounds called *Sycambrians*,[17] named for the German tribe that bred them. Farther east, in the region just north of the Yugoslavian part of Macedonia, were the *Pannonians;*[18] and still farther east, in southern Russia, the *Sarmatians*, or *Sauromatians*.[19] Of the *Paeonians*[20] we know only that they were reputed to have been used as shield-bearers in war and must therefore have been big. Of the *Illyrian, Belgian, Scottish*[21] (to which I can find no classical reference), and

Gelonian hounds, there is nothing recorded of worth. We can tell where they came from, and that is all. Probably they were completely unknown to the Greeks of the fifth century before Christ.

ASIATIC BREEDS

From north of the Himalayas, perhaps from China, but at least from Tibet, came a ferocious breed of hounds known as *Seres*,[22] the name for the people in that part of the world, at least when approached from the south or the west. These hounds may very well have been close to the wolf in size, shape, and character and were either the same as the *Indian* hounds or very closely related to them. Xenophon recommends the latter for hunting both deer and wild boar,[23] obviously because of their size and strength. They were said to be the result of crossing a tiger and a bitch, so we can guess their appearance: they must have been red or tawny in color, short-haired, and with a brindled coat that suggested the stripes on their tiger sires.[24] In many ways they remind us of the *dhole*, the wild red dog of India, which, according to modern reports, is untamable; but the possibility of any connection is surely ruled out by physiological differences that keep the dhole from being classified as a true member of the dog family.[25]

Of Persian hounds there were four kinds: *Elymaeans*,[26] which came from just northeast of the head of the Persian Gulf; the *Carmanians*,[27] which were said to be savage and implacable; the *Hyrcanians*,[28] another savage breed; and the *Medians*,[29] great fighters. There is no further information about them, and we are left wondering if their savage character might not be due to poetic fancy in the same way that the modern cowpony is reputed to be a bucking bronco, wild and difficult to ride. It is a thoroughly normal thing to impute savagery to the hound you hunt with, even though in reality he is an amiable old soul whose chief interest in the chase is to find out what made that lovely smell. At any rate references to all Persian breeds come from the first, second, and third centuries after Christ. Whether any of these particular breeds were among the ancestors of the saluki or not is impossible to say.

In Asia Minor were the *Carians*, used by Arrian as examples of the tracking hound and held up as a standard of nose, speed, and cry.[30] The *Magnesians* were a variety of the Carian hounds and were used as shield-bearers as well as for hunting, so they must have been big and strong. From south central Asia Minor came the *Lycaonian* hounds, reputedly with good dispositions.[31] That is all we know about them.

AFRICAN BREEDS

Egyptian dogs, so many writers say, when thirsty drank by lapping up the water in the river while on the run, in order to avoid being grabbed by the crocodiles. Aristotle gives us one more bit of information. He says that although all other animals in Egypt are larger than their congeners in Greece, the dog is smaller.[32] His observation may be meaningless, but, if true, permits several possibilities. The most obvious one is that the Egyptians did not like big dogs, such as those of the mastiff type, and therefore confined their attention to breeding small greyhounds and whippets, animals which they thought more suitable to their country. It is impossible to tell size from Egyptian works of art, for the artists often made important figures big and unimportant figures small, disregarding the natural scale of objects, so that we have no means of judging true size.

Egypt is not the whole of Africa, of course. There were *Libyan*[33] hounds in Libya and *Cyrenean* hounds in Cyrene. These latter were bred by crossing the dog with the wolf,[34] a thing that was said to have been done in Gaul also. There were hounds, too, in Aethiopia, a country rather vague in extent as well as location; sometimes it corresponds with modern Ethiopia, but at other times it covers all of Central Africa, and at still other times it seems to be located somewhere southwest of India. Wherever it may have been, it contained a tribe of people known as the Cynomolgi, or "bitch-milkers," who lived on the milk of their bitches but fed their hounds on the milk of cows. To get this, the hounds were said to have attacked the Indian cattle.[35]

GREEK BREEDS

Returning to Greece, we find a very large number of breeds and a great deal more information about them than about the European, Asiatic, or African hounds. The first two, mentioned in Latin but not in Greek literature, admittedly do not amount to much. These are the *Acarnanians*,[36] which ran mute, a characteristic considered desirable by the Romans but by no one else until modern times, and the *Athamanians*.[37] Both are from Epirus, in the extreme northwest corner of Greece, and the home of large animals of all kinds. The third breed, the *Chaonians*,[38] were also from Epirus and were, according to Nicander (as quoted by Pollux), "descendants of a dog which Hephaestus forged from Demonesian bronze, put a soul into, and gave as a gift to Zeus. The latter gave it to Europa; she gave it to Minos; Minos, to Procris; and Procris, to Cephalus. It had a nature that was inescapable, just as the Teumessian fox was uncatchable. And for this reason both were turned to stone, the one that it might not catch the uncatchable fox, and the other that it might not escape the inescapable hound." The name of this hound was Laelaps, or Whirlwind, and we shall meet him again when we come to the Cretan hounds.

The fourth breed was also from Epirus, the *Molossian*,[39] and it too was descended from Laelaps. Fortunately we know a great deal about the Molossians, so that we can identify them with certainty and accuracy, for they are not only mentioned more often than any other breed in ancient history but have been well represented in sculpture, both in purebred and in crossbred form. They were the ancestors of the modern mastiff and can be seen in bas-reliefs in the Assyrian sculpture from Assur-bani-pal now in the British Museum, which shows huge dogs hunting wild horses. There is another example, in the Palazzo Torlonia in Rome, which shows a mastiff under a chair. Still others can be seen in the illustrations in G. M. A. Richter's *Animals in Greek Sculpture*.

The origin of the Molossian can only be guessed. Otto Keller, in *Die Antike Tierwelt*, states that the breed traced back to the big dogs of Tibet and thence to the Tibetan wolf and that the big dogs of Tibet lost their shaggy hair when they descended to the plains of Mesopotamia. This theory is as good as any and might very well be true. Fortunately it is easier to trace their descendants than their ancestors, for the former are scattered throughout all Europe where they were taken by Roman soldiers. The modern mastiff is, of course, the prime example, although a less efficient beast for guard duty than his ancestor, except in his homeland, Epirus, where he has a reputation for savagery that may be true or may be due to his well-developed sense of property. The mastiff one sees in the Western hemisphere, however, is extraordinarily good-natured.

Just as the sheep dog of modern Greece is usually a mastiff or Molossian, so were the Molossians of ancient Greece usually sheep dogs. Sometimes they were hunted, just as they had been in Mesopotamia, but more often they were kept to guard the flocks and herds and to keep watch over the house. Sometimes they were crossed with other breeds, particularly with the Laconians, which we shall discuss shortly; and some of these crossbreds have been immortalized in sculpture but labeled Molossians, so that before many centuries it was believed that this was not a breed but just a mongrel. Thus, I think, the name "mastiff" came to mean "mongrel" in the Middle Ages.

Next after the Molossians came a number of unimportant breeds, of which the first was the *Aetolian*, said to be noisy.[40] Next was the *Locrian*,[41] known to Xenophon, who recommended them for boar hunting; they must, therefore, have been big and were possibly related to their neighbors, the Molossians. The *Phereans*[42] and the *Eurytides*[43]—the latter named for Eurytus, one of Homer's Moliones twins—came from Thessaly, as did the bloodstock from which the *Eretrians* of Euboea were bred.[44] *Thracian* hounds, not strictly Greek by classical standards, are also named.[45] None of these breeds are described, so it is impossible to guess what they were like; nor, for that matter, were the *Elean, Arcadian, Tegean, Argive,* and *Glympic* hounds described, all of which were obviously named for the places where they were found.[46] The last of these breeds came from Glypeis, a place on the border between Argolis and Laconia, according to Polybius.[47] All these breeds are mentioned only by late writers and may very well have been nothing but local varieties of the next breed we shall meet.

This next and most important of all the ancient Greek hounds was the Laconian, or, as it was sometimes called, the Spartan hound,[48] the very breed that Shakespeare pictured so mistakenly. In Xenophon's time there were two strains of Laconians, the *Castorians*, named for Castor (one of the Heavenly Twins) because he was said to have taken especial pleasure in raising and caring for them, and the *Vulpines*, a smaller variety, so named because they were supposed to have originated from the crossing of a dog with a fox. Xenophon distinguishes clearly between these two varieties, but later accounts confuse them. According to Nicander of Colophon (as quoted by Pollux), Castor was supposed to have been the first to cross the fox and the dog, so the Castorians were the Vulpines. We may guess that either the two strains became mixed over the years or that one died out and the stories themselves became mixed.

But whatever its origin, the Laconian hound, according to Xenophon, was big. But how big is big? He gives us no idea, so we must find out from some other source. We may make some estimate from the marble hound in the Acropolis Museum in Athens or even from the marble hound in the Art Museum in Basel. The latter is eighty-two and a half centimeters long, that is, about thirty-two and a half inches. We don't know what breed the Basel hound was, but we do know that any hound thirty-two and a half inches long is a big one. Unfortunately statues are almost never made exactly life-size; if they were, they would appear less than life-size. There is, however, no exact scale for statuary. One instructor in sculpture, John Wilson, who taught at Harvard in the 1920's, used to insist that a statue of a man should be made eight feet tall in order to appear six. Others, however, have used other proportions. Paintings are helpful in judging the size of hounds, because we can at least see hounds together with human beings; and yet even vase paintings are not reliable gauges, because artists frequently alter the scale of the figures for artistic purposes or in order to cram several figures into a small space. In view of all the representations, however, we can make a fairly safe guess that the Laconian was about the size of a very large beagle or small harrier. It would therefore have been about eighteen inches high at the shoulder and must have weighed between thirty and forty pounds.

As for its conformation, the Laconian hound had a light head; that is, it was not blocky and mssive like the head of a mastiff; the nose was straight, neither dished like that of a modern pointer nor aquiline like that of a bull terrier (which it otherwise rather resembled) or show collie. The forehead was flat and broad like that of a beagle rather than domed like that of a basset hound; but it had none of the narrowness of the head of the show collie, otherwise it could not have had the deep dividing line between the two halves of the skull which Xenophon mentions. The ears of the Laconian hound, however, were small, upright, prick ears, more like those of a terrier than those of a hound, and were free from excess hair behind. The neck was long and supple; it was rounded and free from throatiness or dewlap. Seen from in front the breast was broad and the shoulders square, so that the points of the shoulder blades were separated slightly—the breadth of breast is not given by Xenophon any more than it is by Arrian. The front legs were short, straight, compact, and firm. They did not splay or bend back at the pasterns, nor did the hounds stand with elbows out. The rib cage was not close to the ground, as it is in a modern dachshund or basset hound, but sloped away obliquely; and the shoulders sloped back well also, showing that the front legs were set on well forward, as they are in a modern race horse or steeplechaser. The loins were muscular but of average length; that is, the back was neither very short nor very long. The quarters were well rounded, so that when seen from behind, the point of the hipbones was well below the croup, as it is in a race horse, and not high, as it often is in a poorly bred draft horse, where it gives the quarters a square, table-top look. Seen from the side, the hound was tucked up in the belly more than a modern foxhound is but less than a greyhound. The hind legs were bent at the hock, as they should be, and not straight, as some American foxhounds of the 1940's were. The stern was long and whiplike and sometimes a little "curly"; that is, it curled over backwards a bit. The coat was fine and dense and soft, with slightly longer hair on the edges of the thighs and on the underside of the stern. The colors were tan with white on the face, throat, chest, legs, and stern; black with tan on the same places; and white with tan markings. Whether the black and tan hounds had any white on their feet or elsewhere is not certain; it is easy to forget such markings when describing a hound. If there was any white on these hounds, however, it was probably not much. And, finally, the eyes were black and sparkling, and the whole aspect of the hound was bold and confident. In its whole appearance it was like no breed recognized by any kennel club in the world today.

In literature we find four other names besides the Castorians and the Vulpines, representing some sort of variants of the Laconian hound. One was the *Cynosuris;* another, the *Amyclaean;* a third, the *Menelaïd;* and a fourth, the *Psyllic.*[49] The first two were probably named for two villages in Lacedaemonian territory; the third probably means no more than that the hounds were popularly supposed to have been first bred by the Homeric hero Menelaus. The fourth is a puzzler. There was a tribe of barbarians in North Africa called the Psylli who were famous as snake-charmers, and we might suppose that they had bred these hounds. But the breed is also called an Achaean breed, a name that either places it in Greece or makes the people who bred it Greek. There is no mention anywhere, so far as I can find out, of any city or people with a name anything like Psylli anywhere in Greece; and the breed, being Laconian, ought to be found in Greece. But as *psylla* means flea, perhaps we are only being told something about the condition of these hounds.

There are a few other lesser breeds, some of which are easy to trace and some difficult. The *Harmodians* were presumably named for the man who first bred them, but was this man the Athenian tyrannicide?[50] *Amorgian* hounds came, of course, from the island of Amorgis;[51] *Seriphian* hounds from Seriphis; and *Sicyonian*

33

from the city of Sicyon.[52] But where did *Azorian* or *Petronian* hounds come from?[53] Were they Greek? Or did they come from the Azores, or run on rocks? And what were Grattius' "*Metagontes*"?[54] They are plainly described as a cross between Cretans and Spartans; Aymard thinks they were a cross between Argolic Molossians and Spartans, which is essentially the same thing, as we shall see when we discuss the Cretans. The word may be only descriptive, an epithet invented or borrowed by Grattius to suggest their ability to maneuver or to change course.

There remains one more breed to account for, and this is the *Cretan*, a most important breed.[55] Cretan hounds were said to be nimble so that they could run well in the mountains, but nowhere is there a description of their appearance, and there is no adequate archeological evidence of their conformation. There is a faint clue to their appearance in the story of Laelaps, the hound forged by Hephaestus from bronze, which was said to have been the sire of both the Molossians and the Chaonians.[56] Laelaps was certainly associated with Crete, for he had been the property of Minos at one time. The Cretan hound may therefore have had Molossian blood, perhaps crossed with something that made it lighter-boned and therefore nimble. This something may have been the greyhound, brought over from Egypt; but as the Cretan hounds are described by Arrian as tracking hounds rather than gazehounds,[57] it seems more likely that the outcross was Laconian. Molossians and Laconians had been crossed; there is a doubtful passage in Aristotle that refers to just such a cross.[58] And as Oppian refers to the *Cnossian* hound,[59] a variety of the Cretan, as famous for its nose, the outcross can hardly have been the greyhound.

Besides the Cnossians, there were two other varieties of the Cretans, the *Workers* and the *Outrunners*.[60] The Workers were so keen they fought and hunted around the clock, but the Outrunners ran along beside the horses during a hunt, never getting ahead and certainly never lagging behind. The Outrunners evidently ran free, under control of the huntsman's voice alone, and were not led on leashes (a difficult thing for a rider to do in the days before saddles and stirrups without being pulled off his horse) as

were all hounds from the earliest times up through the Middle
Ages until modern times. If so, they were the first to do so until
about the seventeenth century.

HISTORICAL DEVELOPMENT
OF THE BREEDS

Five breeds of dog stand out above all the rest. One we can disre-
gard, the little Melitaean table-dog which was never used for hunting anything at any time. The other four are the Cretan, the Laconian, the Molossian, and the Vertragus. The Cretan, as we have
seen, was developed from the Laconian and the Molossian. The
Laconian, judging from its conformation, probably is the breed
from which the large group now known by the misleading and unfortunate name of "pariah dog" is descended. The Molossian was
the ancestor of the mastiff, and the Vertragus was a member of the
greyhound group.

What, however, was the origin of the pariah dog, the mastiff,
the greyhound, and the little Melitaean? Where did they come
from? Where also did all the rest of the modern breeds come from,
particularly the modern hound breeds—the bloodhound, the foxhound, the harrier, the basset hound, and the beagle? What about
the spaniel, the setter, and all the various kinds of retrievers? Is it
possible that two such dissimilar creatures as the chihuahua and
the St. Bernard came from a common ancestor? Or the Old English
sheep dog and the whippet? Or the bulldog and the saluki? Is it not
more likely that they have been descended from different ancestors,
such as the fox, the jackal, and the wolf?

The classical authors thought so, but this belief is not confined
to them. At the beginning of the twentieth century Otto Keller
divided all the dogs of the classical world into five groups:

1. Spitz dogs, descended from the jackal
2. Sheep dogs, descended from the wild Alpine dog
3. Street dogs (pariah dogs), descended from the jackal
4. Greyhounds, descended from the Abyssinian wolf
5. Mastiffs, descended from the Tibetan dog

Keller had no doubt about the multiple origin of the dog.

In *The New Book of the Dog*, published in 1939, by Edward C. Ash, a well-known writer of books about dogs, are three pictures on a plate which faces page 27. The first of these is a drawing made in 1792 of a creature called a "wild dog of the woods"; Ash asks if this might not have been a wolf-dog hybrid. A second drawing shows a creature believed to be a dog-fox hybrid, owned by a man named Hewer, who lived in Reading, England. The third is a photograph of a dog-fox hybrid, thought to have been owned by the late S. E. Shirley, former president of the Kennel Club in England. Not one of these hybrids is properly authenticated. One is just a guess; the second is "believed" to be a hybrid; the third cannot be substantiated because the man who might have owned it is no longer living. There have been many other similar examples, and even a story about such hybrids in the *Reader's Digest* within the past three years.

In contrast with this belief is the opinion of G. M. Vevers, Superintendent of the Zoological Gardens, London, who wrote a chapter on the phylogeny of the dog, *Canis familiaris*, in *The Book of the Dog*, edited by Brian Vesy-Fitzgerald and published in 1948. (The title is similar to Ash's, but the book is entirely different.) Vevers states with assurance that the dog is descended from the wolf, and from the wolf only, and that there is no scientifically attested case of a fox-dog hybrid. He quotes Gerrit S. Miller and F. Wood Jones, both highly respected zoologists, and describes the experiments made by Iljin, the Russian geneticist, in the Moscow Zoo between 1923 and 1930 as partial proof of his belief.[61]

The opinion of such experts ought to settle the matter. However, it does not. Dr. Ernst Mayr, in *Systematics and the Origin of Species* (New York: Columbia University Press, 1942, p. 259), says that hybrids between dogs, wolves, jackals, and coyotes are possible. Indeed, he points out that hybrids can occur not only between subspecies and between species, but occasionally between members of different genera, and, in exceptional cases, between members of still higher categories. Furthermore, he points out that the degree of fertility or sterility of the offspring of such unions is no indication of the degree of relationship of the parents. So in spite of the fact that Dr. Mayr admits that some of these crosses are very rare, we seem to be right back where we started, for even if these crosses are very rare, who can say that they never occurred?

The truth is that nobody can say with absolute certainty what the origin of the domestic dog of today is. The best informed opinion is that the earliest dogs domesticated by man were probably descended from the smaller breeds of wolf—the cave man tamed the wolf cubs which followed him from campsite to campsite, serving as scavengers. Whether the descendants of these early dogs were crossed with the coyote and the jackal is not known. In view of present-day crosses between dogs and wolves, it is entirely possible that they were crossed back to the wolf from time to time.

But such crosses must have been planned by human breeders and can hardly have been the result of sheer chance, for as Mayr points out, species that are perfectly capable of hybridizing often live in close proximity without doing so. We can be fairly sure that the bitch tied to a tree in the forest will not be impregnated by anything except a stray male dog, certainly not by a fox.

As any breeder knows, the genus *Canis* is a most plastic creature that can be changed rapidly (usually for the worse) in a very few generations. While no one can prove that there is no jackal blood in any domestic breed of dog, the chances are slight that there is. The coyote, being American, surely had nothing to do with the earliest hounds of Greece.

So we shall assume, until we learn better, that the pariah dog, the mastiff, the greyhound, and the little table-dog were descended from the wolf, but just how this evolution took place is far from clear. Perhaps the pariah dog did develop from early dogs of the Nile Valley, Nubia, or India, as Keller believes. Perhaps the mastiff did develop in Tibet, come down the slopes of the Himalayas, and shed its long hair in the hot climate of Mesopotamia, to become the mastiff of Assur-bani-pal and later of Molossis. Perhaps the greyhound did develop in the mountains of Abyssinia, follow the Nile down to its mouth, skirt the shores of the Mediterranean, and cross over into Gaul by way of the Balearic Isles. These theories are no more than guesses, but until we can find more, they will have to do.

We are on slightly surer ground when we attempt to trace the three principal breeds from the classical age down to the present. The Laconian hound, so popular as a tracking hound, may have lost favor after the introduction of the greyhound, or it may have been bred in such great numbers that it became a nuisance and degenerated into the street dog which served all cities of the Roman Empire as a scavenger. Indeed, in Constantinople it multiplied so greatly that the Turks, too tender-hearted to put the surplus dog population to sleep, collected them and left them on an island in the Sea of Marmara to starve to death; whence comes the name of the place, the Isle of Dogs. Other Laconians were probably crossed with the tender-nosed Segusiae to produce the hounds kept by the Bishop of Liége, St. Hubert, the patron saint of the chase; and from his kennels came the four royal races: the white hounds of the King, the hounds of St. Hubert, the gray hounds of St. Louis, and the fawn hounds of Brittany. From these four races came all of the modern tracking hounds—the bloodhound, the basset hound, the beagle, the harrier, and the foxhound.[62]

The earliest ancestors of the modern gundogs—the setters, spaniels and retrievers—do not appear in history before Roman times, when dogs that hunted silently began to come into favor and dogs with long coats first began to be mentioned. Could these have come from some earlier breed of dogs, perhaps one of the five groups suggested by Keller? Or were they too related to the Segusiae and the Laconians? It is possible that they came from Keller's sheep-dog group; but in any case, nothing is certain.

Nothing made the horse so fat as the king's eye.
Plutarch, Of the Training of Children

III The Care of the Hounds

THE BREEDING PROGRAM

Everybody loves a puppy. Think, then, how much fun it is to have a whole basketful, or two, three, or even four baskets full of scampering little hound puppies. Imagine them as they tumble over each other, fight with mock fury, and growl with miniature squeaks. There is nothing more cheering than to watch them grow fat and sleek, and when finally they have at last grown to maturity, and you have taught them obedience, and they have begun to display the ability to hunt that you hoped they would, how satisfying a feeling!

Raising puppies is one of the extra pleasures that go along with the chores and duties of keeping a pack of hounds, and it is one which no master can afford to miss, because it is impossible to buy a really good pack excepting in time of catastrophe. No master will part with his best if he can help it, and the only hounds that can be bought will all have some defect or other, no matter how good their bloodlines. Among such hounds, those which are available because of defects in appearance, providing they are not also bad workers, can be the foundation stock of a really first-rate pack; their defects can be bred out and their good qualities strengthened. In any case, a home-bred pack will hunt better than one made up of drafts from different sources, for they will not only have a family resemblance—a pleasant but not indispensable asset—but they will think and therefore hunt alike.

But even when a master has bred a pack for himself, his job is not finished. Death from disease or injury will deplete it, and some hounds will acquire faults that cannot be corrected, so they must be drafted. As a consequence, there must be a steady flow of replacements flowing into the kennels. The number needed will average about 25 per cent of the full strength of the pack each year, so that with a pack of twelve couples, three couples must be available to enter into the pack each autumn.[1] In order to have these six hounds available, there will have to be twelve puppies to raise, for only about half of the puppies kept when they are whelped will live to prove useful; the others will sicken and die or turn out so faulty they cannot be kept. And finally, in order to have twelve puppies to start with, it will usually be necessary to breed four bitches, because some do not catch, and of those that do, some will have only very small litters or inferior pups. Then, if by some strange mischance, everything goes perfectly, and all the bitches have large, healthy litters, the master is well off, for he can always easily dispose of the surplus. To breed a good pack, he must breed a lot.

For the ancient Greek master of hounds, the problem of acquiring a pack and of keeping it up in quality and numbers was exactly the same as it is today. His pack may not have been bred to look as level as ours are today, but, on the other hand, his losses from disease and injury must have been considerably greater. And as the ancient master, like the modern master, had many puppies that looked promising but turned out useless when tried, he had to keep on breeding litter after litter in order to keep his establishment up. What system of breeding did he follow?

He knew nothing, of course, about the modern science of genetics, of chromosomes and genes, of Mendel's laws of inheritance, or of dominants and recessives. He had not heard of inbreeding and its effects, of outcrossing and its effects, or of line breeding and its advantages. Hybrid chicks and hybrid corn were still many centuries away from him. But if he knew nothing of the science of breeding, he also knew nothing of the pseudoscience. Nobody had washed his brain with theories of prepotency, of breeding to the top line of the pedigree, of the importance of the dam or the importance of the sire, or any of the rest of it. The only theory he had was that he ought to breed his best bitches to the best doghounds he could.[2] This theory is the very oldest of all and is fortunately a good one, although too slow to produce a new breed in fifty years, the way the Dobermann pinscher was produced.[3] But it did produce good hunting hounds, and that, of course, was what he wanted.

In order to choose the best sires, however, he went far afield; and in telling about it afterwards, he let his imagination loose; and when the Greek imagination runs loose, it goes a long way. In this case it ran to lions, tigers, civet cats, foxes, jackals, and wolves. All of these, it seems, had been used as sires for breeding hounds.

In Hyrcania, for example, a place which lies at the south end of the Caspian Sea, the natives were said to have crossed the lion and the dog.[4] In India the natives crossed the tiger and the dog.[5] Aristotle explains how it was done: The native who wished to gamble on the experiment—and it was known to be a gamble—took a bitch that had come in heat and tied her to a tree in some remote and lonely place. If the tiger happened to be in an amorous mood, he would couple with her; but if not—and all too frequently he was not—he would eat her up instead. This outcome was unfortunately of frequent occurrence. The first generation produced by this system was said to be too savage to be of use; but by crossing it back with the dog, it was possible by the third generation to obtain a very useful hound, albeit a little too inclined to eat its master's livestock. The proof of its breeding was obvious: Was not its coat short-haired, tawny in color, and brindled with markings

41

like the tiger's stripes? Besides, India was a long way off, and who could say it was not so?

But if the outcross with the lion and the tiger had occurred a long way from Greece, that with *thos* was said to have happened right in Greece itself.[6] And the thos was itself supposed to have been a hybrid produced by crossing the leopard and the wolf. Descriptions of this beast make it seem now catlike and now doglike, so that there is no agreement whether it was really the civet cat or the jackal.

A much more important outcross, however, was that with the fox.[7] The best-known example was the Laconian breed of hounds known as the Vulpines, foxy-looking creatures, we can be sure, created in the heroic age by Castor, so it was said. This was a particularly plausible outcross, and as we have seen, people still believe it possible today. But whatever the truth about the thos itself, or about the outcross with the thos, or about the Vulpine hounds, no one could disprove the stories, not because the outcrosses had happened so far away, but because they had happened so long ago.

The fifth and last outcross reported was that with the wolf.[8] This was said to have been accomplished both in Cyrene and in Gaul, in different centuries, and in both cases within the memories of living men who could vouch for it. Hounds produced by such an outcross were considered leaders of their packs, both by the men who handled them and by other hounds in their packs.

As we have already seen, outcrosses with the lion, the tiger, and the civet cat are for all practical purposes impossible; that with the fox, highly unlikely; and that with the jackal, improbable. The outcross with the wolf, however, has been repeatedly accomplished, although until recently without any attempt at scientific proof. The Eskimos, for example, cross their sled dogs with the wolf in order to produce hardier dogs capable of leading well. But the experiments of Iljin in the Moscow Zoo, conducted in a scientific manner, should now be sufficient to prove the possibility to anybody.

There is no doubt that the hounds of Cyrene were leaders in their packs. But in spite of the success of this cross and in spite of the success of the Cretan hound—no hybrid, but still a cross between two distinctly different breeds—Greek breeders were essentially conservative in their programs and stuck to what they had learned from their forefathers. This, as Oppian said, was to keep the bloodlines pure.[9]

MATING AND PREGNANCY

The age at which the Greeks began breeding their hounds was probably the same as the age at which we do today, although at first glance it might seem that they bred them much earlier, for Aristotle says that dogs and bitches are ready at the age of one year and sometimes, notably in the case of the Laconian hound, at eight months.[10] Obviously, however, he is talking about biological facts and is not attempting to describe current practices among hound breeders.

Xenophon, a hound breeder, does not say at what age to begin breeding, but he does tell us that bitches should be bred so that they will whelp at the beginning of spring, as spring is the best season for raising puppies. He also tells us that bitches should first be hunted at the age of eight months, and doghounds at ten.[11] Thus we see that bitch puppies whelped early in March could be hunting the following November; and those whelped the end of June, not until the end of the following February. If Xenophon did what he recommends, he entered his bitches in the winter—a poor time for a hound to learn, although perhaps not as bad in Greece as in colder climates. But he also says that the bitches should be relieved of work in the winter so that they will be in good shape for whelping in the spring.[12] If they are relieved from work, they can hardly be busy learning to hunt, and it is therefore evident that they were not bred the first winter after they were born but were held over until the master had had a chance to see how well they worked.

The age for breeding the doghounds is even simpler to discover. Doghound puppies whelped in early March could not be hunted until ten months later, that is, in early January; and those whelped the end of June, not until the end of the following April. The spring is a good time for entering hounds (although not good for fox cubs to be hunted—the reason we don't do it then), but by then the bitches would long be past their time and could not be bred until the following year. Anyway, Xenophon states that bitches should be served by "good doghounds," and he would have needed at least one season to find out which were good.

Pollux, no hound breeder, gives us definite figures, for he says that doghounds should first be bred in their fourth year, and bitches in their third.[13] The doghounds, therefore, would have been entered one spring and hunted all through three seasons before being used at stud, and the bitches would have been bred in their third year after they had been entered in the spring and hunted through two years. Pollux gives us no idea where he got this bit of information, but it makes good sense.

Arrian's figures, although for greyhounds, are also enlightening. Bitches should be bred after they are two, and doghounds after they are three;[14] these are, of course, exactly the same as the figures given by Pollux.

The Greeks knew the period of heat of the bitches, the right time during that period for breeding them, and the number of times a bitch comes in heat each year.[15] They knew the period of gestation and were careful to keep the bitches from overexerting themselves as the time for whelping approached.[16] And, finally, when the time came for the whelps to arrive, we know that they offered prayers to Artemis, the goddess of parturition, who heard not only the prayers of women in labor but those offered for her companions of the chase.[17]

PUPPIES

The number of puppies which a bitch will have in a single litter will vary enormously; it may be as few as one or as many as twelve or fourteen—the record for foxhounds is twenty-six, whelped to an American foxhound bitch named Lena in the kennels of the late W. Newbold Ely, M.F.H., sometime in the 1940's. All twenty-six lived and grew to maturity.

Anything approaching such a large number is, however, unusual. The average litter is about eight. But even eight is more than a bitch can feed all by herself for more than a very few days. Four is the ideal number to raise; six is possible; but if the litter is bigger than that, something has to be done about the surplus. If nothing is done by the master, nature will do it in a somewhat less than perfect way: the vigorous puppies will take charge of the food supply, and the weaker will become still weaker, until they die of starvation. In the meanwhile those that do survive will not get quite as much milk as they should, and although they may grow big and healthy later they will not have had as good a start in life as they should. Most breeders, therefore, try either to weed out the poorest puppies at the very beginning or to find some other source of food for them.

Hand-feeding puppies is difficult even under modern conditions; it requires preparation of a formula, and puppies must be fed at frequent intervals all during the day—at night it is possible to put the whole mob of puppies under their dam and pick out a different group for hand-feeding next day (they can be marked with dabs of green vegetable dye to avoid confusion), so that everybody gets some of each kind of food. But in Xenophon's day such a program would have been impossible. No one knew how to prepare a formula; there were no baby bottles; and rubber nipples and medicine droppers were still unheard of.

But there is another solution to the problem and that is to find a foster mother, some mongrel bitch who has just had unwanted puppies or perhaps a purebred who has had only one or two pups. The Greeks knew about this solution too, but they didn't like it. Both Xenophon and Arrian discouraged the use of foster mothers on the ground that the milk of mongrels is not good for the purebred.[18] They were wrong in their reasoning—Nature cannot distinguish a purebred from a mongrel—but they were right in their conclusions: the foster mother is seldom a success. Some bitches will mother anything and everything that is given them, a baby squirrel, a rabbit, or a kitten; but others are not so maternal and will have nothing to do with the puppies that are offered them. Even if a bitch does accept them, there is still the chance that her milk will not agree with them, not because she is a mongrel, but because the milk of one individual can sometimes differ from that of another. Although this possibility is not great, there is still another possibility that can cause trouble. Worm eggs are sometimes carried in the coat of a dog; and if the foster mother has them in her coat—and being a mongrel, she may not have been kept as clean as the pure-bred hounds—the puppies run the risk of becoming infected by a parasite that can go all through the pack and be exceedingly difficult to get rid of later. So the foster mother is not an unmitigated blessing, and both Xenophon and Arrian were wise in suggesting that she be avoided.

The usual solution in most hound kennels today, and perhaps the solution in ancient Greece, is to keep only as many puppies as the mother can feed by herself and destroy the others as painlessly as possible. Choosing which to keep is not easy, for who can say which of two creatures, neither any bigger than a chipmunk, is going to have the better nose, the better cry, the better drive, stamina, and speed? Modern masters frequently choose on the basis of color alone, unless the puppies show marked differences in size and vigor. The Roman writer Nemesianus suggests letting the mother choose.[19] He puts the puppies in a heap apart from her, builds a ring of fire around them, and then watches to see which she chooses to rescue first. He assumes that she will save the best first, but how can he be sure she knows, and on what basis does she judge?

FEEDING

But whatever the method of selecting the best and reducing the litter to a manageable number, eventually they must all be weaned. The food offered them at first may be solid, but it must not be too hard or too rough. In order to soften it so that it was easy for the puppies to digest, the Greeks added milk to the hounds' regular diet.[20] The milk which they poured over the puppies' food may have been cow's milk, but to this day the Greeks do not use cow's milk for human consumption to any great extent, preferring sheep's milk instead. So we can hazard a guess about the puppies' diet: if they were very valuable puppies, they were probably given sheep's milk or goat's milk; but if they were considered very ordinary, then they got cow's milk or perhaps whey. Later, when they were no longer in need of milk, they were sometimes given the blood of the animals they were expected to hunt when grown, in order to make them hunt more keenly.[21]

The diet of the grown hounds (the very food over which the milk was poured for the puppies) was simply bread, sometimes made from wheat flour but more often from barley flour. At times it was given to the hounds dry, broken into chunks which they could tear and gnaw; but at other times it was soaked in a broth made of the water in which meat for the master had been cooked; and sometimes it was soaked in milk like the puppy food.[22]

Often the bread given the hounds was simply the soft part from the inside of the loaf which had been used for wiping grease from the fingers of diners at the master's table. For a large pack of hounds, however, the supply of this sort of bread would not have been adequate, even in a very large household; and therefore another variety of bread was used, prepared especially for the purpose. In addition, the hounds were also fed scraps of meat and bones; and sometimes the liver of an ox was rubbed in barley meal and roasted in the embers of the fire.[23] Also the huntsman cut up pieces of the game he had caught, particularly if the animal was not one eaten by men, and fed that to the hounds. On festival days the hounds were given a share of the general banquet, although, like the gods, they got the parts the men didn't want.

Was such a diet adequate? At first glance it may seem to the amateur heavy in starches and light in protein, for dogs are popularly supposed to live on meat, the rawer and redder the better. On second thought it sounds much like the diet of table scraps most people fed their dogs before the days of prepared dog foods and therefore probably unbalanced and deficient in essential minerals and vitamins.

Before evaluating this diet, let us first consider what the modern foxhound was fed before the days of prepared dog foods. The usual diet was a pudding made from oatmeal into which a little horsemeat had been thrown while it was cooking. After cooking, it was allowed to dry on a wire screen and then at feeding time was cut into chunks, which were thrown into the feeding trough. Over this was poured a hot broth made of horsemeat with vegetables, so that the oatmeal pudding would be rendered hot and tasty. Thousands and thousands of foxhounds have been fed this pudding and have thrived on it.[24] Only since World War II have prepared dog foods taken its place to any great extent, and then not so much for the purpose of improving the diet as to save the extra manpower required to make the oatmeal pudding.

There is such a marked similarity between the oatmeal pudding and the bread and broth that there is every reason to believe hounds did well in ancient Greece. It is not hard to understand why when we consider the diet of the dog in the wild state.[25] In the wild state the dog hunts small herbivorous and graminivorous animals such as rabbits, hares, squirrels, chipmunks, raccoons, and opossums. When he kills one, the first thing he does is to tear open the stomach of his catch and eat the contents, which are largely vegetables and cereals. Next he eats the liver, heart, kidneys, and stomach. Not until then does he eat the flesh, the very meat that is popularly supposed to be his principal diet. Finally, he eats the bones and perhaps even the skin. In this way he gets a diet that is well balanced and full of minerals and vitamins.

The diet of the Greek hound, therefore, was not so very different from the ideal diet and was balanced in much the same way as that of his wild forebears. Certainly if, as Aristotle says, the hard-working Laconian hound could live to be ten or twelve years old and other breeds fourteen or fifteen, the diet fed them must have been satisfactory. Indeed, modern dogs seldom live as long; certainly foxhounds do not. In this respect, at least, we need not feel sorry for the ancient Greek hound.

KENNELS AND BEDDING

The old saw that the Greeks had a word for everything is not quite true. They had no word for doghouse, and none for kennel; neither can be found in Greek literature anywhere, so far as I can discover, and certainly not in Liddell and Scott's big lexicon. There is very little said on the subject in Latin either.

Odysseus found his old dog Argus sleeping on a dunghill, neglected by the household.[26] Where, we may ask, did he sleep when in his prime? Xenophon does not mention the subject of housing and bedding for hounds at all. Cato the Elder, the next writer to tell about the care of hounds, says only that guard dogs should be chained during the day so that they might be more alert at night.[27] Varro, writing about farm dogs, speaks about giving puppies a bed of chaff because it is soft and recommends that on rainy days the kennel—the first time the word occurs—should be bedded with leaves or fodder, both to keep the dogs dry and to keep them warm.[28] Arrian recommends that each hunt servant—there must have been as many servants as hounds—take a hound to bed with him, partly so that the servant might keep closer watch on the physical condition of the hound and partly because, he said, when hounds were bedded together the smell became intolerable, and the hounds mangy.[29] Obviously somebody had tried bedding them together. Arrian also recommends keeping hounds tied up during the day except when they were taken out for exercise; Nemesianus recommends exactly the opposite.[30] If they were not tied up, where were they kept? Hounds, he said, should not be chained up nor should they be shut up, because they would gnaw and tear at the doors. Doors of what? The author of the *Geoponica* suggests straw bedding for puppies in order to keep them warm.[31]

From what is not said about kennels in Greek literature and from the very little said about them in Latin, we can come to either of two conclusions: first, the Greeks had no kennels, but the Romans did; or, nobody had kennels in the early days, but they began to build them later. The first seems most unlikely. Rather, it seems reasonable to believe that originally hounds were simply kept in the courtyard of the house and given a pile of leaves, straw, or chaff on which to lie. They can never have been allowed perfect freedom, for, of all dogs, hounds are the most likely to wander off in search of something to chase.

In later centuries, however, the corner where the hounds had their bed was roofed over, or shut in, and finally both, thus forming the first kennels. We can date the first kennels only roughly. There were evidently none in Xenophon's day; there were definitely some in Varro's day. The first kennels, therefore, must have been built between the middle of the fourth century B.C. and the middle of the first, for Varro's book was written in 36 B.C.

EXERCISE AND TRAINING

As has often been said, every dog loves to go for a walk, and in this respect hounds are no different from other dogs. In the best-managed foxhound kennels today the hounds are taken out for a walk, usually on the roads, every day that they do not hunt, Sundays excepted.[32] When the hunting season has just ended, they are first given a brief rest and then the walks are resumed, but for no longer than an hour each day; and the hunt servants accompany the hounds on foot. But in the six weeks before the beginning of the next season, the walk is two or perhaps three hours long; and the men go out on their horses so that they can get the hounds and the horses used to each other and get all the animals fit by giving them work at speed, thus opening up their pipes and developing their wind.

Three things are accomplished by the daily walk, whether long or short: First, the hounds are given regular exercise in measured amounts, so that they may be kept healthy and in good condition and may be properly prepared for the hard work they will have to do during the hunting season. Second, the kennels are made easier to keep clean, and the chances of infection from worms is greatly reduced; for every time the hounds start walking out, most of them empty, and it is much better to have this happen outside than inside the kennels. Third, the more often the hounds are taken out by the hunt servants, the more readily they will obey, even though the hunt servants do nothing deliberately to teach them. The mere practice of calling them by name and of handling them makes them more obedient and, of course, keeps the hunt servants from becoming self-conscious when training them, a thing that makes the training ineffective.

Greek hounds were taken out in the same way, but with two slight differences: First, they were taken out four times a day instead of just once, so the chance of their emptying in the courtyard was greatly reduced. Second, they were taken out on leashes instead of loose and were let loose two at a time so that they could play and answer nature's needs.[33] Thus they obtained exactly the same benefits that the modern hound gets; for every time they were let loose and every time they were called back and tied up again, they received practice in obeying and at the same time learned their names.

Xenophon has given us a list of forty-seven names that he considered suitable for hounds,[34] some of which had probably been used by other masters, but some, according to Arrian, names which Xenophon had himself invented. They were all two-syllable names, easy to call out, and either indicative of the appearance or character of the hounds, or else with some military or hunting significance. In many ways they are like the names used for English foxhounds today, although not all of the modern names are limited to two syllables. It is possible that the modern names were derived from Xenophon's, for classical education was common among the people who kept hounds in England during the seventeenth century, when the great ducal packs of foxhounds were developed.

But if English hound names are not all disyllabic, neither were all the Greek. Pollux gives fifteen hound names, of which seven are disyllabic and eight are not;[35] Ovid, although writing in Latin, gives the Greek names of Actaeon's hounds, thirty-six in number, of which fifteen are disyllabic and twenty-one are not.[36] Columella, writing at about the same time as Ovid, gives a few examples of both Greek and Latin names, all disyllabic. It is obvious from these examples that hounds were named in much the same way they are today, sometimes systematically and sometimes whimsically, and that the names used were intended to convey something of the appearance, character, or desired character of the hounds, or to suggest the struggle they were engaged in while hunting.

The fact that names were supposed to be short enough to use when calling hounds is in itself an indication that hounds were trained to come when called. They would, of course, soon learn their names when they were slipped and taken up again whenever they went out for a walk, but something more had to be done to teach them to come when called. That something was to feed them near the nets when out hunting and to let no one but the huntsman give them their food at that time.[37] This practice was discontinued at the time the young entry began to show interest in catching its quarry, so we can be sure that this was the time when the young entry learned to come when called. As to how obedient the hounds were, we may have some doubts, for the Greeks did not trust them loose except when hunting. On the other hand, there is no indication that they had any difficulty getting the hounds back when they called them, and for many centuries to come, nobody, excepting possibly the Cretans, ever let hounds loose anyway.

After preliminary training in obedience, the hounds had to learn to hunt. The method used for training them depended on whether they were to be used for tracking or for running at sight. If they were tracking hounds, they had to learn to keep their noses down, regardless of how tempting the things they saw. If they were gazehounds, they had to learn to run by sight, regardless of what temptation came to their noses.

The training of tracking hounds, according to Xenophon, began when the bitches were at least eight months old (Pollux says six) and the doghounds ten (Pollux says eight), that is, some time during the autumn or winter following whelping. This is one year earlier than we start them; but on the other hand, we expect them to learn something when they are sent out to neighboring farmers to be raised. The system was as follows: The huntsman took them on long leashes and followed the older tracking hounds while they ran the trail of a hare to her form. When the hare had been started, he held the puppies back and allowed the hare plenty of time to get a headstart, so that there would be no chance that they would run her by sight. Then he let them go. If they lost her, he called them in quickly so that they would not get in the habit of casting about aimlessly. If, on the other hand, they ran her down, he let them break her up as a reward for a good job well done.[38]

For exercise and discipline, the hounds were taken into rough mountain country and worked there whether there was a hare to be found or not.[39] They were taken frequently to different coverts so that they would learn their way around[40] and learn the habits of individual hares. The running of foxes was discouraged,[41] for the scent of the fox is stronger than that of any animal excepting the deer, and hounds that have learned to hunt the fox will not do well on hare.

The training of gazehounds began at a slightly greater age, according to Arrian, eleven months for the bitches and two years for the doghounds.[42] This difference may have been due to the difference in the breeds used, for Xenophon was discussing the Laconian hound, and Arrian the Celtic greyhound. At any rate, the procedure was exactly the opposite. To make certain the puppy had a good view, the huntsman released the hare from nearby—not so near that the hare would become confused but near enough for the puppy to know what to run.[43] Then, in order to teach the puppy the purpose of the chase, the huntsman slipped an older hound also and let it demonstrate to the puppy how to kill the hare. After that the puppy was allowed to break up the hare, for all hounds enjoy doing so and the practice serves as a reward and incentive for the next hunt.

Although the two types of hounds were expected to hunt in exactly opposite ways, both types were expected to give tongue whenever they were on the line of their quarry[44] so that the huntsman could tell whether they were really running something or just playing. The use of mute hounds that would sneak up silently on their quarry and then grab it before it had warning did not begin until Roman times.[45] Such hounds, of course, were the forerunners, if not the progenitors, of modern gundogs which must hunt in silence.

But if the Greeks had not yet learned to let their hounds run free, as we do, or had no hunting dogs that would work silently, as our gundogs must, they had learned two very important principles of hound management: first, that the way to train hounds is by the system of rewarding for obedience and punishing for disobedience, just as Xenophon explained he did with horses,[46] and, second, that one must never deceive hounds with false promises but must be absolutely honest with them.[47]

DISEASES AND CURES

Although Hippocrates, the father of Greek medicine, lived and flourished in the fifth century before Christ, there was no science of veterinary medicine for several centuries. Xenophon, although an authority on both horses and hounds, says next to nothing about the diseases with which he must have had to contend, remarking only that hounds with poor feet cannot hunt and that overfeeding puppies can make them ill.[48] Aristotle touches on the subject briefly in his *History of Animals*, referring to the three diseases of dogs which he considered worst,[49] but his primary concern was with natural history, not veterinary medicine. That science did not exist as a separate discipline until the first century after Christ, when *hippiatrici* began practicing on the larger farm animals when their ills were too serious for the farmer and his servants to cope with. Before Aristotle's time nothing was said about the ailments for which dogs suffered (barring rabies), although we can be sure that dogs suffered all the diseases that they do today.

The three diseases from which dogs suffer, said Aristotle, were "raging madness," "dog-throttle," and "foot-seize." The words I use here are literal translations of the Greek. There is no question what "raging madness" was: it was rabies. The symptoms were the same as those of the modern disease; the method of transmission was identical; and it was just as serious. Every authority on the subject is agreed that it was rabies. It is true that a few manuscripts of Aristotle exempt man from the certainty of death if he should contract the disease, but most of them do not. The possibility that man might be exempt may have crept into the manuscripts in Roman times, when wishful thinkers had discovered a sure cure, a fetid extract from the beaver, rubbed with flint, mixed with a powder made from chopped ivory, stirred into milk, and then inserted down the throat of the victim through a horn.[50] Whether the victim died from the disease or the cure is not told. In addition to this remedy, the Romans had a preventative. This was to cut the "worm" which can be seen under the tongue and then treat the wound with salt and olive oil.[51] The only other treatment of which we know is that described in the *Geoponica* compiled by Cassianus Bassus, a late work. Mad dogs were to be confined underground, given nothing to eat for one day, and then given hellebore with their drink. When they had been purged, they were given a little barley bread. The same treatment was recommended for persons bitten by them.[52] But in spite of these supposed cures, the disease was usually considered incurable.

Aristotle's second disease, "dog-throttle," has been variously translated as "quinsy," "dog-quinsy" (whatever that is supposed to be), and "sore throat," but the disease that comes to a hound man's mind as the most probable is distemper. There are several kinds of distemper, but one of the most common kinds is a pulmonary distemper which produces symptoms, such as great difficulty in breathing, that make the name "dog-throttle" particularly appropriate. Furthermore, distemper has been (at least until the last ten years or so, when an excellent preventative treatment has become available) one of the most serious diseases with which the owner of dogs has been faced, and thousands of puppies have been carried off by it every year.

At any rate, I inquired of Dr. Hadley C. Stephenson, D.V.M., Consultant to the Research Laboratory for Diseases of Dogs at Cornell University, what he thought these diseases might have been. He told me that there is no doubt whatsoever about the meaning of "raging madness." It means rabies. "Dog-throttle," he said, was distemper; and he advised me that Professor J. F. Smithcors, of Michigan State University, in a history of veterinary medicine, was of the same opinion.

So we can accept the conclusion that "raging madness" was rabies, certainly the most serious disease a dog can have; and be fairly certain that "dog-throttle" was distemper, although there is always the possibility that it might have been canine hepatitis, which closely resembles some forms of distemper and has only recently been distinguished from it. But "foot-seize" is puzzling. The Greek word for it is *podagra*, a word that can be found in most English-language dictionaries, defined as gout. When applied to human beings the word may very well mean gout; but when applied to dogs it must mean something else, because gout, according to Dr. Stephenson, is rarely seen or diagnosed in dogs. It is true, of course, that Dr. Smithcors believes the word means gout, but as Dr. Stephenson explained, Dr. Smithcors is an anatomist, not a clinician, and is not accustomed to diagnosing dog diseases. Dr. Stephenson, a clinician, is strongly inclined to believe the disease is some form of arthritis of the foot or leg. Dogs may, of course, have lame feet for any one of a number of reasons. Sometimes the ligaments of the toes give way, just as the ligaments in the human foot do when humans have fallen arches. This failure is called "toes down," and although common in the earlier part of the century in the English foxhound of the so-called Peterborough type, an animal bred to stand in an exaggeratedly high position on its tiptoes,[53] rarely occurs today. Sometimes hounds step on nails, thorns, cacti, or barbed wire. Sometimes they wear down the pads of their feet, if they have not had their feet hardened sufficiently before running on rocky ground. Another kind of foot trouble, known in England as "kennel lameness," was supposedly due to lying too much on damp floors in the kennels. Possibly this is "foot-seize," for kennel lameness may very well be a form of arthritis. Certainly arthritis is a thing from which few dogs recover, as Aristotle says about "foot-seize." Anyway, the best translation for "foot-seize" which we can offer is "arthritis of the foot or leg."

Another serious problem in antiquity, although Aristotle did not mention it, was mange. There are two kinds, the sarcoptic type, sometimes called scabies; and the follicular or demodectic type, sometimes called red mange.[54] Sarcoptic mange is the commoner and the less difficult to cure; follicular mange is so difficult that it is often thought better to destroy the victim before he infects others than to attempt to cure him—and probably fail. Although both kinds were probably common in antiquity, no distinction was made, and in fact other skin troubles, such as eczema, were probably included under the same general heading. If the mange was very bad, the first victim to get the disease was destroyed; if it was not very serious, there was a treatment available: a compound of bitumen, wine, pitch, and dregs of olive oil was to be rubbed into the skin. Another compound was made of gypsum and sesame, mixed with an equal amount of liquid pitch. The destruction of the first victim, in the bad cases, indicates follicular mange; the compounds rubbed into the skin are very like our own sulphur and lard or sulphur and lime treatments, admittedly not the last word in veterinary medicine, but surprisingly effective. Perhaps the ancient treatments were just as good.

Besides mange, Greek hounds had worms, of course. The earliest evidence of them is Xenophon's remark that "heavy satiety in whelps distorts their legs, creates illness in their bodies, and makes their inner parts go wrong."[55] From this description we can visualize pot-bellied, bow-legged little puppies filled with roundworms. Now roundworms are the commonest of all intestinal parasites in dogs; tapeworms are very common, particularly in dogs which hunt rabbits and hares; and both are visible to the naked eye. Whipworms too can be seen; but the most difficult type of worm with which the modern master of hounds has to contend is the hookworm, for it is so small that it can be seen only under the microscope; and hunt servants therefore will not believe it exists and tend to let it go unchecked.

There are a number of other varieties of worms, but whichever kinds the Greeks had, they lumped them together and gave the hounds either of two treatments. One was to let the hounds eat the awns of standing grain, the whiskers projecting out from the head of a stalk of wheat.[56] The other was to give them wormwood,[57] an aromatic plant used today to flavor absinthe. It is in fact a vermifuge, but it is hard to believe it could have been very effective, because no treatment will succeed in ridding a pack of any kind of worms unless there is also a very thorough cleaning of the kennels at the same time, so that the worm eggs will be destroyed and the danger of reinfection removed. Although the method by which a dog becomes infected with worms varies somewhat with the type of worm, the essential step to prevent reinfection is the destruction of the eggs. Both the knowledge and the sanitary measures available in ancient Greece were wholly inadequate to do so.

Flies, fleas, and ticks were other creatures that tormented Greek dogs. To keep flies off the ears, a solution of crushed bitter almonds was applied,[58] but if the ears were already very sore, they were swabbed with a mixture of liquid pitch and tar, much as they are swabbed with pine tar today. The purpose was, and is, simply to keep more flies from biting. Ticks were taken off with this same pitch mixed with lard, but fleas were treated with cyprine oil, hellebore and water, cumin, and sour grapes, as well as with cucumber juice and sea water.

Treatment for wounds was drastic but probably fairly effective. If it was a big wound, it was sewed up with fine thread,[59] but if small, it was simply smeared with black pitch. Should the wound fester, it was kept open, as it should be. Except for the lack of any good way of keeping infection out of the wounds, a difficult thing with dogs anyway, the treatment sounds reasonable. The one method which was suggested for keeping infection out of a wound was to sprinkle it with the urine of the wild beast which caused it. Fortunately it was a practical impossibility for the huntsman to collect the urine of boars, bears, lions, and tigers, so the hounds escaped this treatment.

Although veterinary science did become a separate profession after Aristotle's time, it remained based largely on his observations and made little if any further progress until modern times.

And when thou hast on foot the purblind hare,
Mark the poor wretch, to overshoot his troubles,
How he outruns the wind, and with what care
He cranks and crosses with a thousand doubles....
  Shakespeare, Venus and Adonis, *679–82*

IV Hare Hunting

BREEDS OF HARES

When Xenophon speaks of hares, many Americans automatically assume that he is talking about cottontail rabbits, which in this country come in fifty-seven varieties,[1] like pickles. They assume that the translators have committed a Briticism for they believe *hare* to be obsolete, or at least obsolescent, in the United States, a literary word, suitable perhaps for translating a dead language, but no longer in good colloquial use here. Besides, they say, aren't hares and rabbits the same? Naturally, there are several varieties; but what real difference is there between a hare and a rabbit? Why not use the more natural-sounding word? It is much less stilted and affected to say "rabbit."

The reason for using different words, as every European knows, is that the hare and the rabbit, although cousins of a sort, are different animals. We in the United States have been confused and have not made the distinction because the common brown hare of Europe is extraordinarily rare here and because the few breeds of hare with which we are familiar are called by misleading names; the jackrabbit is a good example.

It is not hard to tell the hare and the rabbit apart. Rabbits are born blind; hares are born with their eyes open. Rabbits are born naked; hares are born fully clothed in fur.[2] Rabbits live in burrows (whence comes their former name, "cony,"[3] a word derived from the Latin *cuniculus*, which also means "little tunnel"); hares live in the open in shallow nests or squatting places called "forms," or "seats."[4] Rabbits, when chased, run straight for the nearest hole or, if forced to stay above ground, run in little circles while searching for a place to hide; hares run in large circles, depending on their speed to elude their pursuers, but eventually return to the place where they were first found and started. Rabbits run no more than twenty or twenty-five miles an hour; hares run thirty-five or forty-five.[5] Wild rabbits weigh from three to three and a half pounds;[6] hares weigh from seven to eight and have been reported as heavy as eleven.[7] The hare is a clean and fastidious animal and will not eat where rabbits have moved in and soiled the ground; indeed, the smaller animals are more aggressive and actually drive the larger ones away, so no country remains inhabited by both creatures for long; they simply do not get along together well. If we examine the two creatures closely, we see that they do not look as much alike as we thought: hares have bigger heads, longer ears, and much longer legs than rabbits. Futhermore, there is no question of the fact that the two do not interbreed.[8] So if we can be sure that the Greeks could distinguish hares from rabbits, we can be sure that they hunted hares if they said they did.

There is no doubt whatsoever of their ability to distinguish the two animals. Polybius, writing during the second century before Christ, tells about rabbits that lived on the island of Corsica and remarks that although they look like small hares when seen from a distance, they are distinctly different when seen from nearby; he says further that their flesh tastes different.[9] He told about them because they were at that time unknown in Greece. Later writers, like Aelian and Pliny, also refer to the rabbit; and it is from these writers that we learn that the animal was first seen in what is now Spain, lived at first only in the western half of the Mediterranean basin, and was not known east of Sicily and southern Italy until several centuries after Polybius' time.[10] There is only one small doubt to cloud our certainty that Aesop's tortoise raced a hare: Aristotle says that the young of the hare are born blind.[11] Had he by any chance seen a litter of rabbits? If so, where? Was he repeating something that someone else, perhaps someone from Magna Graecia, had told him? Was he simply guessing? We can't tell, but we can still be confident that in this case Aristotle was wrong, whatever may have been the reason.

So we can assume that the animals Xenophon calls hares really were hares and can go ahead and try to discover what kinds they were. Although he speaks of "mountain hares," "plains hares," and "marsh hares,"[12] he does so only to note the different behavior of hares that live in the mountains, the plains, and the marshes. He makes this fact clear because farther on he speaks of two different breeds and describes them carefully. The first of these, he says, was rather large and rather dark (perhaps, as Pollux says,[13] similar in shade to a half-ripe olive, neither light nor wholly black); it had a white star on the forehead, blue eyes, black on the tips of the ears, and spots around the scut. The second was smaller, yellower in color, with a smaller star on the forehead, gray eyes, very little black on the tips of the ears, and spots on either side of the scut.[14]

From these descriptions, it seems probable that both were varieties of the common brown or European hare, *Lepus europaeus*, which some authorities divide into three smaller groups.[15] The first (and largest in size) of these is found in northeastern Europe; the second (and middle-sized), both in England and in central and southern Europe; and the third (and smallest), around the Mediterranean basin. Of course we cannot be positive that two or three thousand years ago the same breeds of hare lived in the same regions that they live in today or that there has been no change in the appearance of any of the breeds during that time. Minor shifts of animal population are always occurring: some areas no longer can support wildlife; places that were barren become stocked by accident or intention; and some areas become depopulated because of disease, predation, too much hunting, or simply starvation, the commonest cause of all.

But we have no evidence that there have been any major shifts in population or that any change has occurred in the species themselves, and Xenophon's descriptions of the two breeds he knew fit both the central and southern European type and the Mediterranean type of common brown hare closely enough. The only other breed of hare that he might possibly have meant is the varying hare, *Lepus timidus*, known also as the blue or mountain hare; but the description which Xenophon gives will not fit, for the varying hare is both smaller and bluer; it has more black on the tips of the ears than the larger hare, not less; and more important still, it usually lives in colder climates than those in which Xenophon was accustomed to hunt, places like the Alps, which do have the varying hare, as Pliny discovered, for he says that this hare is white in winter because it eats the snow[16] but changes its color to brown in summer. It is this change of coat color, of course, that has given the varying hare its name. It is unlikely that Xenophon ever saw one.

FAMILY LIFE OF THE HARE

It is very difficult for anyone to tell the sex of a hare from a distance, for the differences between the jack and the doe are practically invisible on casual inspection. The two beasts are about the same size, shape, and coloring; and there are no distinctive markings, such as there are on many birds, for example. As a result many people have fanciful theories about how to tell the sexes apart at a glance. Some people say that if a fleeing hare holds one ear forward and the other back, it is a jack; but that if it holds both back, it is a doe.[17] In the Middle Ages it was believed that the farther it held its ears back, the more timid it was.[18] There are some who say that

62

only male leverets in a litter have white stars on their foreheads; still others believe this mark indicates only the number of the leverets in the litter.[19] But whatever the truth about these beliefs, none have been scientifically attested, and all can probably be put down as old wives' tales.

In antiquity people had some theories that were even more fantastic. Aristotle says that the female hare is sometimes seen to cover the male.[20] Considering how difficult it is to tell one sex from the other, we may well wonder how he knew. Was he perhaps repeating what he had heard from others? Usually he identifies hearsay, but sometimes he extends a theory to situations in which it does not fit the facts.

But such was Aristotle's reputation that everything he said was repeated for centuries, sometimes with understanding but often without. What he said about the mating of hares led to much confusion about their sex. Aelian, for instance, writing at about the beginning of the third century after Christ, tells a tale related to him by a man whose word, he says, could be trusted absolutely: a male hare had given birth to leverets.[21] If a male could give birth to leverets, it was obvious that the hare could perform the functions of either sex at will, and such was the belief in the seventh century.[22] By the eleventh century, she was thought to change her sex every month.[23] Like compound interest, confusion increased rapidly with the passage of the centuries.

Conversely, the earlier Greeks had more accurate ideas. Xenophon was well aware of the amorous nature of the hare and noticed that the most active breeding season was in the early spring, when the jacks become playful, or, as we say, "mad as March hares,"[24] and, if there are more jacks than does in the neighborhood, they engage in frequent fights, which, so long as the combat is conducted solely with the forelegs, are full of fur and fury, miniature but bloodless boxing matches, but if the powerful hindlegs are brought into action, are likely to be fatal to one of the combatants.[25]

Not only was the hare known to be amorous, but she was given an astonishing reputation for high productivity. Beginning with Herodotus, Greek authors who wrote about the hare all remarked that she superfoetates; that is, she was supposed to be pregnant with more than one litter at a time, so just as she has finished bearing one litter, she has a second still in the making, while a third is just being conceived.[26]

Now there is no doubt that the hare is prolific, but the real reason that she multiplies so fast lies not in her individual capacity as a producer but in the speed with which her young mature and begin producing litters of their own. The hare herself usually has only one or two leverets at a time, sometimes three, but seldom more.[27] She has no more than perhaps three litters in a year—some say that young does have only one—so her year's production could not be over nine at the most and, more likely, only three or four. But these young mature so rapidly that they may have litters of their own before the year is out; that is, doe leverets born in late March may kittle in August. Theoretically, therefore, the original doe will have nine of her own in one year; the second generation will have eighteen; and the third generation, twenty-seven, making a grand total of fifty-four, not including the original doe. Practically, of course, the number will be nowhere nearly so many; but in fact it doesn't matter, because even if she had all fifty-four, the factor that restricts expansion and prevents a population explosion is the food supply, aided by disease, accident, and predation. This limits her considerably.

As to the astonishing idea that the hare superfoetates, it is, even more astonishingly, true, even though the overlapping of the periods of gestation is only from one to five days[28] and cannot really be said to contribute much to the hare's high rate of productivity. What is extraordinary is that Herodotus, Xenophon, and Aristotle knew it so many centuries ago.

The jack is faithful to his mate only so long as his family is growing, and he seems to take some interest in protecting them,[29] but as soon as the leverets are able to take care of themselves, he moves on in search of another mate. The doe is a good mother, and in spite of her apparent carelessness in leaving one little leveret here and another there, she keeps an eye on all. She scatters them for a purpose, and that is to protect them.[30] One little leveret alone keeps absolutely motionless and is almost impossible to see because it blends into the background well—Xenophon observed this same thing about older hares[31]—but two or more are likely to wiggle and then be seen. The doe seems instinctively to know this and to realize that by separating them she ensures the survival of one, should the others be found.

This system of dispersal, this plan of not putting all her leverets in one nest, is probably the thing that made Aristotle believe that the hare gave birth to her young one at a time at different times.[32] At any rate the system does help the race to survive, for the young are beset by many perils. Foxes do catch them, although perhaps not by harrying and chivvying them until they are exhausted, as Aelian believes;[33] and eagles,[34] as well as hawks, do swoop down on them and carry them off; so in spite of all the doe's precautions and in spite of their extraordinarily rapid growth, only a relatively small proportion of those born survives.

HABITS AND CHARACTERISTICS

The hare makes her form wherever there is a projecting tuft of grass or clump of vegetation,[35] preferring the wide open places where she can often find a point of vantage on top of a hill so that she can see approaching enemies from a distance.[36] Still, as Pollux points out, she does not disdain the forests and the shelter of thick bushes. In summer she prefers the cool and shady places; but in winter, the warm and sunny places, unless the ground is covered with snow, in which case she may camouflage her form by picking a hollow spot in the snow where she may lie and there appear exactly like a rounded boulder.[37]

She does most of her foraging by night, not for the sake of finding strange food, as Aelian thought,[38] but simply because she finds the night safer for eating and for nursing her leverets. What she eats, however, either escaped the notice of the Greeks, or else (and more probably) they did not think clover, young shoots of wheat, turnips and carrots, or similar cereals and vegetables worthy of the notice of a hunting man.

They observed her conformation with considerable accuracy. Aristotle, for example, says that the hare has fur on the soles of her feet and on the inside of her mouth.[39] She was, indeed, called "shaggy-foot," and Aristotle was right about her feet. This is what makes it easy for her to run well on ice, but it does hamper her badly on soft snow or in mud, because she collects great balls and blobs on the hair of her feet and consequently tires rapidly. As to hair inside her mouth, there is none, of course, and it is hard to imagine how Aristotle got the idea that there was.

Another idea that originated in antiquity and has persisted for many centuries is the idea that the hare always sleeps with her eyes open.[40] Perhaps we should question what the Greeks meant by sleep, for although the hare is extremely watchful and keeps her eyes open a large part of the time, she does not keep them open when in deep sleep; but, on the other hand, she goes sound asleep very little. Aristotle did not say that the hare slept with her eyes open; he said that all animals that are "red-blooded and provided with legs" close their eyes when they sleep, providing that they have eyelids.[41] Xenophon gives us the impression in one place that he thought the hare has no eyelids,[42] but in another he says that she blinks her eyes when awake.[43] Hares need eyelids to wipe the corneas of their eyes clean (in the same way a windshield wiper cleans the windshield) just as all warm-blooded animals do. Later writers, basing their statements on what authorities had said, repeated the story that the hare slept with her eyes open, so for centuries everybody believed it.

The Greeks had another notion that was even stranger, however, and concerned the use the hare makes of her ears for steering her body. We know, of course, that the horse balances himself with his head and neck[44] and that all four-legged animals use similar means of balancing; the dog, for instance, unless it has been docked, uses not only its head and neck but also its tail. The Greeks had evidently observed this, for Xenophon says[45] that since the hare's scut is too small for steering, she uses her ears for that purpose, not just employing them for balancing, but using them to push herself around a corner, just as we might use a pole to push a raft away from the bank of a stream. Pollux suggests that she uses her ears to row herself along, as if with oars;[46] Aelian even says she uses them to goad herself to greater exertion, as if with spurs.[47]

A few more strange misconceptions occur, but the worst of them are found only in late Greek or Latin authors; the Greeks of the Periclean age knew better. One is the theory that the age of a hare could be told by the number of apertures for elimination which she had beneath her scut.[48] How such nonsense could have originated is hard to understand. Another misconception, however, has a simple enough explanation: Aelian says in two places that the hares of Bisaltia, a part of Macedonia not far from present-day Thessalonike, had double livers.[49] Aristotle, however, had said that the shape of the liver in these animals might conceivably lead people to believe they had two livers.[50] Aristotle had probably dissected these hares; Aelian wrote only what he had read elsewhere. Another theory was that you could predict the weather by observing the number of hares;[51] the modern counterpart of this idea is that the behavior of hares will give you a clue to the weather.[52] Old wives' tales are common to all ages.

On the whole the Greeks had a pretty good idea of the natural history of the hare, and lest any of us feel superior to them, we might note one detail of the hare's natural history which has escaped the notice of all but hare-hunters today, but which the Greeks seemed to know well. Xenophon tells us that hares will sometimes plunge into the sea or into fresh water.[53] Of course they did; the hare, as few people today realize, is an excellent swimmer, and although she hates to get her fur wet, she has been known to cross considerable bodies of water, in some instances as wide as a mile, when she has been compelled by force of circumstances.[54]

SCENT OF THE HARE[55]

The behavior of scent, the mysterious way in which it appears and disappears, getting worse just when the huntsman thinks it should be getting better and suddenly improving for no good reason at all, is a thing familiar to everyone who has ever hunted a pack of hounds. It is a phenomenon as old as hunting. The Greeks and many others before them had the same difficulties we have today, and their huntsmen made observations about scent and its nature that were as accurate as any made by hunting people since.

Of course the Greeks could not know some of the chemical and physical facts that we know today, so they made a few very natural mistakes; but the modern huntsman has made his share of silly errors, too, so we can't afford to be too critical. Indeed, the number of huntsmen who have a scientific knowledge of scent is trivial, and even if the number were large, the difficulty of applying that knowledge during a hunt is almost insuperable. There simply isn't time. Hunting is still an art and not an exact science, and the Greeks had a flair for the split-second decisions necessary for it.

But before we discuss what they knew about scent, let us review the elementary physical facts involved, in order to have a suitable background for our discussion.

The sources of scent in all animals are the glands involved in the production of the waste products of the body, namely, feces, urine, sweat, saliva, the breath, and the horny growth of the hoofs, claws, horns, or nails. The chemicals producing the scent substance vary from species to species and are determined by the food consumed by the animal and by the way the animal lives. Even when the scent substances are similar, the proportions of the chemicals vary. We know that in some animals the scent substance comes from the anal glands; but in others, from the sweat glands; while in still others, from a mixture of the two. Furthermore, even the sweat glands are not located in exactly the same places in all animals. Thus the fox, like the dog, has no sweat glands on the surface of its body but only between the toes; the scent which interests the hounds is probably not the "foxy" smell which humans notice but the pad scent from between the toes, which is left in the footprints. The fox, however, does have a strong scent from its anal glands; this is the "foxy" smell. The deer has a scent which comes from its hoofs, and this too is the scent which interests the hounds the most. The scent of the hare, however, may be something else,

68

for it is not only much more subtle than that of either the fox or the deer but is said to be more persistent. Perhaps it is body scent; we are not sure.

We simply do not know just what chemical substances cause the scents, and even if we did, we would still be faced with the difficulty of determining which are of interest to the noses of hounds. But we do know how the scents behave. Whatever they are, they are carried in an oil vehicle and must also be very volatile so that they will evaporate. Furthermore, they do not evaporate easily and directly from the oil which carries them; the oil must first be spread out thin on the surface of the water so that when the water evaporates the oil will be carried into the air. Since the particles of water that are carried into the air are very small, it is probable that the film of oil on the water is no more than one molecule in thickness, and the particles of scent material carried by the oil must be just as small. Indeed, they must be extraordinarily small if twenty or thirty hounds are able to perceive them in a path perhaps fifteen feet wide and six or eight miles long. All this scent material must be produced by one hare, and yet so little is produced that it is impossible to detect any loss of weight in the hare's body after a run. Her ability to produce scent is, however, not unlimited; her glands run out of material, and the scent she produces weakens or changes the farther she runs, for sometimes the sinking hare seems to leave no scent at all and sometimes her scent seems to stimulate the hounds more than ever.

Because the scent material is distributed by evaporation, the most important factor in determining whether scenting conditions will be good or bad is the ability of the air to absorb the moisture that carries the scent material. This material must be in suspension in the air and not just lying on the ground, for it must reach the inside of the hounds' nostrils and of course it must be suspended at a height the hounds can reach.

The amount of moisture the air will absorb is determined by its temperature; hot air will absorb more moisture than cold. The degree of moisture in the air is called its relative humidity, that is, the amount of moisture relative to saturation, measured in percentage. As saturation varies with temperature, the relative humidity of the air will change with changes in temperature, but inversely: with rising air temperature, relative humidity falls; and with falling air temperature, relative humidity rises. If the air temperature falls enough that the relative humidity reaches the saturation point, it rains; if cold outdoor air is brought indoors and heated without adding water, the relative humidity becomes uncomfortably low.

Now if the relative humidity of the air is very low, the air will absorb scent so rapidly and dilute it so much that it will not be perceptible to the hounds; but if the relative humidity is very high, the air will not absorb the scent at all. A moderate degree of relative humidity is therefore best for hunting so that the scent will be absorbed into the air but not scattered and diluted.

No huntsman can carry a hygrometer with him, and even if he could, he could not take the time to discover the relative humidity beneath every bush or clump of grass. All he can do is to notice the temperature of the air, the probable temperature of the ground, the direction and force of the wind, the pattern of shade caused by trees and various plantings, the moisture-absorbing qualities of the various plants, and make some sort of estimate on the basis of his experience. He will have enough other troubles created by the scents of some plants and of sheep and cattle to prevent his concern with scientific equipment. But with some understanding of the general conditions of the day's scenting, he will be ready to begin hunting.

PREPARATIONS

The preparations which the huntsman makes will depend on the motive behind his hunting; that is, if he hunts for the pot, he will make one kind of preparation; if solely for sport, he will make another. If he hunts for the purpose of destroying predators, he will make still other preparations.

Although originally hare hunting was primarily undertaken for the sake of filling the pot, it probably became a sport in fairly early days. In the classical period it was a mixture of sport and practical necessity, in this respect resembling our modern rabbit-hunters who go out with gun and dog to bring in a cottontail or two. But the possibility of cooking and eating the hare probably played a somewhat larger part in Greek hunting than it does in our cottontail hunting today, for although the Greeks, like most Mediterranean peoples, were cereal-eaters, they liked a little meat as a relish to break the monotony of bread and wheat pastes which they ate every day. So hare, although never a staple, was always a welcome addition to the menu.[56]

Preparations for a hunt varied according to the methods used, and these changed somewhat from century to century. We do not know just how hares were hunted in the heroic age, for although Homer tells us that they were hunted,[57] he does not tell us how; and there is little to be learned from archeology about this particular branch of hunting. Perhaps the heroes simply turned their hounds loose and followed after, hoping either that the hounds would run a hare down or that they might drive one near enough so that the hunters would have a chance to throw a stick or club at her and knock her over. Homer says little about hare hunting for the obvious reason that it was a much less heroic sport than hunting lions or wild boars, and even these sports appear to have been organized no more systematically than the Homeric armies, which, as we all remember, were little better than mobs.

But by the end of the fifth century before Christ, hare hunting was very thoroughly organized. It was normally undertaken on foot, in much the same way as modern beagling, for Xenophon makes it clear that the huntsman must be dressed lightly so that he can run after hounds, winding his cloak around his arm so that he can move easily.[58]

The idea was to find the trail of the hare—that is, the line of scent made by the hare when returning to her form after a night's foraging—follow her trail to her form, start her, and then run her into nets which had been set up in strategic places. The hunt therefore began about dawn, the exact time depending on the time of year.[59] The hounds were first brought to the covert side by hunt servants, who were of course slaves in those days, and tied to trees off to one side; each hound was tied separately[60] so that there would be no danger of the leashes getting tangled and thus delaying a quick start when everything was ready. We have no way of knowing exactly how many hounds were usually brought along, but if we can judge by the length of the hound lists of Xenophon and of Ovid,[61] bearing in mind that people of high social standing and people drawn from mythology would have more hounds than the average man, it seems probable that sixteen to twenty-four hounds —eight to twelve couples, we should say today—were about the usual number. Today we should take about the same number for beagling. To lead sixteen hounds to the covert side would require at least two hunt servants—modern French hunt servants bring up relays of eight big staghounds, led on leashes from horses—although it is difficult for one man to lead more than four hounds without getting all tangled up. So there may easily have been four or even more men leading the hounds.

When selecting a place to tie up the hounds, the huntsman was careful to choose a place downwind from the covert he planned to draw[62] and on higher ground also, if possible.[63] It was important that the scent of the hounds should not be carried to the hare before the hunt began; anyhow, hares, like all hunted animals, prefer to run downwind, in order to keep their own scent from being blown into the hounds' noses; so it was advantageous to be downwind to begin with. As to being on higher ground, hares always seek safety by running uphill,[64] so again the hounds would have the advantage.

While the hounds were waiting at the covert side, the net-watcher and his assistants set up the nets which they had brought with them in big leather bags. We can only guess how many such hunt servants there may have been—perhaps six, perhaps many more, and perhaps only two. The purse-nets were set up in the hare's meuses, that is, in gaps through walls, narrow passages between rocks, and similar defiles[65] through which the hares were accustomed to run, for hares, like many other wild creatures, have their customary paths which they follow when foraging. The road-nets were set up across paths and roads,[66] both the paths made by hu-

72

mans and the game paths made by animals, and particularly in places where such paths approached open fields, for the hare has a fondness for running roads,[67] knowing that roads are bad for scenting, and such places are likely to be the spots where she gets on and off the roads. The long-nets were set up on level ground[68] at the edge of the covert[69] so that the hare would run right into them when she was driven out.

THE CHASE

When everything was ready, a matter of only a few minutes,[70] the huntsman first prayed briefly to Apollo and Artemis, promising them their share of the day's catch—a very necessary procedure—and then slipped the hound with the keenest nose[71] to draw for the trail of the hare. As soon as this hound owned the scent and opened, he slipped a second hound and then a third, letting the rest of the pack follow, one by one, with little interval between. The first stage of the hunt, that of hunting the hare up to her form, was now under way.[72]

When the hounds reached the hare's form, she would usually be waiting for them, hoping that perhaps they would not notice her and would go away. But before they could grab her, she would bound away, leaving them in momentary confusion, but only for an instant, for they would at once be hot after her. Her pace at first was leisurely, for a hare is always confident of her ability to outwit and outrun the clumsy creatures that come after; indeed, she seems often to be saving her strength in case she might need it later, rather than waste it on unnecessary speed at the beginning[73] as a young leveret might do. Then, after a little, when she was comfortably ahead of the hounds, she would sit up and look back at her enemies struggling after,[74] just as she does today.

The hare has many tricks that she has been using for thousands of years in order to throw her pursuers off her track, so it is no wonder she has been called a witch.[75] One of the commonest of these is to stop and run back along her own line, then turn and take a prodigious leap to the side. From the point where she lands she runs still farther to the side and then turns and looks back to see if the hounds can figure out what she has done. They, poor simple souls, run first to the end of the line she first made and then cast frantically for something that isn't there. Even if one of them happens to try back, he is not likely to find the point at which she made her big leap[76] and will probably run back too far. So the huntsman must cast the hounds in ever-widening circles[77] until they again hit off the line of the hare that seems to have vanished into the air.

But the hare is a home-loving creature, and sooner or later she will turn and go back to the neighborhood where she was first found and started. For this reason she was often caught in the nets which were set up for her. Ordinarily there were only two ways to catch her: she must be outmatched in endurance, as she is when pursued by a pack of beagles; or she must be driven into a net, as she was by Xenophon's hounds. There was, and is, little doubt about her ability to outrun almost any hound that can be set on her.[78] Even greyhounds have their difficulties in running her down.

But the use of nets raises a question I have not yet seen either asked or answered: Had Xenophon's hounds been trained to drive their hares into the nets or toward the huntsman, who might be waiting with a harestick to throw at them? Poachers in nineteenth-century England taught their lurchers to do both; so it is possible that Xenophon did the same thing. But it does not seem likely, for any huntsman who did not attempt to teach his hounds to run loose under control of only the voice and horn would not be likely to try such a feat. It is much more likely that he would depend on his woodcraft in the placing of the nets, rather than try such an apparently difficult trick.

HUNTING IN SNOW[79]

When there is snow lying on the ground, hare hunting becomes a matter of a man's tracking with his eyes, rather than hound work. The hare's footprints are visible in the snow, and a man skilled in woodcraft will have no difficulty in following them. When the ground is bare and the weather is cold enough for snow, there is seldom any scent for hounds to follow. The hare's tracks will remain visible longer in snow if the sky is overcast than if it is sunny, because the rays of the sun melt the surface of the snow. But on very cold days when there is sun on the snow, there is scent also, and the hounds can hunt then—my own hounds have hunted fox in snow when the temperature was six degrees below zero Fahrenheit, when the sun was shining. The effect of north or south wind, noted by Xenophon, is a matter of local geography, and we can readily imagine that a wind coming down from the Pindus Mountains would be colder than a wind blowing up from Crete.

When there is a snowstorm or when the wind blows the snow up into drifts, there is obviously no point in taking hounds out, although the cold does not freeze the hounds' nostrils literally; in saying this, Xenophon was speaking figuratively or perhaps using a technical term. But generally his descriptions of conditions found in winter hunting are remarkably accurate. The hare does clap down in the snow, hoping to escape notice, just as she does in grass. And she does tire easily from the weight of the snow that balls up on her feet.

COURSING [80]

Although hunting as Xenophon practiced it was still carried on, particularly by the Cretans and the Carians, and although the Romans hunted in much the same manner as the Greeks (as well as in great hunts of the Persian sort), a new sport was introduced into the ancient world by the Celts some time before the second century after Christ. Although it may have been called hunting, it was in fact almost exactly the same sport as what we call "coursing," and its purpose was not to catch the hare but to watch the hounds race her, and—we may well image—to bet on the outcome. The hounds used were the Vertragi, a breed of greyhounds, as we have already seen. Coursing was conducted as follows: Scouts were sent out to find a hare and to beat up the hedgerows. The hunters then slipped their greyhounds, usually not more than two at a time. The object was to see whose hound gave the hare the best chase. No nets were used; and if we may believe Arrian, the hunters were generally glad if the hare escaped with her life, especially if she had given the hounds a real run for their money.

What shall he have that kill'd the deer?
His leather skin and horns to wear.
Then sing him home.
      Shakespeare, As You Like It, *IV. ii. 10*

V *Antlers and Horns*

THE RED DEER

When Xenophon first settled down to live the life of a country gentleman on the estate at Scillus which the Spartans had given him after he was banished from Athens, he held sacrifices and a festival, and he and his sons, together with those of his neighbors who wished to go along, went hunting. They caught, he says, wild boars, roe deer, and red deer, for the country was full of every kind of game that was hunted.[1]

Just what kind of a creature was this red deer? Was it, as most Americans might imagine, the same deer as that hunted by sportsmen in the United States and Canada? The American deer has a lovely red coat in summer, so it is sometimes called the red deer, and Americans who read about the red deer hunted by European royalty all through the Middle Ages sometimes imagine that it is the same. Unfortunately this so-called red deer, properly known as the White-tail or Virginia deer, *Odocoileus virginianus*,[2] does not exist in Europe;[3] and so far as anybody knows, it never has existed there, for the deer of the Western hemisphere, like the hares and the rabbits, differ from their Old World counterparts; they are distant cousins only. What, then, was the red deer of Scillus?

In the parts of the world usually visited by the Greeks during historical times, there have been only three kinds of deer, as we know from tradition, descriptions, and pictures, as well as from bones and antlers found throughout the area. These three are the red deer, the fallow deer, and the roe deer, none of them known in the Western hemisphere and all of them hunted in Europe from the earliest times down to the present. The red deer, known to zoologists as *Cervus elaphus*,[4] is clearly distinguished from the other two and strictly European in origin. There is only one subspecies of it found outside of Europe, the Barbary deer, *Cervus elaphus barbarus*,[5] which is found in North Africa along the Algerian-Tunisian border, where it may have wandered easily after crossing the Straits of Gibraltar, either by swimming or by being carried across by men. All other present subspecies are found in Europe only: *Cervus elaphus germanicus*,[6] throughout Continental Europe; *Cervus elaphus corsicanus*,[7] in Sardinia and Corsica only (although Polybius says that there were no deer there in his day,[8] so it, too, must have come from Europe later); and *Cervus elaphus hispanicus*[9] and *Cervus elaphus bolivari*,[10] in Spain. It is, of course, impossible to say just what subspecies Xenophon hunted at Scillus twenty-six hundred years ago; and it is quite unnecessary, for the variations between one subspecies and another are slight, so it is enough to know that the red deer hunted by the Greeks was *Cervus elaphus*.

What distinguishes the deer, whatever its species, from the antelope and similar creatures is its headdress. The Greeks were well aware of the fact that the deer alone has antlers and that the antlers are solid throughout,[11] not hollow like the horns of sheep, goats, oxen, antelopes, and gazelles. Furthermore, as Aristotle says, the antlers of the deer are made of a substance similar to bone, while horns are made of something which seems to be derived from the skin. Deer, he says, shed their antlers every year, leaving them in places where they are difficult to discover, so the saying has arisen that no one has ever found the left antler of the deer.[12] They shed their antlers in or about the month of May;[13] and each year, beginning in their second year, they grow new ones. The first set of antlers is straight like a peg; but the second set, which comes in the third year, has in addition to the straight peg a forward-pointing branch with a sharp tip. In the following year another branch is added; in the next, another; and in the sixth year, a fifth.[14] After that, he says, there is no further differentiation, and it is no longer possible to tell the age of a deer by its antlers; although the heads of old deer, the patriarchs of the herd, have no brow antlers, and their points are dull.

During the period when the antlers are growing, he says, they are covered with a thin layer of skin which the deer rub off as soon as the antlers are fully developed. While the deer have no antlers, they stay in hiding, because they are conscious that they have no weapons with which to defend themselves.

The mating season, he says, is during the month of October,[15] and hinds mate only under compulsion.[16] The period of gestation is about eight months, and the hind generally has only one calf, but on rare occasions two. She drops her calf by the side of public roads, where it will be safe from large predators because of their fear of man.[17] Later she takes her calf to a lair in some protected place, arranged so that there will be only one entrance to it, where she can guard her calf easily from harm.[18]

In these observations Aristotle is extraordinarily accurate; his mistakes are not serious, and they are very understandable. Deer do indeed seem to shed their antlers in places where they are difficult to find, but that is because they are fond of eating them, particularly if the soil is deficient in any of the minerals, such as calcium, needed to develop them.[19] But he is not quite accurate in saying that there is no further differentiation in antlers after the sixth year.[20] Further points may and often do develop, sometimes —although rarely—to a number as great as sixteen on each antler;[21] but he is quite right in saying that it is not possible to judge age accurately by counting points from the age of six on. Indeed, the number of points seem to depend as much on the character of food available as on the age of the animal.[22] Then he is not quite right in saying that after shedding their antlers stags go into hiding; the truth is that they seldom stay with the hinds at all except during the rutting season, when every master stag collects as big a harem as he can. But during the rutting season, when they are spent, they disappear for short periods of rest on the mountain tops.[23]

It is quite probable that deer do mate in October in Greece and in Asia Minor. The date varies somewhat with the climate; in Scotland, a place where the red deer has been extensively studied, the rut begins sometime near the end of September and extends through October.[24] The period of gestation is from two hundred and ten to two hundred and thirty days, that is, between seven and eight months. It is unlikely that any hind ever knowingly dropped her calf by the side of a public road, but she makes no great effort to hide her calves in secluded places.[25] The actual birth, however, has seldom been witnessed by human beings. She does not immediately take her calf with her to some lair, but leaves it for perhaps three days and simply watches it from a distance, approaching only to nurse it. Then, as soon as it can stand up, she returns and pays close attention to it, licking and fondling it while nursing it, a thing she does standing up.[26]

The red deer calf grows very rapidly and attains extraordinary speed while still very young, as Xenophon discovered.[27] It stays absolutely motionless when approached by danger, a trick which was observed as early as the time of Homer.[28] When they are chased, the calves slip in among the older deer in the herd and are surrounded, so they are very difficult to catch, as Xenophon says.[29]

Aristotle knew, of course, that only the male has antlers, but he did not come right out and say so; he assumed that by speaking of the deer in the masculine gender he would make his meaning clear, for it was a common although not a universal practice to speak of the deer in the feminine gender when referring to it generically. Examples of this usage can be found, ironically enough, in the very quotations from Sophocles, Euripides, and Pindar which Aelian gives in attempting to prove exactly the opposite.[30] Aelian, however, was a Roman and not a Greek, and although exceptionally skilled in the Greek language, was not aware of this particular usage, which, indeed, even some Greeks in his day did not know. Anyway, he was an armchair observer who probably never saw a deer of either sex.

Aristotle observed how stags wallow in the mud, but he gives the impression that they do so only for sexual reasons.[31] The truth is that both sexes wallow[32] in May and June, evidently because of the irritation caused by ticks, flies, and other skin parasites,[33] as well as because they are shedding their winter coats at that time. But stags wallow again in September and October,[34] usually beginning about two weeks before the rutting season; in this case the motive seems to be to make themselves darker in color and therefore more terrifying—dark colors frighten deer more than light— to the other stags with whom they must compete for the favor of the hinds. This certainly must be the reason, for the hinds do not wallow at that time too, as they would if some sort of skin irritation were involved.

At the beginning of the rutting season—that is, at the time when they are beginning to wallow—stags in Scotland are at their heaviest and average perhaps two hundred and fifty pounds in weight.[35] This is the very time, according to Aristotle, when stags in Greece were heaviest,[36] but Aristotle did not mention the fact that at the end of the rutting season these same stags might weigh a hundred pounds less,[37] although he did note that they were thinnest in winter.[38]

Xenophon makes no such detailed observations of the red deer, but there are few mistakes in the observations he does make. As we have seen, he notices how a herd of hinds will surround the calves when pursued by hounds, thus making it difficult for the hounds to get at them. He observes that deer, when dead beat, will often run into water in an effort to escape,[39] a well-known trick that did not escape Oppian either, for he calls deer "amphibian" because of it.[40] Oppian, however, is not as accurate an observer as either Aristotle or Xenophon—authority rather than experience was the basis of almost everybody's beliefs in his day—and he repeats the story of the inveterate enmity between deer and snakes[41] and the myth of the longevity of the deer.[42] Solinus tells us that Alexander the Great fastened collars on deer and that a hundred years later these same deer were observed still wearing the collars;[43] but Aristotle was too good a scientist to believe such a myth without proof or at least better authority than mere rumor. He doubts it because, he says, the period of gestation and the rapidity with which the red deer calves mature do not warrant the belief that the animal lives a long time.[44] In actual fact, the red deer has a potential life span of about nineteen years.[45]

Pollux was a grammarian and lexicographer, so he repeated many of other people's mistakes, but still he adds one of his own.[46] He imagined that the stag stood guard over the hind while she lay down to nurse her calf. The stag, of course, not only ignores his offspring but does not even know them, for he leaves the hinds long before they drop their calves. The hind does not lie down to nurse her calf; she stands up to do so, just as the cow does,[47] a point Xenophon failed to observe correctly.[48]

THE FALLOW DEER

Other kinds of deer which the Greeks probably hunted, although Xenophon does not mention them, were the fallow deer, *Dama dama*, and possibly another closely related species, *Dama mesopotamica*.[49] The fallow deer is found today in the Mediterranean basin, particularly in Asia Minor,[50] and although now few in numbers, it was never numerous. It is smaller than the red deer, but larger than the roe deer, and it has palmated antlers, that is, the branches are broad and flat, spreading out into separate points at the ends. It was this broad characteristic of the fallow deer's antlers that gave it its Greek name, *Broadhorn*.[51]

The number of fallow deer in Greece must have been very small, and it is possible that in classic times there were none to be found there at all; opinions differ. However, they certainly existed in Asia Minor, even if not in large numbers.

THE ROE DEER

But the roe deer, *Capreolus capreolus*,[52] certainly did exist in Greece in classic times. It was the little creature that Xenophon hunted in the country around Scillus and called the "dorcas." It is about the size of a goat—indeed, the young of the roe deer has sometimes been called a "kid" rather than a "fawn"[53]—and has a red coat in summer and a gray coat with white patches in winter. Its antlers rise from near the top of its head and are erect and forked near the end, so from a little distance the roebuck looks very much like one of the gazelles. The roe deer, unlike the red deer and the fallow deer, is strictly monogamous and lives in small families dominated by the male, rather than in large herds of males and females dominated by the females.[54] It is a woodland creature, and it moves with the gait appropriate to its environment; that is, instead of trotting as the red deer usually does, except in emergencies, it flies through the air in a series of graceful bounds, both hind feet leaving the ground at the same time and both front feet touching down together. It is a gait particularly suited to getting across heavy underbrush.[55]

The roe deer is unfortunately never seen in North America, for it is a European animal only, found today all the way from the British Isles to the borders of Asia and from the Scandinavian Peninsula to the shores of the Mediterranean.[56] There is no evidence that its numbers are either increasing or decreasing; it certainly is in no immediate danger of extermination. It is probable that the number of roe deer in ancient Greece was not much more than the number in the Greece of today.

THE GAZELLE

In Africa and the countries immediately adjacent to it, the place occupied by the deer in the wildlife of Europe is taken by a group of animals that are generally, but vaguely, called antelopes. There are, and were, no roe deer in Asia Minor, Syria, or Arabia,[57] so when Xenophon or some other Greek author refers to the "dorcas" there, he cannot mean the roe deer. But just as we lump a group of very dissimilar animals together under the name "antelope," so the Greeks lumped together two different animals which looked very similar under the name "dorcas." The animal most closely resembling the roe deer is the gazelle, of which one species, *Gazella dorcas*, looks so much like the roe deer that the Greeks might easily have called both by the same name.[58] There are two subspecies of this gazelle today, either one of which might have been the one Xenophon saw in Asia Minor, the dorcas gazelle, *Gazella dorcas dorcas;* and the Isabella gazelle, *Gazella dorcas isabella.*[59]

Other Greeks in later times may easily have hunted some of the gazelles in North Africa, *Gazella cuvieri, Gazella leptocerus,* or *Gazella dama mhorr.*[60] This last, because of the white patch on its rear end, might possibly have been Aelian's "white rump."[61] None of them, however, are likely to have been hunted by Xenophon or his friends.

OTHER ANTELOPES

Among other animals of the so-called antelope group which appear in Greek literary references to hunting are the three species of oryx. First, there is the Beisa oryx, *Oryx beisa beisa,*[62] which was found in Palestine and is by far the commonest kind there now.

Second, there is the Arabian or Beatrix oryx, *Oryx leucoryx*,[63] found at the head of the Persian Gulf; it is white except for its legs and a patch on each cheek, which are brown. Because of its appearance, especially when seen from a distance, it may have been the original of the fabled unicorn, for the two horns would be hard to distinguish in the glare of the desert sunlight, particularly if the observer were already looking for a unicorn. Third, and last, there is the so-called white oryx, *Oryx algazel*,[64] which is actually not quite as white as the Arabian oryx. It is found in North Africa.

Oppian mentions three other animals, in addition to the oryx, which may tentatively be identified as the hartebeest, *Alcelaphus*;[65] the gnu, *Connochaetes gnu*;[66] and the nilgai, *Boselaphus tragocamelus*.[67] The first two are found in North Africa; the third, in India. There is no certainty about these identifications, of course, but there is no certainty that Oppian ever saw any of the animals he mentions. As he was probably a Syrian,[68] however, he lived in a country where it was not impossible for him to see them.

SHEEP AND GOATS

Separating the sheep from the goats is not only proverbially difficult but actually so. Most domestic sheep, however, are easy to identify, as they are usually members of the species *Ovis aries*, and many of the wild sheep were of this same species, too. Most domestic goats in the Aegean region are descended from the wild goat, *Capra aegagrus*, and so these too are easy to identify.

Oppian's *Soubus*, however, is more difficult; it might be almost any kind of yellow animal.[69] One wild sheep, *Ovis ophion anatolica*,[70] a native of Asia Minor, is yellow; but so is the wild goat, *Capra nubiana nubiana*,[71] which lives along the west coast of the Red Sea; and so is *Capra nubiana sinaitica*,[72] a close relative that lives in Israel and Jordan. All three must surely have been among the wild animals Oppian numbered, and the Soubus may have been any one of them.

Finally, there was the yellow sheep of Gortyn, in south central Crete, distinguished by having four horns.[73] In addition, Aelian mentions a four-horned animal that from its description sounds like an antelope. Now a four-horned animal might easily be dismissed as pure myth, and most editors must have thought it was, for they do not mention it; but the fact is that there actually is a four-horned antelope, *Tetracerus quadricornis*,[74] which is so real that it has been exhibited by the New York Zoological Society in recent years. It is a little fellow only about twenty-five inches high at the shoulder, with one pair of horns in the usual place and another pair just above and between the eyes. Although small, it is related to the nilgai. As it comes from Asia, it is probably the animal called "sheep" by Oppian and "antelope" by Aelian.

WILD CATTLE

When Neolithic man migrated from Asia to Europe, he brought cattle with him which he had already domesticated.[75] They were small, scrawny, and short-horned and bore little resemblance to the cattle represented in works of the Bronze Age. This is because there was already a wild species of cattle in Europe, a species that had been there since the Pleistocene era;[76] as this species was huge, measuring six feet high at the shoulder, he upgraded his herds by crossing his little domestic cattle with the big wild ones and thus produced the cattle of Crete and Mycenae and, of course, of classic Greece.

The wild species he found was the "ure-ox," or aurochs, *Bos primigenius*,[77] which wandered at large throughout Europe and parts of western Asia and is now thought to be the foundation stock of all domestic cattle. The aurochs was not only huge and high at the shoulders, but it had horns that were long, spread wide, stood high, and had sharp points that turned up at the ends. The bulls were nearly black in color; the cows, a very dark brown; and the calves, a little lighter brown.[78] Julius Caesar,[79] Vergil,[80] and Pliny[81] all mention the aurochs; it did not become extinct until modern times, for the last one was killed in Poland in 1627.[82] It is quite possible the Greeks hunted the aurochs in Macedonia and Thrace during the classic period, and it is even more likely that they hunted it during the heroic age; but most of the wild cattle, the Egyptian, Phrygian, Aonian, Armenian, and Syrian, all mentioned by Oppian,[83] were probably only domesticated cattle that had escaped from their herds and had reverted to the wild. In any case they were all descended from *Bos primigenius*, but the degree of purity of their bloodlines varied considerably.

Another beast which is now extinct but which the Greeks may very well have hunted was the European bison, *Bison bonasus bonasus*,[84] frequently called by its German name, the "*Wisent*," and even more frequently miscalled the "aurochs," for, like the true aurochs, the European bison was huge and it too stood six feet high at the shoulder, although in appearance it looked nothing like the true aurochs; instead it closely resembled its cousin, the American bison of the prairies, usually miscalled the "buffalo."

The true buffalo, which may have been hunted in later times, came from India. There are two species which may have been seen by the Greeks who accompanied Alexander the Great when he invaded India: *Bubalus bubalis arnee*,[85] which now lives only in the eastern part of India and is therefore the least likely; and *Bubalus macrocerus* or *Bubalus bubalis bubalis*[86]—it is possible that these two were one and the same species. The superficial resemblance of these beasts to cattle makes it possible that the Greeks hunted them when they said they hunted wild cattle.

METHODS OF HUNTING DEER

The Greeks hunted both harts and hinds; the practices of sending a harborer to search for a warrantable stag and of leaving the hinds and the young deer alone did not begin until some time in the Middle Ages, when herds became so depleted that even royalty felt the need to use some restraint in order to preserve the species.[87]

In the heroic age, the age of which Homer writes, hunting was simple, difficult, and inefficient. The hunter and his friends might go out with the intention of bringing home a stag or a hind and actually come back with a lion, a boar, or most likely nothing at all.[88] Their method was to stalk the game, usually but not invariably with the aid of hounds, and when near enough to shoot it with an arrow, just as Heracles was said to have shot the Cernytian hind,[89] or if it was possible to get close enough, to strike it down with a spear. Hounds were useful, for they could not only help a great deal with the business of stalking, but they could hold the quarry at bay until the hunter could come up and dispatch it, or they could chase it and run it down if it were wounded. Hounds were not taken into the covert on leashes the way the medieval harborer took his lymers,[90] but brought to the covert side and turned loose to track the game on their own responsibility, and it was for this reason the hunted animal sometimes turned out to be a lion or boar when a stag had been intended.

Deer hunting, like hare hunting, was undertaken on foot; it was not until the end of the Persian wars that men rode to hounds. It was therefore essential that the deer be caught with as little running as possible, for the hunter on foot had absolutely no chance of keeping up with any kind of deer; hunting for the sake of the chase was unthinkable. The Greek huntsman therefore had to depend on his skill in woodcraft, rather than on the noses and speed of his hounds; he had to know the signs of deer, the places where they might lie, and their habits when found and started.

It did not take the Greek huntsman long, however, to discover that the red deer calf, when closely approached, has the habit of freezing in place and of lying perfectly still in hope of escaping discovery.[91] It was easy to catch such a calf, and when it was caught, it inevitably bellowed lustily for its mother, who promptly responded by coming to the rescue and was therefore an easy victim of the hunter's spears or javelins.[92] By Xenophon's time this method of catching deer was common, but it was good only in the spring, when the calves were very small, for as soon as they were a little bigger, they ran away with the herd of hinds and were surrounded, as we have seen.[93]

It was therefore necessary to devise some other method of catching deer at other times of the year, and the commonest system seems to have been to use the footsnares described in chapter i. Footsnares of this sort, of course, had to be set in places where the deer would be likely to run, and for this reason also the Greek huntsman had to be well versed in woodcraft. We do not know just what methods he used, but we do know what the medieval harborer used, and it is not impossible that the Greeks may have used somewhat the same methods, for many medieval customs were derived from classical sources.

The medieval harborer used six signs.[94] The first of these was the slot, or footprint; it was possible to tell the sex and size of the deer by the shape and size of the slot. The second was the gait, or pattern, of the footprints; it was possible to tell the sex of the deer and the speed with which it was traveling by the manner of putting one foot in front of the other. The third and fourth were the entries and the breakages; the entries were the marks left by the stag's antlers as he moved through the trees, and the breakages were the marks left by other parts of his body; it was possible to tell his size from these. The fifth was the fraying, or marks, left on the trees by the stag when he rubbed the velvet from his antlers; it was possible to tell his size and age by the size of the trees used and by the height of the marks above the ground. The sixth was the fewmet, or droppings; it was possible to tell whether the deer had passed by recently or a long time ago. The medieval harborer made a great deal out of the fewmets, but it is difficult to see how much could be told by such a thing that would be of any importance to hunting, except perhaps what the deer had been eating.

With signs such as these, it should not have been impossible for the Greek huntsman to determine where the deer might run when found and started and to set his footsnares accordingly. When the deer stepped in the footsnare, it would be badly hampered by the clog; then it was easy enough to follow its trail, and the huntsman, even though on foot, would have no great difficulty in catching up with it.[95]

Although Xenophon makes no mention of the use of nets for deer hunting, we know that they were used because others, particularly writers of the Roman era, say so.[96] Just what these nets were like is not certain, but it seems likely that they were simply variants of the long-nets and the purse-nets used for hare hunting, differing primarily in dimensions and weight of materials. Another device, the formido, or scare, was used by the Romans, and the only Greek author who mentions it is Oppian.[97] It consisted of a long cord to which bright-colored feathers were attached so that they would twist and flutter in the breeze and thus frighten the game into the waiting nets or the hands of the hunters.

There is no specific mention of the methods used in hunting the fallow deer, the roe deer, the gazelle, or any of the various kinds of antelope; but it is probable that they were hunted in much the same way as the deer; indeed, they may have been considered inferior game, just as they have been in more recent times,[98] and therefore hardly worth telling about.

Wild sheep and goats must also have been hunted by a similar method, although, of course, the lamb and the kid do not behave exactly like the red deer calf.

METHODS OF HUNTING WILD CATTLE

The aurochs, the bison, and all the various kinds of wild cattle can hardly have been hunted in quite the same way as deer, gazelles, sheep, and goats, if only because of their larger size. Pausanias tells us how the Paeonians caught bisons alive and remarked that they are the most difficult animal in the world to catch and much too strong to be held by any net. The Paeonians, he said, made a sort of toboggan slide on the slope of a hill by covering it with hides freshly skinned or freshly oiled, so when the bisons were driven across the slippery surface, they fell and rolled down the slope into a pit prepared at the bottom. There they were kept without food for about five days and then, being submissive from weakness and hunger, were led away by ropes.[99] We may doubt that nets strong enough to hold the bison could not be made, in view of the evidence from Mycenaean times that nets were used to catch wild cattle, but there was no doubt that they were powerful beasts. Anyhow, the usual method of catching such creatures in the classical era was probably by means of pitfalls or hidden trenches, suitably baited.

O, be advised; thou know's not what it is
With javelin's point a churlish swine to gore,
Whose tushes never sheathed he whetteth still,
Like to a mortal butcher, bent to kill.
  Shakespeare, Venus and Adonis, *615–18*

VI Other Game

SMALL GAME

Some animals, says Oppian, are so small and ignoble that they are beneath the notice of the Muse,[1] but he promptly takes notice of them line after line and verse after verse for a large part of his *Cynegetica;* this sort of trick is old hat to us now, although it probably seemed pretty clever to Oppian's readers. But he took no notice of why and how these contemptible creatures were hunted— and we must assume they were hunted or he would never have mentioned them at all. Some, of course, were edible; others were considered vermin; but still others could hardly have been hunted for anything but sport, and a poor kind of sport it must have been.

There is, for example, the mole, *Talpa caeca;*[2] it was a garden pest. It is still found in Greece, excepting in the Cyclades. There are also two species of mole-rat, *Spalax typhlus* and *Spalax graecus;* the latter is common in the neighborhood of Athens. The hedgehog, *Erinaceus europaeus,*[3] although unknown in the Western hemisphere, is common in Greece; while the spiny mouse, *Acomys,* which looks almost exactly like a small variety of hedgehog, is found in Syria, Israel, and North Africa. The hedgehog is said to be remarkable for its low degree of mental development and for the fact that on the slightest degree of alarm it rolls itself up in a ball and erects its spines for protection—you will remember how Alice played croquet with hedgehogs for balls and flamingos for mallets. The porcupine also has quills and is found around the eastern end of the Mediterranean, although the species there, *Hystrix cristata,* is not the same as the porcupine familiar to all campers in the northern woods of the United States; it is bigger, and it does not climb trees as well as the American porcupine does. In size, however, although bigger than the hedgehog and bigger than its American cousin, it is nowhere nearly as big as the wolf— Oppian compares them—nor does it throw its quills, as many people believe even today. But the quills do fall out very easily and are certainly very terrible weapons, for the surface of each is covered with fine and nearly invisible barbs, so once a quill has entered the body of an animal, it continues to work its way in and can only be removed with great difficulty and greater pain. The American porcupine is edible and is very easily caught because it fears nothing in the world but the skunk, so an unarmed man can walk up to it and kill it with a blow on the nose. For this reason it is protected in many states so that campers lost in the woods without weapons may have it for food and save themselves from possible starvation.

Not edible, but good for their beautiful furs, are the members of the weasel family, both the genus *Mustela* and the genus *Martes,* which include the weasel, ferret, polecat, marten, sable, fisher, and of course the mink. All these were lumped together by the Greeks and called by the name *galē,*[4] which in modern Greek means cat.

At some point in history the meaning of the word appears to have changed animals, so we are left in doubt about several things. Was the hereditary and traditional enemy of the mouse once the weasel instead of the cat? Does Babrius' thirty-first fable[5] refer to war between mice and weasels or mice and cats? And what about the bride in his thirty-second fable?[6] Aphrodite had changed her into a beautiful girl; but at the wedding banquet, when a little mouse ran across the floor, she leaped down from her couch and pursued it. Which had she been before her transformation, a weasel or a cat? This shift in meaning, however, is more apparent than real, because the ancient Greeks thought that the domestic cat, which was rare in their country, was a member of the weasel family; and *galē* in modern Greek is more generic than specific and more literary than familiar.

Two others of this same group are also mentioned: the ichneumon, *Mungos ichneumon*,[7] and the otter, *Lutra*.[8] The ichneumon was not mentioned as game to be hunted, however, but as a hunter used in Egypt for catching reptiles and crocodiles. Crocodiles seem a little large, and the method of hunting them is improbable: the ichneumon smeared itself with mud, rolled itself into a ball, jumped down the crocodile's throat, and ate the creature's insides out. The otter, on the other hand, was apparently hunted; although the number available in such a dry country as Greece must have been very small.

The triple breeds of apes which Oppian mentions are undoubtedly the Barbary ape, *Inuus ecaudatus*;[9] the common rhesus monkey, *Macacus rhesus*; and the Hamadryas baboon, *Papio hamadryas*, the sacred baboon of Egypt. These correspond with the three breeds named by Aristotle, so it is possible that Oppian simply borrowed the names from him.

Other animals beneath the dignity of Oppian's muse are the beaver, *Castor fiber*,[10] which exists throughout Europe; the squirrel, *Sciurus vulgaris*,[11] who shades himself with his tail, as his name implies, and is edible although small; and the dormouse, of which there are three varieties: the European dormouse, *Glis glis*,[12] common throughout Europe; the garden dormouse, *Eliomys*, found in Europe, North Africa, and western Asia; and the Asiatic dormouse, *Dryomys*. The last small creature mentioned by Oppian, the common house mouse,[13] *Mus musculus*, was, as the mouse himself said, not even a mouthful.

BIG GAME

The biggest game of all, of course, was the elephant. It was first mentioned by Herodotus,[14] who spoke of the bigger variety, the African elephant, *Loxodonta*, and said that he believed the elephant's tusks were teeth. Aristotle, who first mentioned the Indian elephant, *Elephas*, was of the same opinion.[15] There were, however, many who disagreed. Aelian[16] denied that they were teeth and stated that those who called them horns were right. Philostratus[17] reported that Juba called them horns because they remained in place after they had grown, whereas teeth fell out and grew again. He himself could not agree with Juba; he was sure they were teeth. Pausanias[18] used almost the same argument to prove the opposite, pointing out that the antlers of deer fell off and were replaced; the antlers were certainly not teeth. Oppian[19] said that only the vulgar believed they were teeth and that the tusks of the elephant grew out from somewhere near the forehead but were concealed under the skin until they came out through the mouth. Anyway, he said, the material of which teeth are made is brittle and breaks easily, that of horns is elastic. If bows could be made from the tusks of elephants, how could they be teeth?

But whatever they believed about the elephant's tusks, they all agreed that the animal was huge, used its trunk like a hand, and although truly wild before capture, could be tamed and trained to be a very useful servant. Unfortunately they did not describe the hunting of the elephant as clearly as we might like, but we do know that they captured it alive by using a tame elephant as a decoy or by driving the wild beasts into places where pitfalls had been prepared; and sometimes natives dropped down upon the backs of the elephants from the trees and captured them that way.[20] The animal must have been known from very early times because the word *eléphas* appears a number of times in Homer, but always means ivory and never the animal itself. If ivory were known, somebody must have been hunting the animal, but the hunters were probably not Greeks.

Next in size after the elephant was the rhinoceros.[21] There are three species today, the Indian animal, *Rhinoceros;* the white rhinoceros, *Ceratotherium;* and the black rhinoceros, *Diceros.* The white and the black species are from Africa. It is probable that the species known to the Greeks was the Indian, for their descriptions do not suggest either a white or a black animal but rather one that was "yellowish," "box-colored," "rather like an elephant in color." Just what is "box-colored"? Is it the color of the raw box-wood, the bark of the plant, or what? Anyway the Greeks tell us even less how they hunted the rhinoceros but a great deal about how the rhinoceros fought the elephant.[22] In spite of the latter's much greater size, the rhinoceros was able to kill the elephant by running under it and ripping its belly open with its sharp nose horn. Occasionally the elephant fell down on the rhinoceros, but usually the latter was able to get out from under in time to escape injury.

One beast which the Greeks may have encountered and hunted in the Roman era was the giraffe.[23] Its shape was so odd that they were convinced it must have been a hybrid between the camel and the leopard, just as they were convinced that the ostrich was a cross between the camel and the sparrow. The giraffe, they thought, got its form and size from the camel, but its spotted skin from the leopard. Just how the cross which produced the ostrich could be accomplished is nowhere told. The camel, of course, was a well-known beast, both the one-humped Arabian camel, or dromedary, *Camelus dromedarius;*[24] and the two-humped Bactrian camel, *Camelus bactrianus.*[25] They were very much more familiar with the former than with the latter, however, so that references to the camel usually mean the Arabian species.

Another large beast which was hunted from the earliest times was the brown bear, *Ursus arctos,*[26] common throughout Europe, Asia, and North America. The grizzly, *Ursus horribilis,* does not exist in Europe at all; and the polar bear, *Thalarctos polaris*, is, of course, found only in the Arctic, a region, by the way, not named for the animal that lives there but for the constellation of the bear. Aristotle, among several others, took note of the bear's habit of hibernation, although he could not explain it.[27] He also remarked that the bear's cubs were smaller in proportion to the size of their parents than the young of any other animal and that they were not well articulated.[28] Many other Greeks believed that the bear cub was born a shapeless mass of flesh and that the mother licked it into form with her tongue.[29]

Oppian gives a good description of bear hunting in Mesopotamia.[30] Some of the hunters took the hounds into the coverts to draw for the bear, keeping them on leashes while they did so; others set up long-nets with a pile of brush at each end of the line of nets, under which the net-watchers lay in hiding. From the wings of the line of nets long cords were then stretched at about waist height, each cord decorated with fluttering feathers of bright colors. When everyone was ready the trumpet was blown, and the men rushed into the covert with a cry and frightened the bear into running. The line of feathered cords guided the bear into the waiting nets; and when it hit them, the men stationed there drew the skirting cords tight and piled more nets on top until the bear was held securely. Then one man tied the bear by the paws and put it in a wooden cage.

ASSES AND HORSES

The horse had been domesticated some centuries before the time of the Trojan War, but it was little used for riding until some centuries later. Homer almost invariably speaks of horses, usually mares, as pulling chariots. The ass, which later became the butt of innumerable jokes, is only mentioned once by Homer;[31] it is fair to infer, therefore, that it was domesticated somewhat later than the horse. The mule, of course, came a little later still but was very very well known by the fifth century, and the differences between the mule proper (the jackass-mare hybrid) and the hinny (the stallion–jenny ass hybrid) were well understood: Aristotle describes these differences, although he is a little optimistic about the fertility of the offspring of such crosses.[32]

The Greeks say that they hunted wild horses and wild asses, and it is possible that they actually did hunt wild individuals of the species *Equus caballus* and *Asinus asinus*, particularly the latter, for the wild asses which the eight-year-old Numidian boys caught, riding bareback and without bridles, as described by Arrian,[33] may very well have been just such. There are others, however, which seem more likely. Oppian describes one which he calls the "orynx,"[34] which, however, is defined as the oryx in Liddell and Scott. But Oppian says there are two species, one striped like a tiger and the other spotted like a leopard. The striped orynx must have been the zebra, *Equus zebra;* and the spotted orynx, one of the ancestors of the Appaloosa—a modern name for a riding horse which has a coat color that has been known perhaps twenty thousand years.[35] On the other hand, Oppian may have made the whole story up and simply used the name of the oryx in different form.

Elsewhere Oppian tells of an animal he calls the "hippagros." This is probably the nilgai, *Boselaphus tragocamelus*,[36] the same creature Aristotle calls the "hippelaphos."[37] It is a native of India. Aristotle also tells of a so-called wild mule which is found in Syria;[38] this is probably the wild ass, *Asinus hemionus*,[39] of Persia, Syria, Palestine, Arabia, and Iraq. A subspecies, *Asinus hemionus onagrus*, is sometimes called the Persian onager.

THE FOX, WOLF, JACKAL, CIVET CAT, AND HYENA

The fox of ancient Greece was the same animal as the red fox of the Western hemisphere, for *Vulpes vulpes* inhabits both Old and New worlds. He was famous in antiquity, just as he is today, for his cleverness and mischief, so he was often called "Wily," the word being used just as if it were a name. Indeed, his cleverness was so great that people enjoyed the occasions on which he himself was outwitted, as he was in many of the Babrian fables, with especial relish.

In Greece the fox was usually spoken of in the feminine gender, in much the way we refer to the cat. He was, as we have seen, supposed to have been crossed with the dog to produce the Laconian hound;[40] but apart from that fact and his reputed wiliness, he was of no great importance. As a beast of the chase he enjoyed a very much lower status than his modern counterpart, perhaps because there were other predators that were more troublesome to the Greek farmer and perhaps because he was not good to eat. He was, in fact, little more than a nuisance, and Xenophon recommends that hounds should not be permitted to get in the habit of hunting foxes lest it ruin them for hare hunting.

The most famous fox hunt of antiquity was that of the Teumessian fox, a huge beast sent by the gods to ravage the countryside around Thebes. By nature it was uncatchable, and when the hound Laelaps was brought by Cephalus to chase it, the gods were faced with a dilemma that could only be resolved by turning both to stone.[41]

The wolf was *Canis lupus*, the same as our modern wolves. He occurs in ten of the Babrian fables, where he appears to be savage and treacherous, the reputation he enjoyed generally.[42] Aristotle said that the wolf could be crossed with the dog to produce hounds good for hunting,[43] just as the Eskimos cross him with local sled dogs to produce leaders of their teams. Oppian lists five different kinds of wolf: the "archer," the "ring," the "robber," the "golden," and the "kite."[44] These may have been subspecies, but it is impossible to identify them.

According to several authors, the wolf when mated with the leopard produced the *thos*. The contexts in which the thos appears vary; in some places it seems to be the jackal, *Canis aureus;* but in others the descriptions make it seem more like the civet cat, probably one of the members of the genus *Viverra* of Asia, but possibly *Civettictis* of Africa. It has even been suggested that it might be the wild African hunting dog, *Lycaon pictis*.[45] In the books concerned with hunting, the thos appears to be the civet cat; in Aristotle's description the animal is long and low and its coat is spotted. As both the leopard and the civet cat have spotted coats, it is easy to understand how the Greeks came to think the latter was descended from the former.

But whatever it was, the thos was hunted either by means of the circular pit described by Xenophon, which had a fence around it and bait (perhaps a live puppy) on a column in the center; or by the pitfall, covered with a fragile roof of twigs over which leaves were laid so that the civet cat would fall through if it tried to cross.

The hyena which Oppian describes was probably the striped variety, genus *Hyena*;[46] it is doubtful if the Greeks had seen the spotted variety, genus *Crocuta*, although they may have heard about it. Aristotle describes the striped species:[47] it is about the size of a wolf and is colored very much like one, but it has a slightly arched back and a mane made of bristles running the length of the spine. It has an unearthly cry with which it lures dogs to their death, although, on the whole, it prefers carrion to fresh meat. Many Greeks believed that the hyena changed its sex each year, being male one year and female the next, but this idea was too much for Aristotle.

THE CATS

The cat family is large and has always been confusing because many species resemble each other very closely, except for very slight differences in size, color, or conformation. The result is that many species are called by one name, and one species is called by many names. In addition, although the American species differ from the European, Asian, and African species, they are often called by names which the early settlers transferred from the cats they knew in the Old World. In order to identify the species which the Greeks hunted and to eliminate all that were unknown to them, it would therefore be well to clear up some of the confusion.

"Catamount," "cougar," "mountain lion," "panther," and "puma"[48] are all synonyms and refer to one and the same beast,

Felis concolor, a native of the Western hemisphere only and therefore unknown to the Greeks. However, "panther" is also used to refer to one of the Old World cats; and sometimes the mountain lion is called simply "lion," although he is far from being the same as the cat we see in the circus or zoo.

"Wildcat," "bobcat," and "lynx" are synonyms when used to refer to an American cat. This cat is *Lynx rufus*. A different animal is called "wildcat" (or "wild cat") in the Old World; and "lynx," in Europe, refers to *Lynx lynx*, related to but not identical with the American lynx. No animal in the Old World is called "bobcat."

The cats which the Greeks knew and perhaps hunted were therefore the following:

1. The wild cat, *Felis silvestris*, a native of Europe.[49] The domestic cat, *Felis domestica*, is descended from the wild cat of Egypt, with an outcross of the blood of the wild cat of Asia and perhaps the wild cat of Europe,[50] all of which are closely related. The domestic cat was still a newcomer to Greece in the classic age and, although known, was far less common and familiar then than now.

2. The lynx, which as we have said, refers to *Lynx lynx* in Europe.[51]

3. The leopard and the panther,[52] the same beast, *Felis pardus*, a native of Asia and Africa. "Panther" has long been a vague term; the Romans made no distinction between a panther and a leopard. The Greeks often but not invariably did; and when they did, the panther seems, by the contexts, to have been smaller than the leopard. It may therefore have been one of the larger subspecies of *Felis silvestris;* it can hardly have been the ounce or snow leopard, *Felis uncia*,[53] a native of Asia, as many editors have suggested, for the ounce is bigger, not smaller than the leopard. And at this point we might remark that *Felis onca* is not a variant spelling or a misprint but a different beast, the jaguar, which is strictly American.

4. The black leopard, which is not a different species but simply a fairly common mutant of *Felis pardus*, and very possibly the "black lion" to which Aelian refers.

5. The cheetah, or hunting leopard, refers to *Acinonyx jubatus*,[54] a native of Africa and of Asia. This beast has been used in Persia and in India for hunting antelopes for so many centuries that it is impossible the Greeks did not know it; besides, there are references to tame leopards in a number of books, although no descriptions of how the beast was used.

6. The caracal, a native of North Africa, *Caracal caracal*. Its identification is fairly certain, although Oppian called it a lynx.[55]

7. The tiger, *Felis tigris*.[56] This is the Bengal tiger, the largest of all the cats. References to the tiger do not give the impression of familiarity, and so it is likely that it was known largely by reputation.

8. The lion, *Felis leo*.[57] The only difficulty about identifying this beast is that nobody will believe it. It is nearly incredible that lions ran wild in any part of Greece.

The Greeks hunted all the smaller cats by tracking them with hounds and driving them toward nets which were prepared beforehand, just as they hunted many other animals. But anyone who has ever hunted mountain lions in Arizona or New Mexico knows that on many occasions the hounds tree the lion. The Greek hounds must surely have treed their cats, too. We shoot mountain lions out of the trees; the Greeks must have speared their cats, and this may well have provided some difficult moments, for even the most peaceful-appearing domestic cat can give a dog a bad time, so *Felis silvestris* must have given the hounds a fearful time. So when the moment came, they had to be quick with their spears or, if they had to shake it out of the tree, kill it at once, or it would maul the hounds unmercifully.

The bigger cats were hunted in the way Xenophon describes; that is, by means of a circular trench with live bait on a column in the middle, concealed from view of the quarry.[58] Sometimes instead they put aconite or some other poison in meat which they left near the watering places which the game frequented.[59] Sometimes mounted men intercepted the animals when they came down to the watering places during the night. This method, however, was extremely dangerous. Sometimes beaters, armed with torches and shields, drove the lion into a long-net by waving their torches and

100

shouting into their shields,[60] for the lion, according to Aristotle, is very much afraid of fire.[61] Still another method of hunting was said to have been used by the Aethiopians: four men, armed only with wicker shields covered with hides and with spears attacked the lion, first on one side and then on the other, until teased and irritated to the point of exhaustion he fell down. Then the men leaped upon him and killed him.[62] We cannot help wondering, however, how exhausted the four men were.

THE LION IN EUROPE[63]

In spite of the reluctance of many people to believe that the lion ever ran wild in Greece or any other part of Europe, there is good evidence that he did. It can hardly be accident that he appears in every period of Greek art and always appears to have been drawn from firsthand knowledge. In later periods, of course, his image may have been only a memory and a tradition. He became a myth to the Greeks, just as he is to us today. We see him in all sorts of representations, in illustrations of fables, in heraldry and other symbols; we read about him in fiction; and we feel that we know all about the lion just because we see him occasionally in the circus or the zoo. But although he is a sort of modern myth, even myths have to have some sort of a beginning in reality, and that beginning, I believe, was in prehistoric Greece.

The lion was real in Mycenaean Greece: in the National Museum in Athens is a bronze dagger inlaid with gold, silver, and niello, depicting a lion hunt in about 1560 B.C. It is full of life and action. There is also a gold rhyton in the form of a lion's head; both were found in the same grave in Mycenae. The Lion Gate in Mycenae is famous. Yet these three examples are only a small sample of the representations of the lion in early Greek art.[64] During the classical period there are many more, the total running into hundreds, and there are still more in Hellenistic and Roman times, such as the pebble mosaic of a lion hunt in the late fourth century B.C., in Pella, Alexander the Great's capital in Macedonia.[65] An examination of these ought to be enough to convince skeptics that the Greeks were familiar with the lion through personal observation until a very late epoch.

In addition, there is literary evidence that the lion was seen in Greece. Herodotus tells us that Xerxes' camels were attacked and killed by lions while passing through Macedonia during the invasion of Greece. Aristotle, although perhaps getting his information from Herodotus, says that lions were numerous between the Nessos and the Acheloüs rivers; an examination of a map will show that the area between these two rivers includes the better part of Greece north of the Gulf of Corinth, excluding Epirus. Pausanias repeats the same tale.

Heracles killed the Cithaeronian lion on the border between Attica and Boeotia; he killed the Nemean lion in the Peloponnesus. Both these exploits belong, of course, to the realm of mythology and must not be taken as fact. They do, however, give an indication. The story is made more plausible by Heracles' own name, which means Hera's Glory and is evidence that there was probably a real man of that name, for purely imaginary figures, such as the gods, would never have been given names derived from the names of other imaginary figures. If Heracles, the lord of Tiryns in the Mycenaean age, was real, is it unreasonable to assume that the stories about him, although of course grossly exaggerated, had some basis in reality? And if so, then why is it not very likely that he hunted real lions, particularly in view of the supporting evidence of the Mycenaean artifacts? Nor should we lose sight of these facts: the Old Testament says that there were lions in both Lebanon and Jordan; lions were seen in Palestine as late as the twelfth century; a lion was killed near Damascus in modern Syria in the 1880's; and lions are said to exist in Iraq today.

The only good piece of evidence that there were no lions in ancient Greece is the fact that the only bones of lions that have been found so far are fossil bones. These do correspond exactly with the bones of the modern lion, so we know that there were lions in Greece at some time. It is not impossible that lion bones may yet be found; and it is equally possible that they may not be. All we have to go on is the artistic and literary evidence. But this to me, is enough; it is sufficient to convince me that there were lions throughout all Greece in the heroic age and in northern Greece even during the time of Xenophon. He said so, too!

THE WILD BOAR

Exciting as lion hunting must have been, particularly with weapons that required close combat with the beast, hunting the wild boar made lion hunting seem tame by comparison, for the wild boar is generally acknowledged to be the most dangerous and difficult animal in the world to hunt (with the possible exception of the rhinoceros), as those who have tried the sport of "pig-sticking" in India in modern times can testify.

The wild pig hunted by the Greeks—for they hunted both boar and sow—is easily identified. It was *Sus scrofa*, a species common only in the Old World and completely unknown in the New, where its place in nature is taken by the peccaries, distantly related, but nowhere nearly as big or as dangerous. The razorback hog is not really a native animal, but a domestic pig gone wild, for the domestic pig is a descendant of either *Sus scrofa* or *Sus cristatus*, a slightly smaller species found in India, or of both.[66] There is therefore no possibility that the ancient wild pig could have been anything other than *Sus scrofa*.

This animal is extraordinarily strong, quick on its feet in spite of its apparently ungainly shape, courageous, aggressive, and perhaps more intelligent than the dog. It has very sharp hearing and a keen sense of smell, so it is not easily surprised. Some individuals weigh more than three hundred pounds. Although omnivorous, its preferred diet is roots, which it can dig out of the hardest ground by rooting with its snout. Individuals confined to zoological gardens have been known to destroy macadam paving in only a few days' time. For weapons the boar has tusks which curve up from its lower jaw and are used with great effect to slash and tear its opponents.

The Greeks hunted the wild pig, whether boar or sow, in three different ways: they tracked it down with hounds and drove it into specially made nets; they ran it down in the open; and they caught it with footsnares similar to those they used to catch the red deer. The hounds they used for the pig had to be the very best of their kind if they were to survive a fight with the wild beast. Xenophon recommends Indian, Cretan, Locrian, and Laconian hounds—the Indian, for their size and strength; and the Laconian, for their excellent tracking ability. The nets used were purse-nets similar to those used for the hare, but very much heavier; the skirting-lines were run through metal rings instead of through linen grommets, so that they would run easily. The footsnares, too, must have been very much heavier than those used for the red deer. The spears which the men carried were as heavy as war spears; their blades were fifteen inches long; and there were teeth projecting from the sides of the socket so that the boar could not rush up the shaft and attack the man when it was speared.

The huntsman drew for the boar by slipping his best tracker, one of the Laconian hounds, and then following after with the other hounds still on leashes. The field followed in single file. When the Laconian hound struck, the huntsman slipped the rest of the pack, and the field spread out in open order, approaching the lair abreast. (This is my belief, although some translators think they kept in file; however, such an arrangement would not only be impractical but extremely dangerous. The text, I think, permits my interpretation.)

The nets, of course, had been set up beforehand. The boar might get tangled in one, but it might also come out again without pulling the skirting-line tight enough to close the mouth of the net. In either event, it was cornered and likely to fight, so the best and most experienced man had to approach and dispatch it with a thrust of his spear to the shoulder. Great care had to be used in aiming, because the spear might strike the shoulder blade and glance aside or the boar might knock the spear aside with its head. If the blow failed to reach its mark, the boar was sure to charge, and then the only way the man had of escaping certain death was to throw himself flat on the ground, cling to the earth, and keep as flat as possible, so that the boar could not get its tusks under his body, for their curvature made it difficult. If the boar succeeded, it would tear the man to pieces. If, however, it failed, or if the beast happened to be a sow, it would only trample him. Three hundred pounds of angry pig with sharp little hoofs trampling on his back could be very painful; but at least the man had a chance of life, for one of his companions could entice the pig away and thus give him a chance to rise again.

Running the wild pig down in the open could only succeed if the chase were long and the weather hot enough for the beast to become exhausted. Such a hunt was always dangerous for the hounds, many of which were killed each hunt. Catching the beast in a footsnare presented much the same problem as catching it in a net: someone still had to approach and dispatch it with a blow from his spear. There was no easy way to kill a wild boar.

The temper of the beast was summarized by stories of the heat of its tusks. These were said to become red hot when the boar was angry; and they would set fire to the coats of the hounds if they came close enough for the boar to touch them. Even the tusks of a dead boar were still so hot they would melt the hairs of a hound.[67]

It was the very danger of the boar hunt that made it fascinating to the Greeks; victory was essential, for there was no safety except through conquest. It was that urge to display courage that made the boar hunt the highest manifestation of the chase for the hunter; that urge to show that he too was made of the same stuff as the heroes of the *Iliad* and the *Odyssey*, his forefathers, that compelled a man to take the risks and face the danger.

Xenophon's CYNEGETICUS

INTRODUCTION

The most useful of all our sources of information about ancient Greek hunting is the little book commonly known as Xenophon's *Cynegeticus*, a treatise on the sport as practiced at the end of the fifth century before Christ.

Xenophon, the nominal if not the actual author, was an Athenian historian, essayist, general, and country gentleman, who was born in about 430 B.C. His father was Gryllus, a member of the equestrian order, who belonged to a family of the deme of Erchia and was a man of means. In 401 B.C., at the suggestion of Proxenus, a Boeotian friend, and in spite of the advice of Socrates, whom he knew and greatly admired, Xenophon joined the expedition of Cyrus the Younger against Artaxerxes, going along not as a soldier but as a civilian, hoping through his acquaintance with Cyrus to make his fortune, for his opportunities in Athens were very limited at the time because the equestrian class to which he belonged was out of favor with the democracy then in power.

After Cyrus was killed at the Battle of Cunaxa, the expedition was pointless; but the Greek generals, while trying to negotiate safe passage home for their men, were treacherously murdered. Xenophon was then elected an officer, and it was largely because of his leadership that the army made its way to the Greek colony of Trapezus, on the Black Sea, and then to Byzantium. After brief service with the Thracian Prince Seuthes, the army was incorporated into that of the Spartans, then fighting the Persian satraps Tissaphernes and Pharnabazus in Asia Minor. Xenophon remained with them for a while and then returned to Greece, where he served under the Spartan king Agesilaus, and was present and possibly fought at the Battle of Coroneia, when the Spartans defeated the Athenians.

Probably because of his presence at this battle, but certainly because of his known sympathy with Sparta and his liking for Spartan political institutions (he had sent his two sons Gryllus and Diodorus to Sparta to be educated), Xenophon was banished from Athens. Fortunately the Spartan government presented him with a country estate at Scillus in Elis, not far from Olympia, where he lived the life of a typical country gentleman, overseeing the operation of his farm, hunting, and writing many of his books. After the defeat of the Spartans at Leuctra, however, the Eleans drove him out of Scillus, and he took refuge in Corinth, where he lived until his death in about 354 B.C.

Xenophon wrote the *Anabasis*, an account of Cyrus' expedition; the *Hellenica; Cyropaedia; Constitution of the Lacedaemonians; Agesilaus; Memorabilia; Apology; Oeconomicus; Symposium; Hiero; The Cavalry Commander; Ways and Means; About Horsemanship;* and the *Cynegeticus.*

The *Cynegeticus* consists of one introductory chapter on the origins of hunting, ten chapters on the technical side of hunting, one chapter about the physical and moral benefits to be derived from hunting, and a final chapter which is largely an attack on the Sophists. Whether Xenophon wrote any of the book has long been debated; it is generally agreed now that he could not have written the introductory chapter, which must have been composed several hundred years after his death. The last two chapters are consistent both with his manner of writing and with his known opinions. The ten chapters on the technical side of hunting may very well have been his, for the subject interested him immensely and he approached hunting as he did everything else: you should learn before you begin. The book shows his usual piety, his keen understanding of animal nature, and his ability to record what he saw. Although the book is not as well organized as his other works, it may have been his; if it was his, however, it must have been written before he left on the expedition with Cyrus, for he makes no mention of things he learned about hunting while in Asia Minor, such as, for instance, the use of both tracking hounds and gazehounds, a practice he mentions in book i, chapter vi, section 40 of the *Cyropaedia*.

But whether Xenophon was the author or not, the book is extremely helpful because the author, whoever he may have been, had a keen eye for nature, a real understanding of animals, and a thorough knowledge of hunting. He wrote from his own experience and observation, not simply from the authority of tradition as so many of the later Greek authors did, so we can have confidence in what he says. Whatever the book may lack in literary merit, it is indispensable to anyone who wants to learn about ancient Greek hunting, and I, for one, find it hard to believe that the author is not the same man who wrote about horsemanship.

There is an excellent translation of the *Cynegeticus* by E. C. Marchant in the volume in the Loeb Classical Library series containing Xenophon's *Scripta minora*. Why, therefore, have I translated it again? Because there are a number of details, particularly those relating to the nets, which puzzled Marchant, just as they have puzzled everyone else. It seemed a good idea to clear these details up in the translation as well as in my own exposition. Marchant's difficulty was well explained by William Blane when he told why he too had written his own translation in 1788: "It is very difficult for a general Greek scholar to translate a Treatise on any particular Art, without being in some degree versed in that Art himself." Marchant disclaimed knowledge of horsemanship and would, I'm sure, have done the same for hunting.

Blane, unfortunately, did not translate the whole of the technical part of the *Cynegeticus*, so we cannot use his version; but even if he had, it is better to do another, because the text Blane used was not as accurate as that which Marchant has prepared for the Oxford Classical Texts. This is the version I have used with a very few trivial changes, each noted by an asterisk, and in each of these I have simply reverted to the reading of the manuscript known as "A." The most important of these changes, that in the last line of chapter x, section 2, I have already discussed.

Xenophon's CYNEGETICUS

I

[1] Hounds and hunting are the invention of the gods Apollo and Artemis. They gave them, honoring Chiron with them for his righteousness. [2] He took the gift, rejoicing in it, and put it to use; and he had as students of the chase and of other good things, too, Cephalus Asclepius, Milanion, Nestor, Amphiaraus, Peleus, Telamon, Meleager, Theseus, Hippolytus, Palamedes, Menestheus, Odysseus, Diomedes, Castor, Polydeuces, Machaon, Podalirius, Antilochus, Aeneas, and Achilles, each of whom in his time was honored by the gods.

[3] But let no one wonder that most of them died even though they were pleasing to the gods, for this is nature; but praise of them grew great. Nor should one wonder that they were not all of the same generation, because Chiron's life was long enough for all. [4] For Zeus and Chiron were brothers, sons of the same father, although the mother of one was Rhea; and of the other, the nymph, Naïs. Thus Chiron was born earlier than they and died later, when he had educated Achilles.

[5] Because of their devotion to hounds and hunting and because of their other education, they excelled greatly and were looked upon with admiration for their character. [6] Cephalus was carried off by a goddess; but Asclepius achieved greater things, raising the dead and healing the sick, and for that reason has fame as a god that will always be remembered among men.

[7] Milanion excelled so in diligence that he alone of those men, the noblest of the time, who were his rivals in love for the greatest marriage of the day, won Atalanta. The prowess of Nestor has been heard by the Greeks before, so they would know it should I tell it. [8] When Amphiaraus fought against Thebes it fell his lot to receive great praise and to be honored with immortality by the gods. Peleus even created desire among the gods to give him Thetis and to celebrate his wedding at Chiron's.

[9] Telamon became so great that he married the woman he desired, the daughter of Alcathus, Periboea, who came from a very great city; and when the first of the Greeks, Heracles, the son of Zeus, took Troy and was giving the prize for valor, he gave Hesione to Telamon. [10] The honors that Meleager won are manifest; and it was not his fault that he was unfortunate, for his father, in old age, forgot the goddess. Theseus singlehanded destroyed the enemies of all Greece and, having made his native country larger, is even now admired. [11] Hippolytus was honored by Artemis and joined with her in converse. He died blessed for his moderation and great piety.

While Palamedes lived, he excelled all those in his time in wisdom. But when he was unjustly slain, he was granted such vengeance by the gods as no other man had been given. But he did not die at the hands of those whom people think; for one of them could not have been almost the best, and the other the peer of good men. Evil men did the deed.

[12] Menestheus so excelled in diligence from the practice of hunting that the first of the Greeks conceded that they came after him in the arts of war, except Nestor, and he, it is said, did not excel but rivaled him. [13] Odysseus and Diomedes were brilliant in every single deed and, in sum, were responsible for the conquest

of Troy. Castor and Polydeuces too displayed in Greece so much that they learned from Chiron that they became immortal for these skills because of their own renown. [14] Machaon and Podalirius, who had been taught all the same things, became good men in arts and letters and war.

Antilochus, who died for his father, achieved such glory that he alone was proclaimed among the Greeks as the Devoted Son. [15] Aeneas, after saving his paternal and maternal gods and after saving his own father too, bore such a reputation for piety that he alone of those in Troy whom the enemy vanquished was spared from being despoiled. [16] Achilles, reared in this education, has handed down such great and good memorials that no one has given up talking or hearing about him.

[17] These men whom good men even now still love and evil men envy became so great from the practices they learned from Chiron that whenever there were disasters to any city or king in Greece, they were always ended because of these men. And whenever there was strife or war against all the barbarians by the whole of Greece, it was owing to these men that the Greeks were victorious, for they made Greece unconquerable.

[18] So I recommend to the young not to scorn hunting or other education, for from such things they became skilled in the arts of war and other arts by means of which they think, speak, and act well.

I I

[1] One who is just emerging from childhood should therefore first take up the practice of hunting and subsequently other studies too, after considering what resources he has. If he has enough, he should use what is worthwhile; if not, then at least let him display eagerness, leaving nothing in his power undone. [2] I shall tell how many and what kinds of things must be made ready in order to undertake it and shall tell the science of each so that he may know them before he begins his task. And let no one think these details trivial, for indeed without them nothing would be accomplished.

[3] The net-watcher must be keen about his work, his language

Greek, his age about twenty years, his figure nimble and strong, and his spirit adequate, so that by mastering his tasks with these qualities he may enjoy his work.

[4] The purse-nets, as well as the road-nets and the long-nets, should be made of fine Phasian or Carthaginian flax. Let the purse-nets be of nine threads with three strands of three threads each. Let their size be forty-five inches, their meshes six inches, and their skirting-lines without knots so that they may be easy-running. [5] Let the road-nets be of twelve threads, and the long-nets of sixteen threads. As to size, let the road-nets be twelve, eighteen, twenty-four, or thirty feet; and the long-nets sixty, one hundred and twenty, or one hundred and eighty feet. If they are bigger, they will be difficult to handle. Each should be thirty knots in height, and the intervals of their meshes should be like those of the purse-nets. [6] In the end-meshes let the road-nets have clinches and the long-nets rings, and let them hold the skirting-lines by bands.

[7] Let the props of the purse-nets be thirty inches in length or less; unequally long ones should be put up in sloping spots so that they will hold up the tops evenly; but in the level places the props should be equally long. It should be easy to pull things off them, and they should be smooth.

The props for the road-nets should be twice as long as those for the purse-nets; those for the long-nets forty-five inches in size, having small forks, their notches not deep. All should be strong, and their thickness should not be disproportionate to their length. [8] In number of stakes, it is possible to use many or few for the long-nets; fewer if they are stretched tight in position; more if they are slack.

[9] And let there be a calfskin pouch in which the purse-nets, road-nets, and long-nets may be kept; and let there be machetes for cutting wood to block up whatever is necessary.

I I I

[1] There are two kinds of hounds, the Castorians and the Vulpines. The Castorians have their name because Castor took especial

pleasure in the task of keeping them; and the Vulpines have theirs because they were bred from both dogs and foxes, although over a long time their nature has blended.

[2] Inferior ones, and the majority are such, are small, swine-chopped, glass-eyed, nearsighted, misshapen, stiff, weak, thin-coated, long-legged, badly proportioned, spiritless, noseless, and without good feet. [3] Now the small ones often quit their work on account of their smallness; the swine-chopped ones have poor mouths and therefore do not keep hold of the hare; the glass-eyed and the nearsighted have very bad eyes; the misshapen are also a disgrace to be seen; the stiff are in bad shape after hunting; the weak and the thin-coated are unable to work; the long-legged and the badly proportioned, because they have their bodies badly put together, wander about clumsily; the spiritless leave their work, hold aloof, escape the sun under the shadows, and lie prostrate; the noseless seldom and infrequently wind the hare; the ones with bad feet, even if they are stout-hearted, cannot hold up in their work, but give up because of the pain in their feet.

[4] The styles of hunting among the same hounds are many. For when some pick up the scent, they go ahead without a sign, so you do not know that they are hunting. [5] Some move only the ears, but keep the stern quiet; and others hold their ears motionless, but wag the tip of the stern. Others prick their ears, look solemn because of the scent, let the stern fall, hold it down, and run around. Many of them do nothing but flash around frantically and babble over the scent; and when they stumble on it, they senselessly trample down what they have found.

[6] There are others that employ many circles and digressions and pick up the scent up forward but overrun the hare; and whenever they run across the scent, they make a guess; and when they see the hare ahead, they quiver but do not approach until they see her stir. [7] There are hounds that frequently search for the discoveries of the other hounds as they run on in their casting and drawing, distrustful of themselves; but there are bold ones that do not allow the wiser of their fellow workers to go forward, but hold them back and make an uproar. Some welcome false scents,

show great eagerness for whatever they hit on, and drive on, conscious within themselves that they are cheating. Others, not knowing this, do the same as they do. Those that do not give up the paths and do not know what is right are poor ones.

[8] Those hounds that do not own the trail of the hare and quickly overrun the line of one running are not well bred. Some chase vigorously when they begin, but on account of softness go back; others cut in ahead, then miss the line; and others stupidly burst out into the roads and miss the line and are very disobedient.

[9] Many leave the chase and go home because they hate the chase, and many do this because they love people. Others, after giving tongue on the line, try to cheat and to make the false true. [10] There are those that do not do this but leave their work and run meanwhile to the place where they hear a cry, harking to it without forethought. Some chase aimlessly, and some very presumptuously, imagining differently. Some by pretense, and others grudgingly, keep casting about near the scent and are carried along with the rest to the end.

[11] Now most of these faults are in their natures; but other hounds are useless because they have been trained unintelligently. At any rate such hounds would turn away keen people from hunting. But what the appearance and other qualities of the same breeds should be I shall explain.

I V

[1] Now first, they must be big. Then their heads must be light, flat-nosed, well-knit, with the lower part of their foreheads sinewy; their eyes raised, black, and bright; their foreheads broad with a deep dividing line; ears small, delicate, and bare behind; necks long, supple, and rounded; breasts broad, not without muscle; shoulder blades standing apart from the shoulders a little; front legs short, straight, compact, and firm; elbows straight; ribs not close to the ground but stretching obliquely; loins muscular, their size between long and short, neither very soft nor hard; flanks between large and small; quarters compact; well-muscled behind,

and not tied together above but tucked up within; the lower part of the belly and the belly itself hollow; sterns long, straight, and flexible; thighs hard; lower legs long, rounded, and compact; hind legs much bigger than the front and bent; feet rounded. [2] If the hounds are this sort, they will be strong in appearance, nimble, well proportioned, fast running, and they will be cheerful in appearance, and with good mouths.

[3] Let them follow the scent, departing quickly from the paths, putting their heads slanting to the ground, rejoicing in the scent, and letting their ears drop. Let them go forward to the hare's form, scrutinizing with their eyes, feathering with their sterns, and making many circles, all together on the trail. [4] When they are close to the hare herself, let them make it clear to their huntsman by casting about, pointing out more by their liveliness, by their heads, by their eyes, by the changes in their postures, by their glances up and into the covert, by the way they turn back to the hare's form, by their plunging forward and backward and sideways, and by their spirits, now truly raised up and rejoicing, that they are near the hare. [5] Let them give chase vigorously without relaxing, with much clamor and baying, all coming out together after the hare on every side. Let them pursue fast and brilliantly, borne along after her in a pack, giving tongue properly again and again. And let them not leave the line and return to the huntsman.

[6] Along with this appearance and activity, let them be courageous, keen-nosed, and with good feet and good coats. Now they will be courageous if they do not leave the chase when it is hot; keen-nosed if they own the scent in bare places, in dry places, and in sunny places when the dog days approach. They will have good feet if their feet do not break down in the very hour when they are running in the mountains. They will have good coats if their coats are fine and dense and soft.

[7] The color of the hounds must not be completely tan or black or white, for this is not well bred; on the contrary, the plain coat is beastlike. [8] So let there be tan ones having white hair appearing around the face and black ones and white ones having tan. On the edges of the thighs and upon the loins and below the stern, there

should be straight, thick hair, but above there should be medium-length hair.

[9] It is better to take the hounds to the mountains often but to the fields less often, for in the mountains it is possible to run cleanly, but in the fields it is not possible on account of the paths. [10] It is good also to take the hounds into rough places without finding a hare, for they acquire good feet and are benefited by exercising their bodies in such places. [11] Let them be taken out in summer until noon, in winter throughout the day, in autumn except at noon, and in spring before evening, for these times are moderate.

V

[1] The scent of the hare lies long in winter on account of the length of the nights, but in summer it lies briefly for the opposite reason. In winter, however, there is no scent of hares early in the morning when there is rime or frost, for the rime holds the heat of the scent by drawing it back with its own strength, but the frost by freezing over it. [2] When it is this way, the hounds become insensitive in the nostrils and are unable to own the scent until the sum melts it or the day advances. Then the hounds catch the scent, for it is carried upwards and is perceptible.

[3] But much dew also keeps it down and makes it disappear; and when rains occur, after a while they bring scent, but make the earth bad for scenting until it is dried out. South winds also make scent very bad, for they soak things and spread it; but north winds, if it has not been dissolved, concentrate and preserve it. [4] Heavy showers and drizzling rains wash it away, and the moon makes it faint by its own warmth, especially when it is full moon, and then it is scantiest, for hares rejoice in its luster and jump high in the air, play together, and separate afar. Scent also becomes baffling when foxes go out ahead through it.

[5] Since spring is temperate in weather, it provides brilliant scenting, except when the earth hinders the hounds by blossoming forth and mixing the scent of flowers with it. In the summer scents are weak and indistinct, for the earth is fiery hot and obliterates the heat which they hold, which is delicate. The hounds catch the scent

less then because their bodies have become relaxed. In the autumn scents are clean, for however many crops the earth bears, the cultivated ones have been gathered and the wild ones destroyed by age, so the scents of harvests do not interfere when mixed with the scent of the hare. [6] In winter and in summer and in autumn the line runs straight, on the whole; but in spring it is confused, for the wild animals are always pairing, but especially at this season. So when they wander with each other because of instinct, they make the line this way.

[7] The scent of the hare's trail lies longer than the line of the running hare, for when going to her form the hare moves deliberately, but when she runs, she moves quickly, so in one case the earth is packed solid with scent and in the other is not filled with it. Scent is better in the wooded places than in the bare, for when running around and sitting up the hare touches many things.

[8] Hares lie on whatever the earth grows or has upon it, under anything, on top, inside and alongside; far away, or a little away, or in between. Sometimes also the hare lies in the sea, plunging upon what she can in the water, if there is anything projecting above or growing in it.

[9] Now the hare that is going to her form generally makes her seat in sheltered spots when it is cold; in thick, shaded spots when it is hot; and in sunny spots in spring and autumn; but those hares that are running do not do this because they are terrified by the hounds. [10] The hare reclines by placing her hind legs under her flanks, generally holding her front legs together and stretched out, and she puts her chin upon the top of her feet, with her ears flying back over her shoulders. And so she covers her soft parts. She has hair good for covering, too, for it is close and soft. [11] When she is awake she blinks her eyelids, but when she lies at rest she keeps her eyelids open motionless and her eyes hold still. When she is resting she moves her nostrils constantly, but when she is not she does so little. [12] When the earth is in full bloom, hares keep to the fields rather than to the mountains. The hare stands altogether still when she is hunted, unless she becomes fearful in the night; when she suffers this, she stirs a little.

[13] She is so prolific that she is always conceiving, bearing, and just finished bearing some young. The scent of the little leverets is better than that of the big hares, for they crawl all along the ground since their limbs are still soft. [14] At any rate those who love the chase dedicate the newly born leverets to the goddess. Those hares that are already yearlings run their first run very fast but run no others so fast, for although they are nimble, they are unable to do so.

[15] You should pick up the scent of the hare by leading the hounds out of the fields from the upper side. Many of the hares do not go to the arable lands, [so draw] the meadows, the glens, the streams, the rocks, and the woodlands. And if the hare stirs, it is best not to shout out, lest the hounds become frenzied and own the line with difficulty. [16] When the hares are found and being chased by hounds, sometimes they cross the streams, double back, and plunge into gullies and holes. They are afraid not only of hounds but also of eagles, for they are snatched up crossing hills and bare places until they are yearlings, while the hounds chase and catch the bigger ones.

[17] Now the fastest running are the mountain hares, those of the plains less swift, and the meadow hares are the slowest. Those that wander everywhere in flight are difficult to run, for they know short cuts. They run mostly uphill or on the level, not usually on uneven places, and least of all downhill. [18] When chased they are most visible when going across plowed land, if they are somewhat red; also they are visible when going through stubble, on account of their shadow. They are visible on the paths and roads, if these are flat, for the light on them reflects; but they are invisible when they withdraw among stones, the mountains, rocky ground, or underbrush, because of the similarity of color.

[19] When they are ahead of the hounds, they stop, raise themselves, and listen to see if there is a clamor of the hounds anywhere nearby; and from whatever direction they hear it, they turn away. [20] Even when they do not hear it but think best or are persuaded by themselves, they run away, jumping hither and thither, imprinting track upon track beside the same things and through the same

places. [21] Those found on bare ground run very far because of their visibility, but in the thickets they run very short distances, for darkness provides cover.

[22] There are two breeds of hares. Some are big, somewhat dark in color, and have much white on the forehead; and some are smaller and yellowish and have little white. [23] The first are pied around the scut, and the second pied on the sides. The first have a lot of black on the tips of the ears, and the second little.

[24] The majority of the islands, both those which are deserted and those which are inhabited, have the smaller of them. The number on these islands is greater than on the mainland, for in the majority of the islands there are neither foxes nor eagles to attack them or their offspring. Big mountains have more such dangers than small; and the mountains on the islands are, on the whole, smaller. [25] Hunting people seldom come to the deserted islands, and in the inhabited islands there are few people, and most are not fond of hunting. It is not possible to bring hounds to the sacred islands. So, since few of those existing there or their posterity are hunted, they are necessarily plentiful.

[26] The hare does not see clearly for many reasons, for she has prominent eyes, and eyelids that are deficient and give no protection from the light. [27] Her vision is therefore dim and dispersed. In addition to these difficulties, the little beast's vision is not much helped because she is asleep a great deal. Her speed in running contributes toward her poor vision, for she slips past each object she sees before she knows what it is. [28] Also the fear of the hounds following after when they are chasing her robs her of precaution. So for these reasons she bumps into many things unawares and falls into the nets.

[29] If the hare ran straight, she would seldom suffer such a fate; but now, because she hangs around, loving the place in which she was born and brought up, she is captured. She is not often caught in her tracks by the hounds on account of her speed, and those hares that are, are caught by accident, in spite of the nature of their bodies, for there is nothing in existence of equal size which is put together in such fashion. For her body is made up in this way:

[30] She has a head that is light, small, held low, narrow from in front; ears that are raised high; neck that is slender, rounded, not stiff, and long enough; shoulder blades that are straight and not tied together above; legs attached to them which are nimble and close together; breast not deep, ribs light, well proportioned; loins rounded; quarters well muscled; flanks pliant, rather slack; hips compactly formed, filled in round, and separated adequately above; thigh bones small, strong, with muscles stretched on the outside but not rounded on the inside; lower legs long, solid; forefeet extremely supple, narrow, and straight; the hind feet firm, broad, and bent out a little; hair short, light.

[31] Thus she cannot be anything but strong, supple, and very nimble, put together out of such elements. Sure proof of how nimble she is, is this: When she is going quietly she jumps—no one has ever seen or ever will see her walking—by putting her hind feet beyond and outside her front feet; and thus she runs. This is evident in snow. [32] She has no need of her scut in running, for it is not adequate to guide her body on account of its shortness. However, she does guide herself with either ear; and when she is started by the hounds, she casts down one ear and holds it aslant on whichever side she is harassed, indeed, supporting herself upon it, and turns quickly aside, leaving the attacker behind in short space. [33] So pleasing is the sight that anyone who has ever seen her tracked, found, chased, and caught would forget whatever he loved most.

[34] When hunting in the tilled fields, you should keep off what the seasons produce and let the streams and freshets be, for touching these is disgraceful and evil; also in order that those who see may not violate the law. When it happens that there is no hunting, you must take off all the equipment of the chase.

VI

[1] Hounds' tackle consists of collars, leashes, and belts. Let the collars be soft and broad in order not to chafe the hounds' coats, and let the leashes have loops for the hand and nothing else, for those who make the collars of the same piece do not watch out

for the hounds well. The belts should have broad straps in order not to rub their sides, and spikes should be sewed on in order to protect the breed.

[2] One should not take them out hunting when they do not cheerfully accept food offered them (for this is proof that they are not fit); nor when the wind blows hard, for it effaces the scent, and they cannot own it, and neither the purse-nets nor the long-nets can stand up. [3] But when neither of these things prevents, take them out every other day. Do not accustom hounds to chasing foxes, for it is the greatest corruption and they will never be on hand when needed. [4] Take them out in different places for hunting so that they may be experienced in their hunting and yourself experienced in the country. Go out early in order that they may not be deprived of the scent, as those who are late prevent the hounds from finding the hare and themselves from profiting, for the scent does not linger the whole day, its nature being delicate.

[5] Let the net-watcher go out hunting wearing clothes that are not heavy. Let him set up the purse-nets in [paths] that are winding, rough, hilly, sunken, and shady;* in streams, cataracts, and everflowing torrents; for to these particularly the hare flees—to what else is endless to say. [6] Let him leave ways by and ways through these places, clearly visible but narrow, at dawn but not too early, so that if the line of nets is near the coverts to be drawn, she will not be frightened by hearing the noise nearby—if they are far apart, being early matters less—and make the lines of nets clear so that nothing is held against them.

[7] He should stick up the props aslant so that when they are put in place they will stand the strain. Let him throw the meshes on the tops so they are even and likewise set the props against them, holding up the purse in the middle. [8] To the foot-line let him attach a long, big stone, so the purse-net will not pull out when it contains the hare. Let him make his line long and high so that she will not jump over.

He must not be overzealous in his casts; for although quick catching in every way is industrious, it is not hunting.

[9] Let him stretch the long-nets in level places, throw the road-

nets up in the roads and from the paths to the adjoining ground, fasten the foot-lines to the ground, bring together the end-meshes, fix the props between the margins, throw the head-lines upon the tops, and close up the gaps. [10] Let him keep watch as he goes around, and if the purse-net pulls out of line, let him set it up.

When the hare is being chased into the purse-nets, let him run ahead and shout as he runs. When the hare has fallen in, let him check the fury of the hounds, not by laying hold of them, but by pacifying them. Let him explain to the huntsman by shouting that the hare has been caught or that she has run past this or that or that he did not view her or say where he had a view.

[11] The huntsman should go out wearing light, simple clothing and footwear for hunting, with a club in his hands; and the net-watcher should follow. He should approach the quarry in silence lest the hare stir upon hearing his voice, if she is anywhere near. [12] After tying up the hounds outside the covert, each separately so that they may be easily slipped, he should set up the purse-nets and the long-nets as has been described. After this the net-watcher should be on guard, and the huntsman should take the hounds and go toward the draw for the quarry. [13] After vowing to give a share of the game to Apollo and to Artemis the Huntress, he should slip the hound which is the smartest at tracking just as the sun is rising if it is winter, before daylight if it is summer, and between these hours at other seasons. [14] When the hound has taken the line straight out of the tangle, he should slip another, also; and if the line goes on, he should send the others away, too, one at a time, not allowing much interval between, and should follow without pressing them, speaking to each by name, but not often, so that they will not be excited before the proper time.

[15] With joy and zest they go forward disentangling the line as it develops, whether double or triple, weaving back and forth through it, whether tangled, straight, or curved, close or spread out, familiar or strange, running past one another, feathering quickly with their sterns, pricking their ears, and flashing their their eyes. [16] When they are around the hare, they will make it clear to their huntsman with their sterns and by lunging backward

and forward with their whole bodies, attacking angrily, racing along in rivalry, running together diligently, gathering quickly, spreading out, and again attacking. Finally they will come to the hare's form and will dash at her.

[17] She will start up suddenly and will make the hounds bay at her and give tongue as she goes away. Let the huntsman shout at her while she is being chased, "Yoi, lads! Yoi! Well done! Smartly done, lads!" Around his arm he should wind what he is wearing, take up his club, and run with hounds after the hare. [18] He should not try to head her, for it is impossible. She, recoiling quickly and getting out of sight again, generally doubles back to where she was found. The huntsman should shout at the net-watcher, "Hit her, boy! Hit her now! Hit her now!" and the latter should make it clear whether she is caught or not.

If she is caught on the first run, he should call in his hounds and draw for another. But if not, he must run with the hounds as fast as possible and not give up but go on persistently. [19] And if, while casting for her, hounds find again, he should shout, "Well done! Well done, lads! Hoick for'ard, lads!"

But if they have gotten a big head start, and he is not able to catch up with them by running after them and is quite out of the running, or also if they are casting about somewhere near or are keeping on the line but he cannot see them, he should inquire of anyone whom he approaches as he runs along, by shouting, "Hi there! Say, did you see the hounds?"

[20] And when he has found out, he should approach them, if they are on the line, calling the names of each of the hounds in turn in as many ways as possible, making the sound of his voice high, low, soft, and loud; among other calls, if the chase is in the mountains, he should call, "Well done, lads! Well done, my lads!"*

[21] But if they are not near the line but are overrunning it, he should call to them, "Try back! Try back, lads!" But when they pile up on the line, he should cast them around, making many circles; and whenever the scent is faint for them, he should set up a pole as a guide for himself and trace it from this, urging and coaxing them until they plainly own it.

[22] As soon as the scent is distinct, they will throw themselves on it, spring forward along it, share it, own it, make it known, marking limits for themselves that are familiar, and give chase quickly; and when they are dashing along the line in a body in this way, he should run with hounds without pressing, so that they will not overrun the line through eagerness. [23] When they are near the hare and reveal her clearly to their huntsman, he should take care lest in terror of the hounds she slip away. They—feathering with their sterns, falling all over themselves, jumping high, giving tongue again and again, and lifting up their heads—look at their huntsman, announcing that this is now the real thing; they will start the hare themselves, give tongue, and attack her. [24] But if she falls into the purse-nets or is let past, either inside or outside, let the net-watcher call out each of these occurrences in turn. If he has caught one, he should draw for another; but if not, let him run after, using the same means of encouragement.

[25] When the hounds are already somewhat tired from running and it is already late in the day, then the huntsman must cast for the hare, for she is sinking, and not neglect anything which grows or lies on the ground, making close turns so that she will not be overlooked (for the little beast lies down in a small space and does not get up because of weariness and fear), bringing up the hounds, calling them, encouraging the gentle one greatly, the stubborn one little, the temperate one moderately, until he either kills her in her tracks or drives her into the purse-nets. Afterward, after taking up the purse-nets and the long-nets and after rubbing down the hounds, he should return from hunting, waiting, if it is a summer noon, so that the hounds' feet may not burn on the way.

VII

[1] You should breed the bitches by discontinuing their work in winter so that by having rest they may be brought into first-class condition toward spring, for that season is the best for raising hounds. There are fourteen days in which they are in heat. [2] As they are leaving off, put them to good doghounds in order that they

may become pregnant more quickly. When they are about to whelp, do not take them out hunting continually but leave time between so that they may not destroy their whelps through diligence. [3] They are pregnant sixty days. When the whelps are born, leave them under the bitch that whelped them and do not put them under another bitch, for nursing by others does not promote growth, whereas their mother's milk and her breath are good for them and her caresses are loved. [4] When the whelps are already wandering around, give them milk for a year, as well as whatever else they live on the rest of the time, but nothing else. For heavy feeding in whelps distorts their legs, creates illness in their bodies, and makes their inner parts go wrong.

[5] Give them names which are short, so that they my be easily called. They should be like this: Vital, Passion, Shield-Ring, Butt-Spike, Spearhead, Ambush, Watchman, Sentry, Tactic, Swordsman, Carnage, Flamer, Valiant, Builder, Woodman, Crafty, Havoc, Hasty, Wrathful, Clamor, Outrage, Prosper, Mighty, Blossom, Youthful, Cheerful, Joyful, Glancer, Daylight, Ranger, Forcer, Linesman, Vineyard, Rugged, Screamer, Deadly, Tumult, Potent, Blazer, Splendor, Spear-Point, Thoughtful, Judgment, Tracker, Impulse.

[6] Take the bitches out hunting at eight months, and the dog-hounds at ten months. Do not slip them on the trail to the form, but keep them fastened up on long leashes, and follow the tracking hounds, allowing the puppies to run along on the line. [7] If they are in good shape for running, do not send them in at once when the hare has been found; but when the hare has a head start in the run, so they can no longer view her, send the puppies after. [8] For if one slips them on the spot when they are in good shape and in high spirits for running, they strain themselves when they view the hare and break down, not yet having their bodies conditioned. [9] So the huntsman must guard against this. But if they are awkward and spiritless in running, there is nothing to prevent sending them after, for indeed, as they are hopeless from the first about catching the hare, they will not be persuaded to do so. Let them run the line of the running hare until they catch her, and when the hare has

126

been caught, give her to them to break up. [10] Whenever they no longer want to stay with the scent, but are scattering, collect them, until they become accustomed to running forward to find the hare, lest they always get out of order drawing for her and become skirters, a sorry lesson.

[11] While they are young, give them their feed at the purse-nets when they are taken up so that if they wander during the hunt on account of inexperience, they may be safe when they return to it. This practice should be given up as soon as they show hostility to the quarry, for then they will be intent on the quarry rather than on the feed. [12] For the most part, too, the huntsman himself should give the hounds their feed when they are in need of it: for when they are not in need of it, they do not think him responsible for it; but when they are eager for it, they love the one who gives it.

VIII

[1] Hunt the hare when it snows so that it conceals the ground, for if the ground is black she will be hard to find. But if it is overcast and there is a north wind, the scent is distinct for a long time, for it does not melt away quickly. But if it is wet and also if the sun shines, the scent lasts a short time, as it dissipates quickly.

But when it snows continually there is no use hunting, for the snow completely covers things; nor when the wind is strong, for the snow drifts and obliterates the scent. [2] So there is no use having the hounds go out for this sort of hunting; the snow freezes the hounds' noses and feet and destroys the scent of the hare with excessive frost. So take your nets and go with someone else to the mountains, pass on from the cultivated fields, and when you pick up the scent, proceed along it. [3] If it is mixed up, go out and around it and come back to the same place again, making circles in some such way while you are trying to find where it may go.

The hare wanders much, for she is uncertain where she may lie; and likewise, she is used to being crafty about where she walks, because she is always being chased from such places. [4] When the line is clear, push forward. It will lead to a thickly grown place or to a precipitous place. For the winds carry the snow to such places, so many good resting places are left; she seeks this sort. [5] Whenever the line runs to such places, do not approach closely but go out around in a circle in order not to disturb her, for there is a good chance she is right there. It will be obvious, for her tracks will lead nowhere from such places. [6] Whenever it is clear that she is there, let her be, for she will remain, and draw for another before the scent becomes uncertain, keeping in mind the time so that should you find others, there will be sufficient time to surround them. [7] When the time comes, stretch the long-nets around each of the hares in exactly the same way as in the bare, black places, enclosing within them whatever she may be near; and when they have been set up, approach and start her.

[8] If the hare has wriggled out of the long-nets, you should run after her along her line. She will reach other such places unless she claps herself right down in the snow itself. So wherever she may be, you must note the place, so as to surround it. But if she does not wait, run after, for she may be caught even without nets, as she gives up quickly because of the depth of the snow and because the lower part of her feet are shaggy and collect big lumps of snow.

IX

[1] For deer and their calves, hounds should be Indian, for they are strong, big, fast-running, and not without spirit. Having these qualities, they are up to the work. So hunt the new-born calves in the spring, for they are born in this season. [2] Go out to the meadowlands first and reconnoiter to see where there are the most deer. Wherever they may be, however, the man who handles the hounds should take the hounds and javelins, go before day to this place, and tie the hounds afar off out of the woods so that they may not give tongue should they see the deer. Then he should watch.

[3] Just at daybreak he will see the deer leading the calves, each hind going to the place where she intends to make her calf lie down. When the hinds have put the calves down, nursed them, and have

looked around in order not to be seen by anyone, each keeps watch over her own calf while she goes away to one side. [4] When the hunter sees this, he should slip his hounds, take his javelins, and approach the first calf, wherever he sees it lying, considering the locations so that he will not go astray, for places differ much when you approach near from what they seem when seen from afar. [5] When he sees the calf, he should approach near. It will hold itself motionless, pressing itself upon the earth, and will allow itself to be picked up, crying loudly, unless it has been rained on. In that case it does not wait, for the dampness which is on it, brought about by the cold, quickly makes it take itself off.

[6] It is caught by the hounds if chased hard, but after the huntsman catches it, he should give it to the net-watcher. It will cry out; and the hind, seeing and hearing this, will run up to him where he holds it, seeking to help it. [7] At this moment, he should call the hounds and use the javelins. And taking this hind, he should proceed similarly after the others and employ the same method of hunting against them.

[8] The young calves are caught in this way; but those that are already big are caught with difficulty, for they graze with their dams and with other deer; and when they are pursued they run away in their midst, sometimes in front, but seldom behind. [9] The hinds, when protecting them, trample the hounds down, so they are not easily taken unless someone gets close to them right away and scatters them apart from each other and so singles one out from them. [10] When hard-pressed in this way, the hounds are left behind in the first run, for the absence of the hinds makes the calves frightened and there is nothing like the speed of deer calves of that age. But on the second or third run they are caught quickly, for the calves' bodies cannot hold out because they are still young for the work.

[11] Footsnares are also set for deer in the mountains, around the meadows and the brooks and the vales, in the thoroughfares and whatever cultivated fields they might approach. [12] The footsnares should be woven of yew without bark, in order not to become rotten, and should have circular crowns, and the nails should

be alternately iron and wood, interwoven in the plaited rope. The iron ones should be bigger so that some of the wooden ones may give way under the foot and others press upon it. [13] The noose of the lasso, which is placed on the crown, is woven of broom, and so is the lasso itself, for this rots the least. The noose and the lasso should be strong. Let the attached clog be twenty-two inches long in size, covered with bark, three inches in thickness, of ilex or oak.

[14] Set up the footsnares by removing the earth to a depth of fifteen inches; make this round and equal in size to the crowns of the footsnares above, but changing to narrow below. Remove also some of the earth for the noose and the clog, which are set on both sides. After doing this, put the footsnare on the hole, level and a little below, and put the noose of the lasso around the top. [15] Then, after putting down both this and the clog, each in its own place, put little twigs of spindlewood on the chamber, not extending to the edge, and upon these put fine leaves of whatever is in season. [16] Next, throw some earth on them on the surface, taking first that from the excavation, and on top of this put some solid earth taken from afar, in order that the position may be completely unknown to the deer. Carry the surplus earth away from the footsnare, for if the deer catches a smell of earth that has just been disturbed, it will be shy—and it becomes so quickly.

[17] Take the hounds and examine the footsnares which have been set up in the mountains, preferably at dawn—you must also do so during the rest of the day—and those in the cultivated fields early. For in the mountains deer are caught not only during the night but also in the middle of the day on account of the solitude. But in the cultivated fields they are caught during the night, because in the middle of the day they fear men greatly. [18] When the huntsman finds that the footsnare has been tripped, he should slip the hounds and run after them, cheering them down the furrow made by the clog, noticing which way it is carried. On the whole it will not be hard to see, for the stones will be moved and the grooves made by the clog will be evident in the cultivated ground; if the deer has crossed rough places, the rocks will have torn off the bark of the clog, and down this trail the chase will be very easy.

130

[19] Now if the deer has been caught by the forefoot, it will be caught quickly, for in the run the clog will strike its whole body and face; but if it is caught by the hind foot, the clog will be dragged after and will be a hindrance to its whole body. Sometimes also in its hurry it falls upon forked sticks of brush, and unless it breaks the lasso, it is brought down right there. [20] But whether the deer is caught in this way or is overcome by fatigue, you must not approach near, for it strikes with its antlers as well as with its feet if it is a stag; but if it is a hind it strikes with its feet. So spear it with javelins from a distance.

Deer are also chased and caught without footsnares in the summer, for they fail rapidly and so can be struck with javelins as they stand. Also they dash into the water if they are hard-pressed, and are helpless in the water; and sometimes they fall when out of breath.

X

[1] For wild boars you should get Indian, Cretan, Locrian, and Laconian hounds, purse-nets, javelins, boar-spears, and footsnares. First, the hounds of each breed must by no means be picked by chance, for they must be prepared to fight the beast.

[2] Let the purse-nets be made of exactly the same flax as those for hares, forty-five threads of three strands; each strand of fifteen threads; the size, counting from the cod-end, ten knots; and the height of the meshes fifteen inches. The skirting-line should be one and one-half times the thickness of the purse-nets. Let there be rings on the edges; let them be put under the meshes; and let their ends extend out through the rings. Fifteen rings are enough.*

[3] Let the javelins be of all sorts, with spearheads of good breadth, as keen as a razor, and with solid shafts. First, the boar-spears should have heads fifteen inches in length, with teeth forged of copper at the middle of the socket; they should be solid; and the shafts should be of dogwood, of the thickness of a war spear. The footsnares should be like those for deer.

There should be several hunters, for the beast is scarcely caught even by many. In what way each of these things must be used for the hunt I shall explain.

[4] Now first, after going where the huntsman thinks to draw for the quarry, slip one of the Laconian hounds, but keep the others tied up, and go around with the hound. [5] When it owns the scent of the boar, the field should follow the leading hound, precisely, one at a time. The huntsman will have many clear signs of the boar— tracks in the soft places, broken branches in the thick parts of the woods, and marks of its teeth where there are trees.

[6] The hound generally comes to a wooded place when it is tracking, for the beast generally lies down in such places, as they are warm in winter and cool in summer. [7] When the hound comes to the boar's lair, it gives tongue, but the boar is not usually roused.

So you should take the hound and tie it with the others, far away from the lair, have the purse-nets put up, throw the meshes on forked stays of wood, make a long projecting bosom out of the purse-net itself, and set up branches as supports inside on each side so that the rays of light enter into the bosom through the meshes as much as possible, in order that the inside may be very light to the beast as it rushes toward it. And fasten the skirting-line to a strong tree and not to a bush, for bushes do not hold in bare places. In setting up each purse-net, block up the poorly anchored places so that the boar will make its run into the purse-nets and not escape.

[8] When the nets are set up, the men should go with the hounds, slip them all, take javelins and boar-spears, and go ahead. The most experienced man should cheer on the hounds, and the others should follow in orderly fashion, separated a great way from each other so that there may be sufficient space for the boar to run between them, for if, when it runs away, it falls upon them when they are close together, there is danger they will be gored, because it turns its fury on whatever it encounters.

[9] When the hounds are near its lair, they will attack. It will be aroused by the clamor, and it will toss whichever one of the hounds attacks it face to face. It will run and fall into the net; but if it does not, you must run after it. If the place where it is caught in the purse-net is sloping, it will get up quickly; but if the place is level, it will stand still at once and hold its ground.

[10] At this moment the hounds will press it hard, and the men

132

must throw their javelins at it warily and cast stones while they stand around far away back, until it thrusts itself ahead and stretches the skirting-line of the purse-net tight. Then whoever is the most experienced and the stoutest among those present should approach from the front and strike with his boar-spear.

[11] If it refuses to pull the skirting-line tight when thrust at and thrown at but withdraws, faces toward the attacker, and makes circles around him, then, when it behaves thus, the man must approach it, carrying his boar-spear, holding it with the left hand in front and the other behind, for the left hand should keep it straight and the right hand thrust it. The left foot should follow the left hand, while the right follows the other.

[12] He should approach, holding the boar-spear before him, with legs apart not much more than in wrestling, turn the left side toward the left hand, and then look into the beast's eye, estimating its movement by the movement of its head. He should thrust his boar-spear and watch out that the boar does not knock it out of his hands by jerking its head aside, for it follows the impetus of the jerk.

[13] If this happens, he must fall on his face and cling to the underbrush beneath him, for if the beast attacks one who clings this way, it cannot lift his body up because of the curvature of its tusks. But if he is off the ground, he will certainly be gored. Therefore it will try to lift him up. If it cannot do so, it will straddle and trample on him.

[14] There is only one escape from these animals when held in this painful way. One of his fellow hunters should approach near, holding his boar-spear, and provoke the boar by acting as if he were going to throw it; but he must not let his boar-spear go lest he hit the man who has fallen.

[15] When it sees this, it will let go of the man under it and will turn with wrath and temper on the man who provoked it. The other should jump up quickly, remembering to hang on to his boar-spear as he rises, for safety is no good except to one who conquers.

[16] He should again use his spear the same way and thrust it

inside the shoulder blade where the throat is, stand firm, and hold it stoutly. The boar will come on impelled by rage, and if the projecting teeth of the spear did not prevent, would come rushing up the shaft upon the man holding the spear.

[17] So great is its strength that you would not imagine what properties it has. For when it is dead, if anyone immediately puts hairs on its tusks, they are so hot they run together. In a living one they become red hot when it is roused to anger, otherwise it would not singe the tips of the hounds' hair, when it missed them, with a blow from its body. [18] Thus when a boar is caught, it causes all this trouble and even more.

But if it is a sow that has fallen into the net, the hunter should run up and strike it, watching out that he is not knocked down, for if he suffers that misfortune, he is bound to be trampled on and bitten. So he must not fall underneath if he can help it; but if he should come to this extremity accidentally, the ways of getting away are just the same as from under the boar. He must stand up and strike it with his boar-spear until he kills it.

[19] They are also caught as follows: The purse-nets are first set up for them at the passages from the valleys to the woods, in the ravines, in the thickets, and at the entrances to meadowlands, marshes, and the water. The man appointed holds his boar-spear and guards the nets. The others lead up the hounds, drawing the most likely places, and when the boar has been found, it is chased. [20] Then, if it falls into the purse-net, the net-watcher should take his boar-spear, approach, and do as I have explained. But if it does not fall in, he should run after it.

It is caught also when the heat is stifling and it is being chased by the hounds, for although it is exceedingly powerful, the beast fails when it gets out of breath.

[21] Many hounds are killed in this sort of hunt, and the hunters themselves are in danger, at least when they have to go forward holding their boar-spears in pursuit of a boar that has become exhausted or is in the water or against one that has stopped beside a precipitous place or one that refuses to come out of covert. For neither a purse-net nor anything else prevents it from attacking

anyone who approaches near. Nevertheless, of course, they must approach it when it is this way, and they must display the high courage that made them chose to practice this thing they desire. [22] They must use the boar-spear and the forward positions of the body which have been explained, for if a man does get into trouble, he should at least not do so on account of doing things wrong.

The footsnares are set up for them just the same as for the deer, in the same places; and there are the same methods of inspection, pursuit, approaching, and uses of the boar-spear.

[23] It is difficult to catch the newborn pigs, for they are not forsaken as long as they are little; and when the hounds find them or the little ones see something, they quickly disappear into the woods, and both their parents generally follow and are dangerous then, for they fight more on behalf of their young than of themselves.

X I

[1] Lions, leopards, lynxes, bears, and other such wild beasts are caught in foreign countries, around Mount Pangaeus, and in Cittus beyond Macedonia, some on Mysian Olympus and Pindus, some at Nysa beyond Syria, and some on other mountains where it is possible for such animals to live.

[2] Because of the roughness of the country in the mountains, some are caught with a drug made of aconite. Those who are hunting mix this with whatever the animal likes and put it down around the watering places and near anything else they might approach.

[3] When the animals go down to the plain at night, some of them are intercepted by mounted and armed men and are caught, but the men that catch them are in danger.

[4] For some animals the hunters make very deep circular ditches in the middle of which they leave a column of earth. Upon this they fasten a goat which they tie up toward night, fencing the ditch in a circle with wood and leaving no entrance lest the animals see what is in front. The beasts, hearing the goat's voice in the night, run in a circle around the enclosure; and when they do not find a way through, they jump over and are caught.

XII

[1] I have told about the actual practices of hunting. Those who are diligent in this work will be benefited in many ways, for it provides health for their bodies, better sight and hearing, and keeps them from growing old; it also educates, especially in things useful for war. [2] In the first place, when they are marching on rough roads while bearing arms, they will not give out, for they will endure their labors because they have been accustomed to capturing wild beasts with arms. Next, they will be able to sleep on hard beds and will be good guards of whatever they are put in charge. [3] In approaches against the enemy they will be the kind who attack, and at the same time they will execute orders passed on to them, because by doing the very same thing they caught their game. [4] When stationed in the forefront they will not leave the ranks, because they can be steadfast. When the enemy is in flight they will pursue their opponents straight and unfailingly in every sort of place, because of habit. When their own army has misfortune in places that are wooded and precipitous or otherwise difficult, they will be able to save themselves and save others, too, without disgrace, for their familiarity with the work will better provide them with the knowledge. [5] And indeed, a few such men have ere this forthwith renewed the battle when a big host of allies has been put to flight and have routed the victorious enemy by their own fitness and courage when he has gone astray because of difficult ground. For those who are fit in body and sound in mind can always be close to success. [6] Our forefathers, knowing they were fortunate against their enemies because of such qualities, looked after their young men. For although they were in need of harvests from the beginning, they believed just the same that on no account should they hinder hunters from hunting over growing crops; [7] and besides this, they believed that those who already had this skill should not hunt at night within many miles, so they would not deprive the young men of the game. For they saw that this pleasure of the young alone does much good. [8] It makes men wise and just by educating them in the truth. Indeed, they perceived that they were

fortunate in affairs of war and in other things because of these men. And if those who hunt wish to make a practice of any other good occupation, this skill will not hinder them in any way, as would evil pleasures which they should not learn.

[9] Of such men, therefore, good soldiers and good generals are made. For those whose labors remove shameful and wanton feelings from the soul and body increase their passion for manliness; those are noblest, for they would not overlook the wronging of their own city or the suffering of ill by their own country.

[10] Some people say that one should not love hunting lest one neglect one's own property, not knowing that those who do well for their cities and their friends are all very careful of their own property. [11] So if the lovers of hunting prepare themselves to be useful to their country in the most important matters, they will not neglect their own private affairs, for the property of each is saved or destroyed along with the city; and so, besides saving their own, such men save the private property of others. [12] But among those who say such things there are many people who are thoughtless because of envy and prefer to be destroyed by their own wickedness rather than to be saved by the virtue of others. For most pleasures are evil, and when men yield to these, they are being persuaded for the worse in their words or their deeds. [13] Then by their frivolous words they make enemies, and by their evil deeds they bring sickness and death on themselves, their children, and their friends, being insensitive to the evils but more sensitive to the pleasures than others. [14] Who would employ them to save the city? Those who love what I recommend will certainly refrain from these evils, for a fine education teaches one to obey laws and to speak and to hear about righteous things. [15] So those who give themselves over to perpetual toil and learning have for their portion hard lessons and exercises, but hold safety for their cities; while others who refuse on account of the bother of it, but wish to continue untimely pleasures, are men who are utterly evil by nature. [16] They obey neither laws nor good words, because, as they do not work, they do not find out what a good man should be, and therefore cannot be either God-fearing or wise. But because they are ignorant they

censure greatly those who have been educated. [17] So, because of these men, nothing goes right. All benefits to human beings have been due to the better sort, and the better sort are those willing to work.

[18] This fact has been proved by a great example. Among the ancients those who were with Chiron, to whom I referred, learned many fine things when they were young, beginning with hunting. From these lessons they acquired great virtue, on account of which they are admired even now. That all love Virtue is obvious; but because only through effort is it possible to achieve her, most men stay aloof. [19] Achieving her is uncertain, but the labors involved are obvious. In truth, perhaps men would be less careless of Virtue if her body were visible, for they would know that they are seen by her just as she is visible to them. [20] For when one is seen by his beloved, he is nobler in every way, and he neither says nor does shameful things lest he be seen by his beloved. [21] But thinking they are not seen by Virtue because they do not see her, men do many evil and shameful things instead. But she is everywhere present because she is immortal, and she honors men who are good to her and dishonors the bad. [22] So if they knew she were watching them, they would hasten toward the labors and the education with which she is barely to be won, and they would win her.

XIII

[1] I am amazed at those called Sophists, because most of them say that they lead the young toward virtue but lead them contrariwise. For we have not seen any man anywhere whom the present-day Sophists have made into a good man; nor have they produced writings from which men might become good, [2] but have written many things about frivolities that offer empty pleasures to the young but have no virtue themselves. The Sophists cause instead a waste of time for those hoping to learn something from them that prevents learning other useful things and teaches evil. [3] So I find fault with them the more for their great evils and with what they write, because their phrases are farfetched; and maxims guiding

138

straight, by means of which the young might be educated in virtue, cannot be found in their writings. [4] I myself am a layman, but I know that it is most important to be taught what is good from nature itself, but next, to learn from those who truly understand what is good, rather than from those who have skill in deceiving. [5] Now perhaps I do not speak in the terms of a Sophist, but I do not try to do so: I do try to speak of those things known to be right which those well educated in virtue need to know. Indeed, words teach nothing, but maxims do if they are good.

[6] Many others also blame the present-day Sophists—and not the philosophers—because they are clever with words but not with thoughts. It does not escape me that someone, perhaps one of such men, will say that what has been well and methodically written is not well and methodically written, for quick and false blame is easy for them. [7] And yet it was written this way in order to be right, and to create not quibblers but wise and good men. For I do not wish it to seem useful but rather to be so, in order that it may forever be impossible to refute. [8] The Sophists talk to deceive and write for their own profit and help no one a bit; for none of them was, or is, wise. On the contrary, each one is even pleased to be called a Sophist, a name that is a reproach among sensible men. [9] So I recommend that the precepts of the Sophists be guarded against, and the arguments of the philosophers be not despised; for the Sophists would hunt out the rich and the young, but the philosophers are partners and friends of all, and neither pay honor to nor slight the fortunes of man.

[10] Do not envy those who push ahead rashly for their own advantage, either in their private business or in public affairs. Remember that the best of them, although well thought of, are envied, while the evil ones are both ill thought of and badly off. [11] For they make off with the property of private citizens and that of the city and are more useless than private citizens for the common defense. They keep their bodies in the worst and most disgraceful condition because they are incapable of toiling. But hunting men offer their bodies and their property, which they keep in good shape, to the community for the benefit of the citizens.

[12] These war against wild beasts; those against their friends. And while those who war against their friends have ill repute among all, hunting men who war against wild beasts have good repute. If they make a catch they are victorious over hostile forces, but even if they do not make a catch they are praised, first, because they go out neither to harm a man nor for love of gain. [13] Besides, from this very attempt they become better in many ways and wiser, and we shall explain why. For unless they excel in toil and invention and great pains, they would not catch their game. [14] For the forces contending with them for life, fighting in their own homes, are very strong. Therefore the hunting man's labors are vain unless by greater industriousness and sagacity he conquers them.

[15] So those who wish to gain advantage over a city take pains to vanquish friends, but hunting men take pains to vanquish common enemies. This practice also makes these braver against other enemies; and those, worse. And these take prudence with them on the hunt, and those take shameful audacity. [16] These can despise bad manners and shameful gain; those cannot. Some speak with eloquent voices and others harsh. In religion nothing keeps the one from being profane, while the other are most reverent. [17] Ancient stories have it that even gods rejoice in this work, both as participants and as spectators. And so the young should begin to consider these things, do what I recommend, and be both dear to the gods and reverent, knowing that some one of the gods sees what they do. These will be good also to their parents and to the entire city and to their friends and fellow citizens. [18] Not only have all such men who loved hunting become good, but also the women to whom Artemis showed these things, namely Atalanta and Procris and any others there may be.

Excerpts from the
ONOMASTICON *of Julius Pollux*

INTRODUCTION

A second very valuable source of information about Greek hunting is the *Onomasticon* of Julius Pollux (Polydeuces in Greek) of Naucratis, Egypt, written toward the end of the second century after Christ.

Of the author we know very little. He was a Greek scholar, rhetorician, and lexicographer who lived in the Greek city of Naucratis on the Canopic branch of the Nile, a city which was established by treaty in the seventh century before Christ as headquarters for the Greek traders who brought merchandise to Egypt from all the ports of the Mediterranean. It had already begun to decline in Pollux' time, as Alexandria had superseded it, perhaps because the delta of the Nile had grown farther out into the sea, leaving Naucratis inland. The Egyptians permitted it to keep its Greek constitution, and a number of Greek scholars still lived there.

Although Pollux presumably wrote other books, he is known only for his *Onomasticon*, a dictionary in ten volumes written during the reign of the Emperor Commodus, sole emperor from A.D. 161 to 193 and eldest son of Marcus Aurelius. We can estimate the date of the *Onomasticon* by the facts that the first eight books were written before Pollux was appointed to a chair of rhetoric in Athens, an event which we know could not have occurred before 178, and that the last two books were written afterwards.

The text which we have is not exactly what he wrote but is a reconstruction made from four incomplete, abridged, and interpolated copies of an earlier manuscript, written about A.D. 900, which was itself only an epitome (with interpolations) of something written still earlier, probably tracing back directly to Pollux' original manuscript.

But although it is not the original, it contains a great deal of useful information. To those who have always believed that Dr. Samuel Johnson was the author of the first dictionary, it may be a shock to discover another so very much earlier. There is, however, very little resemblance, for the purpose of Johnson's *Dictionary of the English Language* was to establish correct usage while the purpose of Pollux' *Onomasticon* was to list all the terms relating to various topics. As a consequence it was not arranged alphabetically but according to the topics covered, and within each category Pollux gave synonyms, antonyms, and words related to each other because of identical or similar roots. Because he did not intend it as a reference book, he made no attempt to collect facts, but in the process of illustrating the use of his many terms, he necessarily included a great deal of information. None of this was obtained by personal observation (except, of course, accidentally) but was gathered from the writings of earlier authorities. Among these, of course, was Xenophon, and for that reason the *Onomasticon* has been of immense help to editors in reconstructing the text of Xenophon's *Cynegeticus*. But Pollux includes details not to be found in the *Cynegeticus*, details obtained from other sources which he does not always name. Because of that detail, as well as other information, parts of the *Onomasticon* are of interest to anyone investigating ancient Greek hunting.

THE TRANSLATION AND THE TEXT

Any translation of the *Onomasticon* can, however, be no more than an attempt. The reasons become obvious as soon as one begins: long lists of words are about as interesting to read as the telephone directory; sometimes Greek has more synonyms for a word than English, so the translator is driven to forced and ridiculous paraphrases; sometimes Pollux has included lists of words based on the same or on similar roots in Greek that cannot be translated into English lists with any etymological relationship.

I have purposely included one horrible example of this sort of thing in section 36 of book v. In this section there are five words that in Greek are very much alike, with English equivalents that are etymologically unrelated. I list them here in the order in which they occur and have added a sixth taken from the same section.

stoichos	a line	(of nets on poles)
stochos	a setting	(of nets on poles)
stochas	an erection	(of nets on poles)
stochasmos	a fixing	(of nets on poles)
stoichismos	a surrounding	(of nets on poles)
stoichas	a row	(of olive trees)

Stochas also means an erection of stone or wood needed to level a hollow spot in order to set up the nets.

These are all bad translations, I know, but do give some approximation to the meanings of the words, and at the same time are not mere repetitions. The truth is that the Greek language is no less subtle than the English; indeed, it is frequently more so, so the translator of a Greek thesaurus such as this runs out of words no matter what English thesaurus he may consult.

There is another kind of difficulty involved in this translation, but it is fairly obvious, for it resembles the perpetual problem of translating puns. An example of what I mean appears at the beginning of section 81. Here the Greek word for *bear* is, of course, *arktos*, whence comes our word *arctic*. Because of the impossibility of proper translation, the whole point of this section is lost in English.

Because of these difficulties I have confined my translation to the most pertinent and entertaining parts of book v, the book which includes the subject of hunting. The text is that edited by Bethe, published by Teubner in Leipzig, 1900.

Excerpts from the
ONOMASTICON
of Julius Pollux

Julius Pollux to Commodus Caesar, greetings:

Now hunting is also something with which it is fitting that you be concerned, because this heroic and royal practice makes for a healthy body and a healthy spirit and is an exercise both in peacetime patience and in wartime courage, leads to manliness, and trains one to be strong, swift, skilled in riding, shrewd and industrious if one intends to conquer by strength that which opposes, and by speed that which runs away, and by riding that which draws off, and by wisdom that which is intelligent; and by reflection that which escapes notice, and by time that which is hidden; staying awake at night and laboring by day. So it is needful also to explain something about the chase. . . .

Let the clothing of the hunting man be a chiton hanging down to the thigh, not white or conspicuous like any other bright color, so it won't be observed by the beasts; [18] and in like manner he should wear a chlamys which he must wind around his left arm whenever he runs after the animals or fights against them, and a cudgel or a club, and boots reaching to the middle of the lower leg, bound round with a thong. He should be young, nimble, light-moving, good at running, keen, fond of work, willing to work, diligent, adventurous, competitive, bold, sleepless, not one to give up, not one to quit, not one to give in before the kill. . . .

[19] The tools for hunting: swords, machetes, javelins, bows, boar-spears, purse-nets, road-nets, long-nets, props, stakes, stays, footsnares, cords. Swords, so that should he fall in with a beast,

144

he will have something to defend himself with; machetes, so that should he have to cut some of the brush for unobstructed placing of the nets, machetes may be at hand. For the same reason axes must be provided, if he should have to cut tree-trunks. [20] Hunters also use bows and javelins for deer and for beasts they shoot from afar, and boar-spears for boars and other hard-fighting beasts. And the javelins should be of ash or beech, solid, strong, their heads of good breadth and as sharp as a razor. Let the boar-spears be of dogwood, solid, and as thick as a war-spear, says Xenophon, and let their heads be of the sharpest cutting iron. [21] The part of the head around the wood is called the "flute," of which the outside is called the "circumference," and the inside the "wall," and the part next to the hollow flute is the "spit," whence it is widened, forming wings, defenses on either side. The end, the point of the spearhead, is called the "tongue." And each of the wings, being widened and thickened, must be fined down and also narrowed, terminating gradually, little by little, all the way up to the tongue. It is useful not only for the point but also for the wings to be hardened. [22] Now for beasts other than the boar the boar-spear must be prepared thus: for boars, down at the end of the flute, before coming to the wings, let there be teeth of hard iron, forged together on the flute on both sides, projecting from each side, so the boar may not reach the man when it thrusts itself forward with rage and boldness and strength the length of the spear, but may be hindered in its vehemence when the teeth stop its rush and may not continue forward. [23] Now the javelins must be fitted with thongs for throwing, but the boar-spears do not need a thong because of their use from near at hand. The use of the boar-spear: Advancing the left foot and keeping the right foot back so that the measure of the stride is as great as in battle, let the man keep his advancing side at an angle corresponding with his foot, stretch his hand over backward, grasping the middle of the boar-spear, and hold it firmly, with the right hand turned back. And with the left hand let him aim the iron for the mortal blow, [24] and let the right hand thrust the boar-spear with all its strength. The eye must be directed toward the beast. And if the beast is a wild boar, let him aim the boar-spear and throw it either at a point between the eyes or at the shoulder blade, for both are suitable. If the spear came down on the boar's jaws, it would use its tusks less. When the boar leaps, he should draw his sword and present it. But he must be on guard lest the boar turn aside the boar-spear with a violent knock of its head, a vehement blow on the iron, and the impetus of its leap. [25] For if this happened, the boar would at once be upon the man, and he would have to lie prone, clinging close to the brush. For it cannot use its tusks because of their curvature, nor toss his body, but it walks around on him, and the female also bites him. But if the huntsman were to attack another beast, he should not stand with his feet so far apart but should stand straighter, because these beasts, [26] such as leopards, use a run as they approach the huntsman, and jump; and it is necessary for him to aim at the breast and the heart, for this is appropriate for them.

Now as for purse-nets, long-nets, and road-nets, the flax for these should be Egyptian, Phasian, Carthaginian, or Sardian. Herodotus says the Phasian, which is the same as Colchian, is called "Sardinian" by Greeks, and that from Sardinia is just as good, hence perhaps the Carthaginian also is esteemed because it is obtained from the west. Anyway, all woven hunting gear should be called "nets," but Pherecrates said the same also about toils. [27] The distinction in names in hunting-use calls those set up in the even and level places "long-nets," but those set up in the roads "road-nets." The purse-nets are smaller than these in size and resemble a woman's hair-net in shape, ending in a point. According to Xenophon's book they must be twined together from three strands. The strand is also called a "member"; the strand is twined from three threads. [28] In the purse-net is something called a "mesh"; the mesh is the continuous four-sided interval in the nets, formed by four knots, which becomes rhomboidal when the purse-net is stretched and through which the beasts thrust their heads as they are trying to escape, and becoming entangled in it, are caught. The skirting-line is a little cord on each side of the purse-net that is drawn through the last meshes both above and below, by means of

146

which the nets are drawn together and again released. [29] The skirting-lines must be without knots, says Xenophon, so that they may be easy-running; they are applied to the long-nets by bands. Nowadays some call these same things "head-lines," but others, since there are two, call that coming from the botton a skirting-line and that from above a head-line. There is also a part of the purse-net, the end-meshes, which are the very ends of the purse-nets; some call them "borders" and some "winglets." And besides, in the road-nets are some things given the name "clinches," braids of thread in a circle, attached to the end-meshes; [30] and in the long-nets are rings having the same shape as the clinches, but eyelets of iron are added to them because the long-nets are bigger. For this reason also Xenophon attaches one more member, which he calls a "strand," to the road-nets than to the purse-nets; and he says you must attach a strand more to the long-nets than to the road-nets, making the road-nets twelve threads and the long-nets sixteen threads, the purse-nets being nine threads. He increases the size proportionately by the addition. [31] Margins, which are the edges of the net, are attached to these strands, holding up the net in the middle of the last mesh, above which the skirting-line, or head-line, lies in the fork upon the props. The hollow part of the purse-net is the "cod-end," which some also call the "pocket." A "pouch" is a calf's hide which has been made just like a stitched purse in shape and in which the long-net is put. Stakes and props and stays are straight pieces of wood, set down in the earth, which hold up with forked ends the meshes of the nets and also the skirting-lines. [32] These supports must be unequal so that the net-watcher, when adapting the position of these nets (which is called the "net-line") to the high and low spots of the ground, may level up the unevenness according to need. The props are set up sloping, leaning considerably toward each other.

The foot-trap is set up sometimes for deer and wild boars and should also be called "footsnare." It is a ring of yew wood, and the ring is called the "crown." [33] It is held together by iron and wooden nails alternating with each other, and the plaited rope is woven in the middle, so the beast steps on it when hurrying, for instance, and trips the footsnare and is caught in the firm mesh artfully made for this very thing. The footsnare is put in a trench, and from the mesh around the crown a cord, which they also call a "line" or a "string," extends. The line is a firm braid made of broom, and from this hangs a clog, which is laid in another trench nearby, so if the beast steps on the footsnare and trips it on itself and is held in the mesh, it will be handicapped in running by the string, and the clog will be dragged after it, especially if one of its front feet is held. [34] And it will be possible for the huntsman to run after it, down along the furrow made by the clog, the more easily if it is dragged along on soft earth. The rougher earth itself gives the indication that he should go after the beast down along the abrasions made by the clog. Sometimes also the clog itself is caught in the roughness of the brush or rocks and stops the beast. It is necessary to lay some solid earth in the trench and some grass or leaves and to carry the fresh earth from the trench as far away as possible, lest the beast, smelling the newly moved earth, be made shy.

[35] And this is the preparation which the huntsman must make: let him set up the nets in all places—roads, beaten paths, copses, marsh-meadows, plains, mountains, waters, woods, glens—where he suspects the beast can be found, leaving intervals for passages through, which are called "gaps." Let him have small nets too, if it should be necessary to block up the intervals also. These nets some hunting people have named "inserts," as they are inserted in the line of those put up before.

[36] You should say, to set the purse-nets, to set in, to set around, to cast around, to spread around, to put around, to stretch around, to stretch upon, to set up, to set in a line, to set a line around, to have a line set around. Their setting is called a row, a setup, an erection, a fixture, and a surround. An "erection" is also what something is called that is made by hand, built of stone, or something of wood set up on the earth, for use in setting nets evenly if there should be a hollow around the line of nets. Solon also called certain olive trees "colonnades," contrasting them with the sacred olives; probably they had been planted in a row.

[37] Well-bred hounds are: Laconian, Arcadian, Argive, Lo-

crian, Celtic, Iberian, Carian, Cretan, Molossian, Eretrian, Hyrca-
nian, and Indian. The hounds called "Psyllic" are named for a city
of ancient Achaea, just as the Elymaeans are named for a nation
lying between the Bactrians and the Hyrcanians. Castorians,
Menelaïds, and Harmodians were named for those who raised
them. [38] They say that the Laconians, originally bred from foxes
and dogs, were called "Vulpines," and the Hyrcanians were bred
from dogs and lions and were called "Leonines." Aristotle says
that the Indian hounds were the third generation from a dog and a
tiger, for the first two were savage animals. Nicander the Colopho-
nian says that the Indian hounds were descendants of the hounds of
Actaeon, which, after their madness, became sane, crossed the
Euphrates, and wandered to the Indians; [39] just as also, they say,
the Chaonians and the Molossians are descendants of a dog which
Hephaestus forged from Demonesian bronze, put a soul into, and
gave to Zeus. The latter gave it to Europa, she to Minos, Minos to
Procris, and Procris to Cephalus. It had a nature that nothing could
escape, just as the Teumessian vixen was uncatchable; and for that
reason both were turned to stone, the one that it might not catch
the uncatchable vixen, and the other that it might not escape the
inescapable hound. The Castorians are the creatures of Castor, the
gift of Apollo. [40] And this very same poet says that these are the
Vulpines, for Castor had crossed the breed with a fox. There are
the Eretrians, and Apollo gave these; but he says that those who
took them and raised them are the Eurytides. And further, he says
that the Menelaïds are the same as the Psyllics, for two sister
hounds from there were raised by Menelaus somewhere near the
Argive country. Somewhere near Cyrene a breed of hounds was
bred from wolves and dogs, Aristotle says. Some of the Cretan
hounds are called Workers and some Outrunners; [41] the Workers
are those which, they say, spend the nights as well as the days in the
battle against the beasts and often, after sleeping beside the beasts,
begin the battle after it's day. The Outrunners run beside the
horses, neither running ahead nor being left behind by any means.
The Bitch-Milkers' dogs are around the marshes during midday,
make the milk of cows their food, and fight with the Indian cattle
that approach them in a herd in summer, as Ctesias relates.

[42] Esteemed dogs: That of Pyrrhus the Epirote, which, when Pyrrhus cried out in his sleep, walked around and guarded him, and when Pyrrhus died and his body was being burned, charged into the fire. Those of Hesiod remained behind with him when he was slain and betrayed his slayers with a bark. Icarius' dog also showed Icarius' body to his daughter; and, if one must believe the poets, Sirius is this dog. Notable too is the Epirote, Cerberus, and Alexander's Peritas, the Indian creature. For this hound conquered a lion, was bought for a hundred minas, and Theopompus says that Alexander founded a city for it when it died. [43] They say that the better-bred Indian hounds deem it unworthy to chase another beast, but fight with the lion as being alone worthy of battle, and that they hang on to it by biting, implanting their teeth, so even if the beast is taken, the huntsmen have many difficulties in dragging the hounds away from the beast. And that Alexander, as a test against this sort of Indian hounds, took some Sopeithan hounds and hazarded many kinds of beasts against one of them, and that it lay stretched out on the ground motionless, as if the despised prey was not for it. [44] But when a lion was provided, it roused up, knowing that it had an honorable antagonist. And when, after locking in combat, the beast had had a workout, the hound bit and held it; but someone cut off the hound's foot with a knife. The hound, holding up under the pain of the cut, did not let go its bite but, with spirit, ignored what was done. A hound from Poros was given to the king as a gift, and it is said to have conquered two lions. The marvelous achievement of Argus, Odysseus' dog in Homer, is well known. And Alcibiades also had a notable dog, its price seventy minas, its beauty marvelous; [45] he removed its tail and said to one who censured him for ruining the beauty of the dog that he had mutilated the animal on purpose so that the Athenians would say this and nothing else about him. Notable also was Atalanta's bitch, its name Aura, which the Calydonian boar slew; hence comes the Tomb of the Dog in Calydon. In this way also they have named another tomb on the Hellespont for a famous dog, unless we believe it was named for Hecuba's transformation into the form of a dog. [46] Geryon's dog, which guards his oxen,

was a brother of the Epirote, Cerberus, but was killed by Heracles; its name was Gargettius, and it has a monument in Iberia. Well known also is Triakas, the Paeonian bitch; Dapanis, the Paeonian satrap, gave her as a gift to Alexander. Yet again there is the Magnesian dog, the property of Hippaemon, the inglorious Forgetful, who was buried with his master, just as the epigram declares:

[47] Hippaemon was a man's name, Fleetfoot a horse's,
    Forgetful a dog's, and Babes a servant's.

The names of Actaeon's hounds, in the opinion of Aeschylus, were Raven, Snatcher, Bright-Eye, and Wolf-Howl; and some say that Xenophon, the son of Gryllus, had a notable hound, Horse-Centaur its name. Also they say, in fact, that the Magnesians on the Maeander raise dogs as shield-bearers in war; and the Paeonians also had the same sort of hounds hunting with them. Simonides also made Lycas, the Thessalian bitch, notable, writing this epigram on the bitch's grave:

[48] Truly, I'm sure your white bones in this tomb
    Make even dead beasts tremble still, huntress Lycas.
    Great Pelion knows their virtue, as does far-seen
    Ossa and Cithaeron's lonely lookout places.

And indeed Anyte, the Tegean woman, has covered Locris, about whom she wrote, with glory, inscribing upon her grave:

    You too indeed once perished beside the many-rooted bush,
    Locris, fleetest of noisy puppies;
    A viper with a spotted neck
    Put such cruel poison in your nimble limb.

[49] Moreover one should hunt in every season, and one should make trial of the hounds' ability in cold to see whether they become weak in the nostrils; and in summer, to see if they bear the sun and are aware of the tracks, for the sun makes the scent faint; and in the spring, to see if they can distinguish the scents in the great quantity of emanations from the flowers. At any rate the spring season is more suitable than the wintertime or summertime for hunting, as the air is more temperate, except insofar as the flowers

give them trouble in distinguishing the scents. [50] The autumn is nearest to spring in its temperature, and neither the emanations from the flowers nor those from the crops already harvested attract the hounds' noses. Nevertheless the tracks are very conspicuous through snow, and the hare is not hard to track, but easy to find, inasmuch as the mass adhering to the thick hairs under her feet impedes the ease of her running.

Now the food for the puppies, after the milk of their mothers—for this promotes growth, says Xenophon, as does also the maternal breath itself—[51] but at least after this they should have blood of animals which have been caught, so they may become accustomed to the hunting way of life. Breeding, be it noticed, is on the one hand the raising of puppies, but on the other hand the origin of puppies. And to breed hounds—you must do it in winter—is to fill up with puppies and to cover. But they should be worked out before; and then, after they have rested, they should be coupled, their bodies having become firm from the work and grown in strength from the rest. They should then eat to surfeit, since when they are hunting, it is not good to eat their fill. The food of those in whelp is bread soaked in wine. [52] They are pregnant two months; and one should not take a bitch out on a hunt when she is about to whelp and is approaching birth. One bitch is pregnant about two months, and the whelps do not see before twelve days; but another is pregnant for seventy-two days, and the sight of the puppies is foreordained the fourteenth day. The pregnancy of another is three months, and the eye-opening of the puppies goes on to the seventeenth day. The best time for breeding hounds and for conceiving begins the fourth year for the doghounds and ends the eighth; the bitches should be coupled from three years up until six years.

[53] The diseases of hounds, of course, are three: rabies, distemper, arthritic foot. But arthritic foot is not wholly incurable; rabies is difficult to cure; but distemper leads to death. Everything bitten by a dog afflicted with rabies passes away, and man alone survives, not without dangers.

[54] One must take the puppies on a hunt when the bitches are six months old and the doghounds eight months old, fastened to a

long leash fitted with a thong. When the beast is within your grasp, allow them to catch it at once so that they may enjoy the hunt, allowing them at first to give tongue from the leash and a little later also releasing the thong so that they may not break loose while straining.

[55] The gear of hounds: A broad strap around the neck, stiff, which is also called "neck-strap" and "neckpiece," let sheepskin be sewed inside it so that the hound's throat may not be chafed by the thong. Now the belt itself also is a broad strap on each side, running crosswise from the collar around the sides, so as to cover the parts of the back behind the points of the shoulder blades and the flanks. [56] There are also nails or spikes on the belts; and the belts are also stretched out around the pubic region so that the bitch may not be covered, so that they will not be filled up with the low-born, the spikes restraining the boldness of those attempting to mount. The neck strap is fastened by a little strap which is tied in a loop, like a choke-collar; and the hound is led by this. Some also cover the backs of the hounds with some strong hides, fastening the hides around the base of the necks of the animals so that with this sort of protection they may be less vulnerable when they fall in with one of the fighting beasts.

[57] Excellences of the bodies of hounds: Big, not unsymmetrical or out of proportion, level-mouthed, well knit. The lower parts of the forehead fibrous. The forehead flat, having distinct separations. Heads light and well carried. Eyes raised, black, bright; the pupils shining; the glance, fiery. Ears fine and small and bare behind. Neck long, pliant, rounded. Breast well muscled, rather broad. [58] The shoulder blades of the shoulders should stand apart a little. Each of the legs should be long, but the hind legs bigger; however, the latter should be crooked, and the forelegs straight, solid, compact, not standing out at the elbows. And let the ribs be tucked up and not depressed toward the earth. Although the loins should not be lean, let softness and hardness alike be absent, wholly and in every way. Of flanks the average is best, as bigness and smallness also are to be avoided. [59] With quarters that are rounded, let the parts behind be fleshy; but the parts above, un-

connected, tucked up from within. The flanks themselves, hollow, also the parts below them; sterns, elongated, straight, pointed, flexible; thighs, hard. The second thighs, rounded, elongated, and firm. And the feet, rounded also. Let them have good coats, and let their fur be thick with light, dense, soft hair. [60] Being this sort they appear fleet of foot, nimble, fast-running, and with good mouths.

And here in detail is the story about excellences of the spirit, displaying the hounds as courageous, naturally clever, skilled, with good noses, keen senses, good feet, sharp, industrious, willing to work, stout-hearted, steady, strong, able to catch the scents, to distinguish the smells, to lead to the tracks, to find the quarry, to go after, to run after, to chase after, to follow after, to go on foot, to find out what has been hidden beneath, to pursue what has been seen from in front, to seize what has been left behind, [61] to take care about searching for the scents, but to take it easy about finding the tracks, to lead the way for the huntsman, and if he should be near the find, to indicate it, to make a sign, to show it privately, to make it manifest by the joy of its spirit, by the bounding of its body, by the brightness of its face, by the brilliance of its eyes, by the changing of its expression, by the glancing-up of its look, by its leaps of hope, by the position of its ears, by the wagging of its stern, by the complete agitation of its body. [62] Bad qualities of the bodies of hounds: Small, or high and unsymmetrical, glass-eyed, near-sighted, swine-chopped, weak, hairless, ugly, shapeless, badly put together in the body, twisted in the feet, with no mouths, sluggish, faint-hearted, slow, mute, lame, heavy in the head, fleshy in the front, excessively shaggy in the stern, stiff in the neck, chests narrow, shoulder blades touching each other at the shoulders, ribs deep, loins fleshy, flanks out of proportion to the body, [63] hips elongated and bare of flesh, thighs soft, the second thighs not round, the feet longish. For with such a body the bad quality of spirit would necessarily be present, and the hounds would necessarily be stupid, senseless, unable to divine the scents, noseless, slow, lazy, sluggish, skirters, easily deceived, deceptive, disobedient on the draw, losing heart on the find, spiritless, hating hunting,

154

fond of people, withdrawing from the chase, abandoning the quarry, betraying his fellow hunters, skirting, overrunning, [64] heading the quarry, babbling, not seizing opportunities, rejoicing too soon, turning back in vain, leaping precipitously, heedlessly standing in the way of the wiser hounds, giving up in the sun, sneaking away in the shadows, showing cowardice in the cold, standing out in the rain, not departing from the beaten paths, growing weary, giving up, trembling a little when near the quarry, becoming timid, not smart at finding, not competent at chasing, without sense, with little sense, intemperate, whining.

[65] The color of hounds: One must allow neither wholly white nor excessively black nor entirely tan; but with each color let others be mixed in, either along the forehead or over the top of the nose or along some other part of the body.

[66] A hare's forms: Thickly covered bushes and enormous woods and deep clefts; in winter, sunny places; in summer, shady places; in snow, dark places (these are the hollow places in which the snow has melted away, called "black" because alongside the other earth, which is white from snow, these alone are black). Straight tracks are easy to distinguish; those woven together are hard to distinguish. They become especially so if foxes go forward through them. [67] As to straight tracks, now it is a fact that whenever the hares hear a noise they stand up straight on their hind legs and would like to learn the truth about the noise attacking them. Or else, rejoicing in the light of the moon when it is full, they play with each other, and jumping far, jumping across, and jumping in all directions, they make the tracks appear confused. The form and nature of a hare: the color is somewhat dark—it has the appearance of a dark olive, not one still green, nor one already blackened —[68] size not big, nimble of nature, shaggy of hair, and hairy not only on the top of the feet, but on the bottoms, a thing which Aristotle denies is present in any other animal. So because of this, I suppose, Cratinus and others call the hare "shaggy-foot," making its nature a name for the animal. Now the bigger hare also has more white on its face; and the little one has less white, and its color is reddish. [69] The hare is blue-eyed or gray-eyed, wide-

eyed; and its eyes do not have eyelashes, hence it is also dim-sighted. Often it is asleep; and this too is not a little harm to its eyes. It has a head that is small, light, sloping down, ending narrow; ears raised high; neck narrow, rounded, supple, longish; shoulder blades straight, not tied together above; the forelegs light, close together; breast not fleshy; ribs not heavy or unsymmetrical; the ham fleshy; flanks supple; [70] hips big, rounded, well muscled, not joined together; thighs short, compact, muscular, the inner sides not rounded; second thighs long and solid; the forefeet narrow and long; the hind feet firm and broad; the forelegs much less in length than the hind. The hind legs are crooked so that they bend in beside the forelegs; and on the run they put them in front of the latter and jump, standing firmly on the hind feet, in no way hinder-ing the forefeet by the passing of the latter on the inside. [71] The animal is a leaper and a jumper rather than a runner, but otherwise both nimble and exceedingly light. And since it has a tail not ade-quate to guide its body, it uses its ears for leading, casting them down beside it and rowing the body along as if with some oars. It is caught more on the downhill slopes, as it is urged forward onto its head by the length of its hind legs. On the uphill slopes the unequal length of the legs makes its body level for the run, accord-ing to the unevenness of the locations, for the length of its legs restores its notion of a level place however much the slope is cut away behind. [72] In cowardice this animal excels, becoming terror-stricken and exceedingly scared easily, whence it is also called "cowerer." It goes to sleep, and during its rest it puts its hind legs under its flanks, and it stretches its forelegs out, and holds them together, and puts its head down on them. But if it shuts its eyes and also keeps its nostrils motionless, it is not sleeping but is per-haps resting after work. But if it keeps quiet with its eyes wide open and breathes out while twitching its nostrils, strict sleep holds it. [73] And truly, for the most part this beast is prolific, being always doubly pregnant at all seasons, so it has just now given birth to one, is about to give birth to another, is conceiving another, and is forming another. You would also say it is prolific, very produc-tive, has many offspring, superfoetates, is always filled up with offspring. It gives birth each month. And it is all covered with hair, so even inside its jaws it has hair. Under its scut it has as many holes, insofar as its body allows, as it has years. [74] It is the only one of the animals which has milk even before it gives birth and the only one of the animals with toes which has rennet. And some of the Elymaean hares are no smaller in body than the foxes around us, but their colors turn dark, and they grow to be elongated, and the white around the tip of the scut is longish also. The scent of the track of the "calves" (as they are called) of the hares is very sharp and easily perceived, so the hounds become quite mad about it. [75] Ithaca alone of the islands is barren of hares. The Carpathians, since formerly there were no hares in their island, introduced a pair, but because of their fecundity they increased to a great number and destroyed the crops; and some made a byword on the self-induced evil the Carpathians brought on themselves, "the Carpathian has his hare." And Sicily, too, as Aristotle says, had been barren of hares hitherto, but Anaxilas the Rhegian introduced them and raised them, and at the same time he was also a winner in the chariot race at the Olympian Games, so he had the coinage of the Rhegians embossed with a chariot and a hare.

[76] The hind of the deer is hornless, but the stag is horn-bearing, or bears horns, or is horned, well antlered, broad-antlered, or antlered beyond measure; and one caught by Heracles was gold-antlered. And Anacreon erred when he called a hind "horned" and Sophocles when he called the nurse of Telephus "horned," but Homer correctly says, "near a horn'd hart." Deer have a tawny color spotted with white lines. The females have more markings [than the males], and the calves of the deer have the most. [77] They are caught with nets when anyone trails them and drives them together, but caught with footsnares when anyone lays an ambush and catches them by the foot. The deer brings forth, for the most part, one calf; it is pregnant for eight months and gives birth, after completing its term, at the beginning of autumn. The parents take the calf to their bed so that the surrounding line of precipitous rocks may provide safety on either side; the mother throws herself down and nurses her infant, but the father stands

guard above and defends it from whatever approaches it. Even if you were able to drive the calf away from its parents, to hunt it with hounds, you and your hounds too would be outdistanced, but the calves give up one at a time. Also many grown deer are caught in continuous pursuits because they are out of breath. Both bows and javelins are needed for them. . . .

[80] And if he [the wild boar] were to touch the hounds on the flanks with his teeth, he would set fire to their coats. If, when he is dead, you apply hairs to his tusks, the hairs run together as if from fire. Thus very fiery heat exists in the beast.

The bear gives birth to flesh and forms and articulates the product with its mouth and molds the limbs into the likeness of an animal. [81] And the northern mountain was named for a bear, and the Attic people used to say that maidens served Artemis as "bears." Helice and Cynosure are two bears in heaven; the one was Zeus's nurse, but some say both were. But some say the one was his nurse and the other his darling. And the Arctic is the exact opposite part of the world from the south. The beast is caught with nets, in combat, and in certain pits which some of the hunters have had dug under the fruit trees, [82] over which they have stretched little beams of reed or of some other easily broken wood, have put some undisturbed earth, and have thrown on grass—as the bear hurries, scrambling up the tree after the fruit, the ditch awaits it when the little beams break.

They catch the leopard in the aforesaid ways and mix a drug, aconite, with its food, and the beast is made to empty from diarrhea and is often easy for them to catch. [83] You would say of the leopard that it has its body spotted, all spotted, saffron-colored, fair of face, of good color, fair of form, of many kinds, lithe, twisting easily, of many forms, good at springing, good at wrestling.

And you would say the lion is fierce, royal, with good mane, with good hair, with good beard, overproud, noble, high-minded, arrogant, overweening, immensely big, violent, quick, strong, courageous, stout, powerful. [84] The grown lion is hunted very little with woven gear, but with mechanical contrivances and clever devices; but the cubs are hunted with such things when their parents, with confidence in the difficulty of attacking them secretly and with courage from being powerful, are separated from them on a hunt.

They pursue wild asses on horseback—they go in herds of great numbers—and whenever they become arrogant and very out of breath and the dust, becoming stirred up because of their numbers, annoys them, the men spear some of them with javelins and catch others alive by lassoing them with twisted cords. Some, becoming senseless from the chase, often follow without objection when someone catches them and turns his horse away.

[85] Let the huntsman call his hounds and cheer them on, encourage them, cry out, shout out, indicate, urge on the hounds, exhort, rouse up, push on, start out, urge along, call on, raise up. . . .

[86] The voices of animals: Of dogs, barking and baying, and howl and howling, and whine. You would also say growl and growling and snarl and snarling. According to Xenophon, "tongue," too, for he says, "giving tongue again and again." Some of the poets have also said that hounds cry; and to yip is to speak in an undertone while sleeping. . . .

Arrian's CYNEGETICUS

INTRODUCTION

Approximately five hundred and fifty years after Xenophon wrote his *Cynegeticus*, another little book with the same title appeared; its author called himself "Xenophon the Younger." The book was intended, it said, as a supplement to the other and earlier book, and its author called himself Xenophon because he, like the son of Gryllus, was an Athenian and was interested in the same things—military affairs, philosophy, and hunting.

The real name of the author was Flavius Arrianus, a Greek born in Nicomedia in Bithynia in about A.D. 96. As a young man he had been a pupil of the Stoic philosopher Epictetus (*circa* A.D. 55–135) and had taken notes of Epictetus' lectures, a fortunate thing for us, because Epictetus did not write anything.

Arrian, as he is generally called, was appointed governor of Cappadocia by the Emperor Hadrian, a great distinction because this was the first time a Greek was appointed to a major military command. He served in this position from 131 to 137, and in 134 he distinguished himself by defeating the great Alan invasion. In 147 or 148 he was archon of Athens. In his later years he is said to have returned to his native city of Nicomedia and spent the remainder of his life writing. He died in about 180.

He has an important position in literary history for two accomplishments: one is his recording of the teachings of Epictetus, the other is his history of Alexander the Great. His writings include the *Discourse of Epictetus* (his lecture notes); the *Manual*, a summary of Epictetus' teachings; the *Anabasis of Alexander;* the *Indica; Circumnavigation of the Euxine Sea; Tactica; Acies contra Alanos; the Cynegeticus;* and two lost works, a *History of Parthia* and *Affairs after Alexander*.

161

In his *Cynegeticus* Arrian points out that hunting methods and hounds themselves had changed since the days of Xenophon largely because of the introduction of Celtic hounds and Celtic methods of hunting. He therefore proposed to add to what Xenophon, from lack of knowledge, had been compelled to omit. This he does very well and gives an entertaining and accurate picture of a sport that today we would call "coursing" rather than hunting. In addition, however, he gives us useful information about feeding and bedding hounds down for the night and inadvertently gives us insight into the differences between his own and Xenophon's times.

Just where or how Arrian became acquainted with Celtic hounds is not known. We may hazard a guess that it was not in Gaul or the West that he first saw them, but in Galatia, the territory between his own home province, Bithynia, and Cappodocia, the province of which he became governor, for Galatia owes its name to the fact that it was occupied and settled by Celtic peoples, the Gauls who had crossed the Hellespont in 278 B.C. and laid waste to Asia Minor until they were confined to the area that was then named Galatia.

In 1788 William Blane translated part of the *Cynegeticus*, and a complete translation is said to have been made in 1831, but I have not seen it. In any case, it is time for a new one. The text which I have used is that of A. G. Roos, published by Teubner, in Leipzig, in 1928. I have omitted the table of contents with which this text is prefaced.

Arrian's CYNEGETICUS

I

[1] Xenophon, the son of Gryllus, has told how many benefits
there are for men in hunting, and how those who were taught this
accomplishment under Chiron's guidance were dear to the gods
and held in honor throughout Greece. He has also told us in what
respects the science of hunting is like that of war and at what time
of life one should begin the practice and what sort of figure and
character he should have and about what sort of purse-nets, long-
nets, and road-nets must be prepared, as well as what snares to set
up for those wild beasts which are caught in a snare.

[2] Also he has told about hares, and what their nature is, and
how they feed, and where they lie, and how to draw for them. And
about hounds he has told which ones track smartly, and which
with difficulty, and how you should judge each of them by their
appearance and their work. [3] There is also that which he has told
about hunting boars, deer, bears, and lions, and how they are
caught by craft and cunning.

[4] Whatever I think he omits from his book—not from carelessness, but from ignorance of the Celtic breed of hounds and of the
Scythian and Libyan breeds of horses—these things I shall tell,
as I am a namesake of his and from the same city and because I
have been keen about the same things since youth—hunting, gen-
eralship, and philosophy. [5] For he himself too thought it necessary to write down what had been inadequately told by Simon
about horsemanship, not in disagreement with Simon about it, but
because he thought it helpful to men.

I I

[1] I myself certainly think no evidence is needed that he did not
know the Celtic breed of hounds, because it was not then known
how many the peoples of Europe were or how many were settled

there, because the Greeks did not occupy much of Italy or have dealings with many in trade by sea.

[2] But the evidence that he did not know any breed of hounds like the Celtic in speed is given by the following: he says that whatever hares are caught by hounds are caught in spite of the nature of the hares' bodies, or by accident. [3] But surely, if he understood Celtic hounds, I think he would have declared this very thing about the hounds: that whatever hares the hounds do not catch in their tracks, they do not catch in spite of the nature of their own bodies, or by accident. For they are bred so well in body and in spirit that a hare would never escape them unless some difficult ground or concealing wood hindered, or unless a hollow deep descent did not remove the danger, or there was a ditch to run through in which the hare made herself invisible.

[4] After that, I think, he relates in his book how you must drive the hare into the purse-nets, and if she should run past the purse-nets, how you must run after her and find her on her line until you catch her sinking from fatigue. [5] But in no way did he make it clear that for one who has acquired greyhounds, nothing is needed in the way of purse-nets, or in drawing for an escaping hare, but described only the hunting which the Carians and the Cretans do.

III

[1] Those Celts who do not make a living by hunting dispense with the purse-nets and hunt for the sheer pleasure of it, for there exists a breed of hounds for hunting in this way that is no less clever than the Carian or the Cretan breed, although its appearance is wretched and wild. [2] And these hunt with a clamor and baying as great as the cry of the Carian hounds. [3] But they become even more frenzied whenever they own the scent, so I, for one, have found fault for the most part with them for their cry, which is the same on every scent, the scent of the running hare no less than the scent of the trail. [4] But at running and at finding a lightly moving one, they are no worse in speed. At any rate you must be content if you kill even one hare in the season of winter. These hounds furnish

164

great sport for you up to the end unless, of course, the hare is caught right away by becoming frantic from the clamor of the hounds. These hounds are called Segusiae, getting their name from a Celtic tribe where first, as at least I imagine, they bred and esteemed them.

[5] But whatever anyone may relate about these hounds in his book, he will tell things which have been told by the Xenophon of old, for they display nothing peculiar or different in their drawing or running—except indeed, if one wished to speak about their appearance—so it really doesn't seem to me worthwhile to tell about just that alone, for they are rough and sorry-looking, and whichever among them are the best bred are the sorriest, so it is popular among the Celts to liken them to people begging by the roadside. For, indeed, they have a pitiful and mournful cry and therefore do not give tongue on the line as if they were furious at the beast but pitifully and entreatingly. [6] Indeed, it seems to me that it would not be worthwhile for anybody to write anything about them.

The fast-running Celtic hounds, on the other hand, are called "Vertragi" in the language of the Celts, not from any tribe, as the Cretan, Carian, or Laconian hounds are named, but in the manner in which the Workers among the Cretan hounds are named because of their love of work, the Hasty because of their keenness, and the Cross-Bred because of both qualities; thus the Vertragi too are named because of their speed. [7] The best bred of them are rather good in appearance, both as to their eyes and as to their whole body, their hair, and their skin. Thus in the pied ones the mottling is bright, and in the plain ones the coats shine, and this is a very pleasant sight to a hunting man.

IV

[1] Now I myself shall tell by what means you should judge the fast and well-bred ones; and again, turning your attention to them, how you should distinguish the badly bred and slow ones among them.

[2] First, then, let them stand long from head to stern, for when you think it over, you will find no such proof of speed and good breeding in the whole appearance of a hound as its length and, contrariwise, its shortness as proof of slowness and poor breeding. Thus I, for my part, have seen hounds before this having many other faults, but because they happened to be long, they were fast and high-spirited. [3] Then truly, too, the bigger ones, if they happen to be similar in other respects, are from their very size more suitable than the little ones. Of the big ones such as are not sturdy and symmetrical in form are poor. For this reason alone they would be poorer than the little ones if other faults were equally present in them.

[4] Let them have light and well-knit heads, although if they are swine-chopped or undershot it will not make a great deal of difference, nor will it if they have the parts below the forehead sinewy, but this last fault must not occur in a big one. But the heavy-headed alone are useless, as are those with thick muzzles not coming to a point but cut off short, even if these have good heads.

[5] Let their eyes be big, raised, clear, bright, astounding to the beholder. The best are the fiery-eyed and those with eyes flashing like lightning, like those of leopards, lions, or lynxes. Second to these are the black-eyed, if their eyes happen to be open and terrible to look at; and third are the gray-eyed. For gray eyes are neither bad nor tokens of bad hounds if they also happen to be clear and terrible to look at.

V

[1] For I myself, you know, raised a hound with eyes as gray as the grayest, and she was both fast and diligent and of good spirit and had good feet, so at one time before this in youthful vigor she even held out after chasing four hares. [2] And as to other qualities, she is very gentle (for she was still mine when I was writing this) and very fond of people; never before did any other hound yearn as she did for either me or my companion and fellow hunter, Megillus. For when she quit her course she still did not leave either of us.

[3] But if I were at home, she would pass her time with me and escort me when I went out somewhere and follow closely after me when I went to school. She would sit beside me while exercising; and when I returned, she would go ahead, frequently turning around so as to make sure that I didn't perhaps turn off the road. But when she saw me, she would smile and at once go ahead again. [4] Then if I should go out upon some civic task, she would join my companion and do the same things for him. Then if she should see him after even a little time, she would jump gently, just as if greeting him, and respond to his greeting, showing great affection; and when staying with him while dining, she would lay hold of him with her feet, first this way and then that, reminding him that some of the food must be shared with her also. And truly there would be such a great outcry as I think I have never before known in another hound, for whatever she wants she indicates with her voice.

[5] And because when she was a puppy she used to be punished with a whip, if anyone even now mentions a whip for this purpose, she approaches him who mentions it, cringes, and entreats him, puts her face to his face as if to kiss him, jumps on him, clings to his neck, and will not let go until she stops the wrathful man from his threat. [6] And so I think I should not hesitate to record the name of the hound, as later I was parted from her, because truly Xenophon the Athenian had a most swift, most wise, and most wonderful hound, Impulse by name.

[7] Let the hounds have ears that are big and soft so that they appear to be broken because of their bigness and softness. This way they are the strongest. But of course even if they were upright they would not be bad unless they were small and stiff. [8] Let the neck be long, rounded, and supple, so that if you hold the hounds back by their collars, the neck will seem to bend from suppleness and softness. [9] Broad breasts are better than narrow; and let them have shoulder blades standing apart and not fastened together, but as free as possible from each other. Let them have legs that are rounded, straight, compact; excellent sides; loins that are broad, strong, not fleshy, but solid with sinews; belly slack; quarters not tied together; flanks pliant; sterns fine, long, the hair rough, soft,

flexible, and the tip of the stern rather shaggy; lower legs long and firm. And if a hound had hind legs bigger than the front, it would run uphill better; [10] while if the front legs were bigger than the hind, downhill; and if both pairs were equal, on the level. And since it is difficult not to be beaten by a hare on an uphill place, because the hare runs uphill better, those hounds seem finer which have hind legs bigger than the front. Rounded and fine feet are the strongest.

V I

[1] It will make no difference what sort of colors they are, or whether they are entirely black or tan or white; nor need you suspect the plain in color of being wild. But truly, let them be glistening and clean; and let the hair, whether it happens to be the rough kind or the smooth, be fine and thick and soft. [2] The best doghounds, such as are big and compact, are like the bitches in suppleness; but the bitches, because of their excellence and the muscular appearance of their bodies, are like the doghounds. [3] Certainly it seems to me that one who examines these parts of the body will make sufficient proof of their excellence, and contrariwise, of the opposite.

V I I

[1] And the intelligence of the hounds about each thing will also be no less evident to one who observes as he should. For example, such hounds as are sullen toward everything are not good; however, there are some you would find difficult with strangers, although friendly with the man who is raising them. This is good rather than bad. [2] Once I knew a hound which was dejected at home and greeted none of those who came near; but when let out on a hunt, it rejoiced exceedingly and smiled on everyone who approached and fawned and made it clear that it was displeased at remaining at home. This too was good.

[3] The most excellent are those that are fond of people and those to whom the face of no man is strange. But those that fear men, and are startled by a noise, and are uproarious, and are

stirred up a lot and without purpose (for these things are characteristic of the unreasonable and not of the sensible), exactly like wretched and senseless men, such hounds would never be good. [4] Those also are bad which, when released from their chains some place, do not return when called back by their handler but bound away. And if you call them back gently, they are contemptuous, but if with a threat, they become frightened and do not approach. [5] But the hound which jumps away and runs around must return to the huntsman, even if he should not call, and must give an indication that it is willing to hearken if by this time he wants it to. But if it should not yet be accepted by him, let it bound away and return. [6] When they have been trained, they submit when the huntsman calls, not from fear, but with affection for him who raised them and to honor him, just as do those who make obeisance to the Great King. Nor is it good for a hound which has been let loose in flat country to stand still, unless it happens to be very old, for this indicates sluggishness. [7] In the best-bred, superciliousness is also present, and they appear haughty, and their walk is light and strong and graceful, and they turn their sides and stretch out their necks just as horses do when they are proud.

VIII

[1] Now some eat greedily and others moderately, and moderation is better than the lack of it. [2] Those are good which are not fastidious, but enjoy wheat bread or barley bread, for this food is best for a hound and there is no fear lest they be filled too full of it. Then, it is better if they like their food dry, but even if you soak it in water and they like it, it is not bad.

[3] To a hound that has been working, give either water from fat meat or the liver of an ox after roasting it in hot ashes and then sprinkling it with barley meal, rubbing it, so to speak. [4] Also for those nursing puppies this food is good for hardening the limbs when they leave off giving milk. But for a hound that is working and also for one that shows signs of weakness, both food and drink are good. Fasting is good too for one that is working.

IX

[1] There is nothing like a good warm bed. The best is that with a human being, because hounds are made fond of people this way, and they rejoice in human skin and love the person they sleep with no less than the one who feeds them. And you would notice which of the hounds was unhappy, so as to provide for one which was thirsty in the night and for one urged on by its necessities, and you would know also how it rested. For if it were wakeful or if it dripped frequently in its sleep or threw up some of its food, taking it on a hunt would not be safe. The man sleeping with it would know these things.

[2] But the worst is the sleeping of hounds with hounds, much more so if they should touch each other when they rest; a man sleeping with a hound removes the trouble from its skin, but hounds resting in the same place will increase whatever trouble there is in the skin by coming near and getting warm. So for the most part they are covered with mange whenever they sleep in the same place. [3] The cause and the smell would be evident whenever you went near where many hounds were sleeping, as it is unpleasant and pungent.

X

[1] Rubbing the whole body is also a great help to a hound no less than to a horse, for it makes the limbs firm and the hound becomes strong. It makes the hair soft and the skin glistening, and it cleans off from the skin whatever is bad. [2] Rub the back and the loins with the right hand, putting the left under the flank so the hound is not pressed down from above and made uncomfortable by squatting. [3] Rub the sides with either hand, and the buttocks down to the tips of the toes and shoulder blades the same way. [4] When these seem to have had enough, take hold of the stern, lift it up, and let it go. It will keep wagging when it is set free, and it will be evident that the hound loved having this done.

XI

[1] Tying up a well-bred hound during the day is, like anything else, good; otherwise they are bound to become unmanageable, and if at any time they should be tied up, they would be distressed and would chew their leashes. [2] So bind some iron on them, just as upon criminals. Also a hound which has been left loose eats all that falls to it, and walking around throughout the day takes the zest for running out of them. It is necessary, however, that some walking be planned, although mostly resting.

XII

[1] Take the hounds out at least four times during the day to a level, clean place. There put aside their chains on account of their necessities and for jumping and running around. [2] If they happen to be unemployed at hunting, do this same thing even more often and release two at a time so that by competing and playing they will be gladdened and exercised together. [3] But do not release many at the same time, for they attack each other, and sometimes great evils are done. [4] Also do not release a sturdy and toughened hound at the same time as a bitch in whelp, for the former is bothersome and hard to get along with and when pursuing, kills; and when fleeing, gets away easily; so one can't help being fearful that the whelp in either case will be carried too little time. [5] But do not release those that hate each other, not at the same time, lest they ruin each other. For truly there are hounds hateful to each other, just as there are men; and, indeed, doghounds are especially hateful to doghounds and bitches to bitches, generally from jealousy. One must not keep any of these carelessly.

XIII

[1] In winter, feed the hounds once, at an hour a little before evening, for the day is short and they should be trained so that if they have to work far through the day on a hunt, they will bear up

against hunger. [2] In summer it is good to give a little at dawn to eat hastily, so they will not be worn out by a long wait. And indeed, if they should be thirsty, it would be less uncomfortable if they drank while eating. Also if you would give salted fat to your hound, this also would be good. [3] But if the scorching heat is great, put an egg in your hand, hold it out, and put it in the hound's mouth, so it will drink it down all at once. This and bread will be enough for it, and will relieve its panting, and will quench its thirst.

XIV

[1] Go out hunting often in spring and autumn, for these seasons are safest for the hounds. [2] But in summer go out seldom, and for the most part leave off if it is stifling, for hounds do not hold up under scorching heat, and many before this have choked from panting while chasing with all their might. [3] Indeed, because of this the huntsman should carry eggs so that if his hound pants excessively, he can give one at once, for there is nothing else that both refreshes them more from the heat and stops their panting. [4] But if a hound which is panting hard drinks immediately, it is not safe either. Indeed, on this account you must be cautious when taking them out in the scorching heat.

[5] But even in winter do not take them out if the frost happens to be severe, and, indeed, particularly if the earth happens to be frozen, for hounds are badly frozen on the ice, and some ruin their claws and tear the pads of their feet. [6] If they are very stouthearted, they may even shatter the bones of their feet on the ice by running without regard. The hare, on the other hand, is nimble and has shaggy, soft feet, and so runs painlessly on the hard ground.

XV

[1] Whoever has greyhounds should neither slip them near the hare, nor slip more than two at a time. In fact, if the hare should happen to be exceedingly fast, and has often escaped many hounds, but is roused from her form by the cry of the hounds that are being laid

on, it is bound to make her panic-stricken and to make her heart beat. And in this way fine hares often perish ingloriously, having neither done nor shown anything worth remembering. [2] Allow her then to flee her form and to take courage. If she happens to be good at running, she will at once prick her ears and jump far from her form. But others also fling their bodies about just as those jumping do and then direct their course away. And then at once the spectacle is worth the efforts of those who had to work with the hounds.

XVI

[1] The best of the hares are those which have their forms in the obvious and wide-open places, for it seems to me that they do not hide themselves away but challenge the hounds out of audacity. [2] When they are chased, these same hares do not run to the ravines or to the woods, in this way readily saving themselves from danger, but press on into the plains, competing against the hounds. And if slow hounds follow them, they run just as long as they are being chased; but if fast ones, as long as their strength permits. [3] Often after they have turned aside into the plains, if they notice that a greyhound is following so closely as to be in their shadow, they frequently shake it off as they double back; or, if perhaps they know a way down, some turn again to the ravines. [4] And this proof must be made: that the hound has beaten the hare. For, you know, those who are truly hunting men do not take out the hounds to catch the little beast, but for the competition of the race and as a contest. They are well pleased if the hare succeeds in coming through safely; [5] and when some see her running for refuge, perhaps to a few thistles, cowering and failing, they even call off the hounds, especially if the hounds have put up a good contest. And so I myself ere this have often followed the run closely on a horse; and coming up to her when she was caught, I took her away alive, took the hound away, tied it, and let the hare escape. If I arrived too late to save her, I beat my head, because the hounds had just destroyed a good antagonist. [6] Because of this thing alone I do

not agree with my namesake, although I do agree that whoever saw the little beast found, pursued, and chased would forget whatever he most loved. But I declare that seeing one caught is not a sight that is pleasant or wonderful but rather distressing; and it is not on this account that one would forget whatever he loved. [7] It is pardonable, however, if a hare that was even caught seemed a spectacle to the former Xenophon, as he did not know gazehounds.

[8] That a hound which is following on a run should give tongue even if I do not cheer him on is, I know, very necessary. So a mute hound which breaks out in cry is, with reason, no less than the son of Croesus.

XVII

[1] Cheering your hound on is good too, for hounds rejoice in knowing the voice of their master, and they get encouragement in their work by knowing that they have a spectator present and that it is not unnoticed that they are exerting themselves well. [2] And indeed, on the first run I do not refrain from cheering one on as often as it pleases me; but on the second or third run, when it is likely that the hound may be tired out, I think it hinders to call it often by name, lest it might even wish to court favor with its master and so, with courage and eagerness, might be strained beyond its power and then injure something inside it; for many of the best hounds have been destroyed in this way before now. [3] So under these circumstances send them off to struggle as they wish; for in truth the contest is not equal between hare and hound. On the contrary, the hare runs wherever she wishes, shakes the hound off, and hurries forward; while he, if shaken off, wanders around, and must run after and overtake her again, and catch up with her, however far he has been carried out of his course. [4] The difficult places, too, favor the hare rather more than the hound—things such as rough spots, light stony ground, hills, and uneven places— because she is nimble and her feet are not torn in the rough places because of their shagginess. Running for her life, too, keeps her from noticing the difficulties.

174

XVIII

[1] You should stroke the hound that keeps to its course or has succeeded in some other way by getting down from your horse and praising it. Pat its head, draw out its ears, and speak to it by name: "Well done, Tawny! Well done, Bonna! Good work, Impulse!" and call whatever name each one has, for hounds enjoy being praised, just as well-bred men do. [2] And unless the hound happens to have quit, it will approach, smiling and affectionate. At this point it is good for the hound to roll around, just the way we see horses do, for clearly it did not quit its course; and at the same time this puts an end to their fatigue.

XIX

[1] Those of the Celts who are wealthy and live sumptuously hunt at early dawn, sending out men to the suspected places to scout out where a hare chances to be resting. And there is one man who sends word in case he gets a view or reports how many hares there might be. [2] Then they come and send the hounds after, start the little creature, and themselves follow on horses.

XX

[1] But some of those who do not have men scouting bring out more men to hunt in company with them and go out on horses. When they come to suspicious places where a hare might perhaps be started, they send their hounds after her. Others, who are even more modest followers of the chase, go out on foot, but some one person follows on their behalf on a horse, and this man is appointed to follow along with the hounds.

[2] They go out and around, drawn up in line; then they go straight forward as far as it is fitting to go, turn around again, and at the same time work up along through the same ground, leaving none of the suspected places behind, as far as possible. [3] But if they were to lay on more hounds, they should not go out in random arrangement, for, you see, if the hare is roused from her form, there

is no one who would refrain from sending in his own hound—one man from eagerness to see his own hound running, and another man, startled by the cry, from excitement—and the hare would be caught without a struggle because of the uproar of the hounds, and whatever advantage there was in the spectacle would be lost. [4] On the contrary, a leader should be appointed for the hunt; let him couple the hounds and arrange so that if the hare jumps this way, you and you only are to slip hounds—and let no one else do so—but if this way instead, you and you. But let them agree upon what has been arranged.

XXI

[1] The Celts also hunt by mixing the gazehounds in with those that track. Some of the men draw, while they themselves stand aside, and lead the greyhounds in hand to the place where it is most likely the hare will direct her course, and then lay on some hounds in order that she may go that way. [2] These are the hounds on account of which the former Xenophon had nets. In this way, however, the runs become disorganized; and the hare, even if she happens to be exceedingly good, is generally panic-stricken by the cry of the hounds; and unless she should happen to bound forward far in front, and so can settle her mind, she is easily caught, as she becomes frantic. [3] So whatever good man slips a hound should not send after her while she is confused by the noise, but should allow the hare to unfold her first turns, and send his hounds after in this way, unless he wishes to spoil the spectacle.

XXII

[1] Let it not be your custom to slip hounds on a new-born hare; on the contrary, you should let them go free for the goddess. So you must call off the tracking hounds if possible. But these are ugly when called off, and intractable from hunger, and terrible; they eat up completely what they have caught, so you can barely turn them away by beating them with a stick.

XXIII

[1] You should hunt deer or anything else that approaches such a creature in size this way and slip the greyhounds. For the beast is big and generally runs, and it is not safe to struggle with it. Also the danger is not small that a greyhound may be destroyed on account of a deer. [2] But on plains fit for riding, some of the Mysians and some of the Getae pursue them on Scythian and Illyrian horses, both in Scythia and throughout Illyria. For in the first place these horses are not good for riding, and if you saw them, you would wholly scorn to compare them with a Thessalian, Sicilian, or Peloponnesian horse; but on the whole they are hardy and hold out. [3] And then you would see the fast, big, and haughty horse give out, while the thin, mangy one first outruns it, then outdistances it, and then leads the wild beast away. [4] Thus it holds up until the deer gives out. The deer stands exhausted and gaping from confusion; and at that time it is possible, if you wish, to strike it with a javelin from nearby, as it is held fast; but if you like, you may lead it away alive by throwing a noose around it.

XXIV

[1] In Libya, with Libyan horses (which, you know, are called Numidians, both the men themselves and their horses), I do not say that they catch deer or gazelles, for even after a long struggle good horses do not seem able to catch any such thing, but they do catch wild asses, which are of course different in speed and hold out for a very long distance when running. [2] For example, when the Greeks with whom Xenophon campaigned along with Cyrus, the son of Darius, were marching against the Great King, Xenophon said that where the plains of the Arabians ended, herds of wild asses appeared before them, and that a wild ass was never caught by a single horseman, but that one after another attacked it separately, and that some asses, after holding out against many men, at last failed from fatigue. Thus then even Cyrus, the son of a great king and brother of a great king, had no horses good for pursuit.

[3] But children of the Libyans, some of them possibly eight years old and some not much older, ride on their stripped-down horses, using a stick on them much as Greeks use a bridle, and in this manner follow the wild asses very far, and in this way end by throwing a noose on the beast and by leading it; and it follows, defeated. [4] In this way, then, those who have good hounds and horses hunt, not by fooling the beasts with snares, nets, or nooses—not with clever contrivances and devices at all—but by competing straightforwardly.

[5] There are no sights, I think, resembling this, for in some ways it is like piracy or theft, and in others like war fought out at full force. Some, like pirates, sailing up stealthily, are carried toward the beasts, while others conquer the beasts openly, just as the Athenians conquered the Medes in a sea battle near Artemisium, or the battles near Salamis and Psyttalia, or again near Cyprus.

XXV

[1] The age of a hound for running: Take a bitch out on a hunt after the eleventh month or even before the tenth month if she happens to be strong and is not weakly formed. Let the hare go from your hand in an obvious place, and let the bitch go after the hare from nearby, so as to give her her fill of a view and so that when she sees the hare is nearby, she may work with good hope. [2] But send another well-bred bitch later so that the puppy will not be in distress for long and quit from fatigue. The older bitch frequently unrolls the hare easily and hands her over to the puppy. But you should not allow the bitch which caught her to tear her with the teeth until the puppy kills her.

[3] When presently it is time to take them out, first walk whichever roads are rough, for the practice is good for hardening the feet of the hounds. [4] Then station the person holding the bitch in a place that is conspicuous and high and do not send her away on the first hare that comes along and gets ahead if she does not see; for this, mind you, the former Xenophon recommends about hounds trained for tracking. [5] Should you slip a gazehound bitch

if she does not see she will be led astray and may jump and become frenzied and be frightened. [6] Therefore, if the hare should ever escape her when she reaches maturity, she will not keep still, or return to the huntsman, or hearken when called, but will stray aimlessly from the habit of running to no purpose and will resemble a mad dog. [7] So station the person who holds the puppy in a place of the sort I have already described, hidden where you would best judge the hare when hard-pressed will come when she doubles back. [8] When the hare sees and is exhausted, set the bitch on her from nearby, not face to face, or the opposite, for when the bitch starts out, she will immediately be carried beyond, while the hare will draw off easily and will outrun her. She will necessarily be left far behind and will turn back with difficulty, just as triremes sailing straight do not turn about easily unless some of the rowers back them until they are turned around. [9] But if you have allowed the hare to run away to the side, you should lay the bitch on. When the hare is caught, let someone quickly follow before the bitch has taken her fill of the blood, not because the meat is of much account to a man who hunts for pleasure, but because it is a bad lesson for a well-bred hound to eat hare. Also many hounds have been destroyed this way ere this, since while panting from a long run, they get filled full and then choke and die.

XXVI

[1] Do not take the doghounds on a hunt before they have become two years old, for, mind you, the limbs become strong much later in the doghounds. [2] And the danger is not small; on the contrary, many before reaching maturity have already perished from competing before their time, especially those that are the best-bred, for they run with as much courage as they can. [3] As to other things, watch out similarly, for all the things I have already told concerning the bitches must be done.

[4] Guard also against their mating within this period of life, for somehow the seed is not planted securely by them but is evanescent

and uncertain, just like that of boys, and they themselves are ruined utterly, so nothing you do later straightens out the mistake. But after the third year it would be a suitable time to put them to.

XXVII

[1] Let them be put to in this way: You should watch when the bitch is clean of blood, for if they receive the seed sooner for the most part they do not catch, and instead the seed is washed out with the blood, just as with women. [2] Take heed of this: a short time intervenes in which blood is no longer produced in her, but she still keeps in heat.

A good age for the bitch is that from two to seven years.

XXVIII

[1] It is best to confine the doghound in the same place with the bitch, but he should be invisible to the hounds, for matings in plain sight are not fruitful, if you must believe hunting men. Inasmuch as such things have been zealously pursued in secret by hounds, it has succeeded in becoming a rule. [2] Afterward take them out hunting, for walking around is good for making the hounds strong; but do not let them go for a hare yet, for there is danger of their being ruined by overstraining and fatigue. [3] And likewise, do not send a doghound after a hare before resting from fatigue and being strengthened no less than sixty days. Then nothing will prevent sending them into the contest.

XXIX

[1] The best season for breeding is that of spring, for in this season frosts and hot spells keep temperate. Frost is not so good for raising puppies, and besides, there is a scarcity of milk; but heat is difficult for the mothers in their nursing; and autumn is worse than spring for breeding, because winter overtakes the puppies before they have become strong.

180

XXX

[1] If you still wish the mother to resume her former speed, do not allow her to nurse, because for the most part bitches are not free from milk for such a thing. Accordingly, take away the puppies and give them to other hounds, choosing well-bred ones, for milk from mongrels is not the right kind for the well-bred. [2] But if the bitch should not yet seem fit for running, it is best to leave the puppies under their mother and not put them under another bitch, for nurture by others, just as the former Xenophon declares also, does not promote growth; but their mother's milk and breath are good.

XXXI

[1] And whenever the whelps are already wandering around, he advises correctly that you should raise them on milk and that heavy feeding distorts their legs and creates illness in their bodies. [2] Also that names which are short and easy to call must be given to the hounds, and in this respect you should be persuaded by him. He has even described such names, discovering some, but making some up himself, and has described them cleverly.

[3] If you do not yet wish to breed them, watch the hounds with the greatest care possible when they are in this condition. The udders of those which have left off nursing are full to bursting and are full of milk, and the parts under the belly are stretched. [4] Under these circumstances it is not safe to slip a hound on a hare, for their flanks would be torn. Nor should you let them loose to jump around with another hound, for sometimes when they are competing and straining beyond their strength they put themselves in equal danger. So it is best for them to wait until their udders become slack. It is proof that they are already safe when their hair falls off in masses when they are lightly stroked. For then they are freed, I think, from their former condition and are by that time ready for the run.

XXXII

[1] A bitch is faster than a doghound, but a doghound is better for hard work than a bitch. Also, because a doghound runs for years, its possession is more honored by almost anyone; and because many bitches are good but it is not easy to happen on a well-bred doghound, the latter is more honored in this way also. [2] Also, with the bitches you must be content if they keep their speed even up to the fifth year, but the doghounds keep it even up to the tenth. And so it seems to me that a doghound is a great possession, truly noble, and not to be gained by a hunting man excepting with the grace of the gods.

XXXIII

[1] But you should sacrifice to Artemis the Huntress for this possession. You must also sacrifice upon doing well on a hunt and must dedicate the first fruits of what you catch to the goddess and cleanse the hounds and the huntsman, according to the rule of our fathers, as is customary.

XXXIV

[1] It is the custom of the Celts too to sacrifice annually to Artemis. Some also deliver a treasure chest to the goddess, and into the treasure chest they throw two obols for each hare they have caught, but a drachma for a fox because it is a treacherous thing and destroys the hares; because of this they throw in more for it, as if for an enemy that has been caught. And for a roe deer they give four drachmas, because the animal is big and the animal is more honored. [2] When the year comes around and the birthday feast of Artemis comes, the treasure chest is opened, and with what has been collected they buy a victim for the slaughter—some a sheep, some a goat, some a calf if it goes that well. [3] Also, after beginning the sacrifice of their offerings to the Huntress, as is the custom of each of the Celts, both they and the hounds feast sumptuously.

Also they put wreaths on the hounds that day, so it will be clear that they are holding festival on their account.

XXXV

[1] I too, with my fellow hunting men, follow the custom of the Celts, and I declare that without the gods nothing good can be accomplished by men. [2] For even those who go sailing are led by those gods whose care is their preservation, and those who return safe sacrifice thank offerings to the sea gods—Poseidon, Amphitrite, and Nereus. Those who till the soil sacrifice to Demeter and her daughter and to Dionysus; those laboring over the arts, to Athena and Hephaestus; those over education, to the Muses, Apollo Musagetes, Mnemosyne, and Hermes; those over love affairs, to Aphrodite, Eros, Peitho, and Charis. [3] Thus, you see, those also who are zealous about hunting must not be careless about Artemis the Huntress or Apollo or Pan or the Nymphs or Hermes, the Wayside God and Guide, or about whatever other mountain gods there are. [4] Otherwise the things they are keen about must turn out half done, for their hounds will be disabled, their horses lamed, and their men overthrown.

XXXVI

[1] Homer makes this clear in his poetry too. For he denied that Teucer, most skilled for the Greeks with the bow, missed the mark in the contest because his bowstring was cut in two but because he did not pray to Apollo; while Meriones, a man not skilled with the bow, had prayed to Apollo and hit the mark when the bird had already flown away. [2] Even the descendants of those campaigning with Polynices against Thebes for the purpose of seizing Thebes "were urged by portents of the gods, or else by help from Zeus."

But their fathers, who were not a bit worse than they in prowess, were destroyed in Thebes because they would not obey what was indicated by the gods. [3] Even Hector, who did not listen to Poly-

damas when the latter would not allow him to charge the ships of
the Greeks—pointing to the serpent overthrown before the eagle—
on the ground that they would not return to the charge in good
order, changed his mind a little later about the deed, because it
was not good to be disobedient to divinity. [4] It is needful that we
be obedient to these just as in any other task and thus be led by the
gods even on a hunt, sacrificing thank offerings when we have done
well, make libations, give honor, reward with a wreath, and dedicate the first portions of what has been taken, no less than the first
fruits upon a victory in war.

Notes and References

(For abbreviations see bibliography)

I: EQUIPMENT FOR HUNTING

CLOTHING

1. Poll. v. 17–18.
2. *O.C.D.*, "Dress."
   D.C.A., "Clothing," "Himation," "Chlamys."
3. Houston, chap. ii.
4. Opp. *Cyn.* i. 97–105.
5. *O.C.D.*, "Ephebi."
See also:
   Xen. *An.* vii. iv. 4.
   Grat. 338–40.
   Butler, chap. iii.
   Manns, chap. iii.
   Liddell-Scott, *passim*.

WEAPONS

6. *Anth. Gr.* vi. 152.
   Theoc. 4. 49; 7. 128.
   Xen. *Cyn.* vi. 11.
7. *Hare*, p. 64.
8. *Anth. Gr.* vi. 176.
   Opp. *Cyn.* i. 152–54.
9. *O.C.D.*, "Arms and Armour, Greek," "Hoplite."
10. Poll. v. 19–22.
11. Poll. v. 23–24.
12. Opp. *Cyn.* i. 91.
13. *D.C.A.*, "Weapons," "Gymnastics."
    Gardiner, chap. xvi.
14. *D.C.A.*, "Swords."
15. Robert, pp. 271–76.

16. Hom. *Il.* i. 37; iv. 105–26; viii. 266–329.
17. Paus. i. xxiii. 4.
18. Xen. *An.* iv. ii. 28.
19. McLeod, "Unpub. Bow, Brkln"; "Egpt. Bows, N.Y."
20. Xen. *An.* iv. ii. 28.
21. McLeod, "Trig."
22. Xen. *An.* iv. ii. 28.
23. "Anc. Treat."
24. Xen. *Cyr.* vii. iv. 15.
See also:
   Xen. *Eq.* xii. 11–13.
   Grat. 108–47.
   Butler, chap. iii.
   Manns, chap. iii.

HOUND TACKLE

25. Xen. *Cyn.* vi. 1.
    Poll. v. 55–56.
26. Anderson, pp. 43, 59.

NETS

27. Xen. *Cyn.* vi. 26.
28. Opp. *Cyn.* i. 150 ff.
    Poll. v. 26–35.
    Xen. *Cyn.* ii. 4–8.
29. *Hare*, p. 69.
    Rabbit, p. 139, *passim*.
30. Petrie, p. 147.
31. *Enc. Brit.*, "Knots," "Net," "Seining, Netting and Trawling."
    Shaw, *passim*.
    Verrill, *passim*.

32. *Master of Game.*
33. Marinatos-Hirmer, Pl. 181.
34. Manns, chap. iii.
35. Xen. *Cyn.* x. 2, 7.
    Enc. Brit., "Pig Sticking or Hog Hunting."
See also:
    Xen. *Cyn.* vi. 7, 9.
    Anth. Gr. xii. 146.
    Grat. 24–60.
    Paus. v. v. 2.
    Tryph. 222.

36. Xen. *Cyn.* ix. 11–16.
    Poll. v. 32–34.
37. Xen. *Cyn.* xi. 4.
38. Nemes. *Cyn.* 299–308.
See also:
    Grat. 75–94.
    Opp. *Cyn.* i. 156.
    Butler, pp. 91, 93.
    Manns, chap. iii.

OTHER EQUIPMENT

39. Xen. *Cyn.* ii. 9.
    Manns, chap. iii.

II: THE BREEDS OF HOUNDS

THE HOUNDS OF ANTIQUITY

1. Opp. *Cyn.* i. 398–400.
2. Xen. *Cyn.* vii. 3.
3. Paus. vii. xviii. 5–6.

EUROPEAN BREEDS

4. Opp. *Cyn.* i. 371.
   Poll. v. 37.
   Nemes. *Cyn.* 228.
5. Opp. *Cyn.* i. 371.
   O.C.D., "Campania."
6. Varro ii. ix. 5.
7. Opp. *Cyn.* i. 396.
   Nemes. *Cyn.* 231 ff.
8. Grat. 172–94.
   Verg. *Aen.* xii. 753.
9. Arr. iii. 1–7.
10. Butler, *passim.*
11. Buchanan-Jardine, p. 4.
12. Holder, II, 1457.
    Meyer-Lübke, III, 247.
    Letter from Professor Eric Hamp, Department of Linguistics, University of Chicago: "Generally the word is glossed as 'swift-footed dog,' even though the etymology of the component parts is clear enough: *ver-* is a superlative prefix, and *trag-* is good Celtic for 'foot.'"
13. Godefroy.
14. Xen. *Cyr.* i. vi. 40.
15. Opp. *Cyn.* i. 468–80.
16. Strabo iv. v. 2 (C 199).
    Claud. iii. 301.
    Grat. 174–78.
    Nemes. *Cyn.* 225–26.
17. Grat. 202.
18. Nemes. *Cyn.* 227.
19. Opp. *Cyn.* i. 373, 397.
    Grat. 157.

20. Opp. *Cyn.* i. 371, 395.
    Poll. v. 46–47.
21. Keller.

ASIATIC BREEDS

22. Grat. 159.
    O.C.D., "Seres," "Sinae."
23. Ael. *N.A.* iv. 19; viii. 1.
    Poll. v. 37–38.
    Xen. *Cyn.* x. 1.
24. Arist. 607*a*. 3.
25. *Enc. Brit.*, "Dhole."
26. Poll. v. 37.
27. Ael. *N.A.* iii. 2.
28. Ael. *N.A.* vii. 38.
    Poll. v. 37.
    Grat. 161–70.
29. Grat. 155.
30. Ael. *N.A.* vii. 38; *V.H.* xiv. 46.
    Arr. iii. 1 ff.
    Dio Chrys. xv. 30.
    Opp. *Cyn.* i. 371, 373, 396.
    Poll. v. 37, 47.
31. Grat. 160.

AFRICAN BREEDS

32. Ael. *N.A.* vi. 53; vii. 19; *V.H.*
    i. 4.
    Arist. 606*a*. 22–24.
    Opp. *Cyn.* i. 374.
    Pliny VIII. 148.
    Solin. xv. 12.
33. Nemes. *Cyn.* 229.
34. Arist. 607*a*. 2.
    Poll. v. 40.
35. Ael. *N.A.* xiv. 21.
    Poll. v. 41.

GREEK BREEDS

36. Grat. 184–85.
37. Grat. 182.
38. Poll. v. 39.
39. Ael. *N.A.* iii. 2; x. 41.
    Arist. 608*a*. 28.
    Athen. v. 201*b*.
    Opp. *Cyn.* i. 375.
    Poll. v. 37, 39.
    Claud. ii. 215; iii. 292.
    Grat. 181, 197.
    Hor. *Ep.* 6. 5; *Sat.* ii. vi. 114.
    Luc. iv. 440.
    Lucr. v. 1061, 1063.
    Nemes. *Cyn.* 107.
    Sen. 32, 33.
    Stat. *Ach.* i. 747; *Silv.* ii. vi. 19;
        Theb. iii. 203.
    Verg. *Geo.* 3. 404–5.
    Bk. of the Dog, pp. 32, 330,
        351, 476, 560–70, 662, 672.
    Nat. Geog., pp. 246–49.
40. Grat. 186–92.
41. Xen. *Cyn.* x. 1.
42. Grat. 183.
43. Poll. v. 40.
    O.C.D., "Moliones."
44. Poll. v. 37, 40.
45. Opp. *Cyn.* i. 371, 396.
46. Grat. 214 ff.
47. Polyb. v. xx. 4.
48. Arist. 574*a*. 16 ff.
    Opp. *Cyn.* v. 372, 396.
    Poll. v. 37–40.
    Xen. *Cyn.* iii. 1 ff; x. 1, 4.
    Grat. 212.
49. Poll. v. 40.
50. Poll. v. 37.
    O.C.D., "Aristogiton."

51. Opp. *Cyn.* i. 373.
52. Keller, no citation.
53. Grat. 183, 202.
54. Grat. 209.
    Liddell-Scott, *passim.*
    Aymard, *passim.*
55. Ael. *N.A.* iii. 2.
    Arr. iii. 1–4.
    Opp. *Cyn.* i. 373, 395; *Hal.* iv.
        274–78.
    Poll. v. 37.
    Xen. *Cyn.* x. 1.
    Claud. iii. 300.
    Grat. 211–12.
    Luc. iv. 441.
    Sen. 33, 34.
56. Poll. v. 39.
57. Arr. iii. 1–4.
58. Arist. 608*a.* 25–33.
59. Opp. *Hal.* iv. 274–78.
60. Poll. v. 41.

HISTORICAL
    DEVELOPMENT OF
    THE BREEDS

61. Iljin, quoted in *Bk. of the Dog*,
    pp. 5, 20.
62. Buchanan-Jardine, p. 406.

III: THE CARE OF
THE HOUNDS

THE BREEDING
    PROGRAM

 1. Hull, chap. vi.
 2. Xen. *Cyn.* vii. 2.
 3. *Bk. of the Dog*, pp. 432–33.
 4. Poll. v. 38.

188

 5. Ael. *N.A.* viii. 1.
    Arist. 607*a.* 1–8.
 6. Opp. *Cyn.* iii. 1.
    Grat. 253.
 7. Poll. v. 38.
    Xen. *Cyn.* iii. 1.
 8. Arist. 607*a.* 1–8.
    Poll. v. 40.
 9. Opp. *Cyn.* i. 398–400.
See also:
    Ash, *New Bk.*, Pl. facing p. 27.
    Whitney, chap. v.
    Enc. Brit., "Animal Breeding."

MATING AND PREGNANCY

10. Arist. 545*b.* 3–9; 574*a.* 16.
11. Xen. *Cyn.* vii. 6.
12. Xen. *Cyn.* vii. 1.
13. Poll. v. 52.
14. Arr. xxvi. 4; xxvii. 2.
15. Arist. 574*a* ff.
16. Xen. *Cyn.* vii. 2.
17. *Anth. Gr.* ix. 303.
See also:
    Ael. *N.A.* xii. 16.
    Grat. 263 ff, 287.
    Nemes. *Cyn.* 103 ff.
    Pliny viii. 151.
    Varro ii. ix. 11.
    Verg. *Geo.* 2. 323 ff.
    Hull, chap. vi.
    Whitney, chap. v.

PUPPIES

18. Arr. viii. 1–4.
    Xen. *Cyn.* vii. 3.

19. Nemes. *Cyn.* 127–76.
See also:
    Ael. *N.A.* vii. 12; ix. 5; x. 45.
    Arist. 574*b*. 8–13, 25–27.
    Colum. vii. xii. 14.
    Grat. 287–309.
    Geop. xix. ii.
    Opp. *Cyn.* i. 436–43.
    Hull, pp. 163–64.

FEEDING

20. Arr. viii. 1–4.
    Xen. *Cyn.* vii. 4, 11–12.
    Nemes. *Cyn.* 151–56.
21. Poll. v. 51.
    Colum. vii. xii. 10.
22. Arr. xiii. 1–3.
23. Arr. xiii. 1–3.
24. Brock, chap. iii.
    Hull, pp. 161–62.
25. Merrick, *passim.*
See also:
    Athen. iii. 109–62.
    Call. Hymn 3. "To Artemis."
    Geop. xix. 1.
    Varro ii. ix. 8–10.
    Verg. *Geo.* 3. 404–5.

KENNELS AND BEDDING

26. Hom. *Od.* xvii. 296–98.
27. Cato cxxiv.
28. Varro ii. ix. 12–13.
29. Arr. ix. 1–3; xi. 1.
30. Nemes. *Cyn.* 165–71.
31. *Geop.* xix. ii.

EXERCISE AND TRAINING

32. Hull, chap. vii. p. 3.
33. Arr. xii. 1–3.
34. Xen. *Cyn.* vii. 5.
35. Poll. v. 42, 45–48.
36. Ovid. *Met.* iii. 143–253.
37. Xen. *Cyn.* vii. 11–12.
38. Xen. *Cyn.* vii. 6–10.
39. Xen. *Cyn.* iv. 10.
40. Xen. *Cyn.* vi. 4.
41. Xen. *Cyn.* vi. 3.
42. Arr. xxv. 1; xxvi. 1.
43. Arr. xxv. 2–9.
44. Arr. xvi. 8.
    Xen. *Cyn.* iv. 5.
45. Luc. iv. 441.
    Pliny viii. 147.
46. Xen. *Eq.* viii. 13.
    Plut. 961D.
47. Xen. *Cyr.* i. iv. 19.
See also:
    Opp. *Cyn.* i. 481–513.
    Grat. 326–30.
    Nemes. *Cyn.* 165–92.

DISEASES AND CURES

48. Xen. *Cyn.* iii. 3; vii. 4.
49. Ael. *N.A.* iv. 40.
    Arist. 604*a*. 4–9.
    Poll. v. 53.
50. Nemes. *Cyn.* 216–23.
51. Grat. 383–95.
52. *Geop.* xix. iii.
53. Hull, p. 124.
54. Arr. ix. 1–3.
    Nemes. *Cyn.* 195.
    Garbutt, *passim.*
    Merrick, *passim.*

55. Xen. *Cyn.* vii. 4.
56. Arist. 612*a*. 31.
57. Ael. *N.A.* ix. 33.
58. Colum. vii. xiii.
    Varro ii. ix. 14.
59. Grat. 352 ff.

See also:
    Ael. *N.A.* viii. 9.
    Arist. 612*a*. 5.
    Plut. 963E, 974B.
    O.C.D., "Hippiatrici."

IV: HARE HUNTING

BREEDS OF HARES

1. *Enc. Brit.*, "Rabbit."
2. Bourlière, p. 171.
3. *Enc. Brit.*, "Rabbit."
4. *Rabbit*, p. 8.
5. Bourlière, p. 7.
6. *Rabbit*, p. 13.
7. *Hare*, pp. 5–6.
8. *Rabbit*, pp. 17–18.
9. Polyb. xii. iii. 9–10.
10. *Rabbit*, pp. 2–4.
    Ael. *N.A.* xiii. 15.
    Athen. ix. 401*a*.
    Polyb. xii. iii. 9–10.
    Enc. Brit., "Rabbit."
11. Arist. 580*a*. 5.
12. Xen. *Cyn.* v. 17.
13. Poll. v. 67.
14. Xen. *Cyn.* v. 22–23.
15. *Hare*, pp. 4–5.
16. Pliny viii. 81.

FAMILY LIFE OF THE HARE

17. *Hare*, p. 20.
18. *Master of Game*, p. 17.
19. *Master of Game*, p. 18.
20. Arist. 539*b*. 22–23.
21. Ael. *N.A.* xiii. 12.
22. *Geop.* xix. iv.
23. *Master of Game*, p. 219.
24. Xen. *Cyn.* v. 4.
25. Paget, p. 135.
26. Hdt. iii. 103.
    Xen. *Cyn.* v. 13.
    Arist. 579*b*. 30.
27. *Hare*, p. 15.
28. Bourlière, p. 167.
29. *Hare*, p. 21.
30. Plut. 971D.
    Paget, p. 147.
31. Xen. *Cyn.* v. 18.
32. Arist. 579*b*. 31—580*a*. 5.
33. Ael. *N.A.* xiii. 11.
34. Xen. *Cyn.* v. 24.

HABITS AND CHARACTERISTICS

35. Xen. *Cyn.* v. 8–14.
36. *Hare*, p. 18.
37. Poll. v. 66.
38. Ael. *N.A.* xiii. 13.
39. Arist. 519*a*. 22.
40. Ael. *N.A.* ii. 12; xiii. 13.
    Xen. *Cyn.* v. 8–14.
    Blane, p. 133.
41. Arist. 536*b*. 24–30.
42. Xen. *Cyn.* v. 26.
43. Xen. *Cyn.* v. 11.
44. Littauer, p. 39.

45. Xen. *Cyn.* v. 32.
46. Poll. v. 71.
47. Ael. *N.A.* xiii. 14.
48. Ael. *N.A.* ii. 12.
Poll. v. 73.
Pliny viii. 81.
49. Ael. *N.A.* v. 27; xi. 40.
50. Arist. 507*b*. 16.
51. Ael. *N.A.* vii. 8.
52. *Hare*, p. 23.
53. Xen. *Cyn.* v. 8.
54. *Hare*, p. 23.

SCENT OF THE HARE

55. *Enc. Brit.*, "Smell and Taste."
Hull, pp. 35–38.
Pollard, *passim.*

PREPARATIONS

56. Athen. ix. 299*d.*
57. Hom. *Il.* x. 360–62.
58. Xen. *Cyn.* vi. 17.
59. Xen. *Cyn.* vi. 4, 6, 13.
60. Xen. *Cyn.* vi. 12.
61. Xen. *Cyn.* vii. 5.
Ovid. *Met.* iii. 143–253.
62. Opp. *Cyn.* iv. 56–76.
63. Opp. *Cyn.* iv. 425–38.
Xen. *Cyn.* v. 15–17.
64. *Hare*, p. 217.
65. Xen. *Cyn.* vi. 5–6.
66. Xen. *Cyn.* vi. 9.
67. Paget, pp. 150, 176.
68. Xen. *Cyn.* vi. 9.
69. *Hare*, p. 69.

THE CHASE

70. *Hare*, pp. 72–73.
71. Xen. *Cyn.* vi. 13.
72. Xen. *Cyn.* vi. 14.
73. Paget, p. 138.
74. Ael. *N.A.* xiii. 14.
Xen. *Cyn.* v. 19.
Arr. xvi. 2.
75. Beckford, x.
Blane, p. 130.
76. Paget, pp. 150–51.
77. Xen. *Cyn.* vi. 21.
78. Xen. *Cyn.* vi. 29.

HUNTING IN SNOW

79. Xen. *Cyn.* viii. 1–8.

COURSING

80. Arr. *passim.*

V: ANTLERS AND
HORNS

THE RED DEER

1. Xen. *An.* v. iii. 10.
2. Bourlière, *passim;* Simpson,
passim.
3. Simpson, *passim.*
4. Simpson, *passim.*
5. Harper, p. 457.
6. Miller, p. 965.
7. Harper, p. 459.
Miller, p. 969.
8. Polyb. xii. 3.
9. Miller, p. 969.
10. Harper, p. 456.

11. Arist. 500*a*. 6–13.
12. Arist. 611*a*. 29.
13. Arist. 611*b*. 9.
14. Arist. 611*a*. 31 ff.
15. Arist. 578*b*. 13.
16. Arist. 578*b*. 7; 611*b*. 32.
17. Arist. 578*b*. 17.
18. Arist. 578*b*. 21.
19. Darling, p. 160.
    Red Deer, p. 34.
20. Twici, p. 50.
21. *Master of Game*, p. 204.
22. *Red Deer*, pp. 39–40.
23. Darling, p. 168.
24. Darling, p. 164.
25. Darling, p. 75.
26. Darling, pp. 181–82.
27. Xen. *Cyn*. ix. 10.
28. Hom. *Il*. xxii. 191–92.
29. Xen. *Cyn*. ix. 8–9.
30. Ael. *N.A*. vii. 39.
31. Arist. 578*b*. 32.
32. Darling, p. 64.
33. Darling, p. 145.
34. Darling, p. 163.
35. *Red Deer*, p. 271.
36. Arist. 579*a*. 5.
37. *Red Deer*, p. 30.
38. Arist. 579*a*. 10.
39. Xen. *Cyn*. ix. 20.
40. Opp. *Cyn*. ii. 217.
41. Opp. *Cyn*. ii. 233.
42. Opp. *Cyn*. ii. 291–92.
43. Solin. xix. 18.
44. Arist. 578*b*. 23.
45. Bourlière, pp. 207–8.
46. Poll. v. 77–78.
47. Darling, p. 181.
48. Xen. *Cyn*. ix. 3.

THE FALLOW DEER

49. *Enc. Brit*., "Fallow Deer,"
    "Deer."
50. Miller, p. 970.
51. Opp. *Cyn*. ii. 293–95.

THE ROE DEER

52. Miller, pp. 972–75.
53. Twici, p. 39.
54. Darling, pp. 92–93.
55. Darling, p. 53.
56. Miller, pp. 972–75.

THE GAZELLE

57. Harper, *passim*.
    Miller, *passim*.
58. Liddell-Scott, *passim*.
59. Leister, "Antelopes," *passim*.
    Harper, p. 688.
60. Harper, pp. 683, 687, 689.
61. Ael. *N.A*. vii. 19.

OTHER ANTELOPES

62. Leister, "Antelopes," p. 87.
63. Leister, "Antelopes," p. 88.
64. Leister, "Antelopes," p. 88.
65. Leister, "Antelopes," p. 67.
    Harper, p. 642.
66. Leister, "Antelopes," p. 78.
67. Leister, "Antelopes," p. 90.
68. Opp. *Cyn*. Introduction, p.
    xix.

SHEEP AND GOATS

69. Opp. *Cyn*. ii. 382.
70. Harper, p. 559.
71. Harper, p. 618.

72. Harper, p. 621.
73. Opp. *Cyn.* ii. 377.
74. Leister, "Antelopes," *passim.*

WILD CATTLE

75. *Enc. Brit.*, "Cattle."
76. *Enc. Brit.*, "Aurochs."
77. Simpson, *passim.*
78. *Enc. Brit.*, "Aurochs."
79. Caes. *B.G.* vi. 28.
80. Verg. *Geo.* 2. 374; 3. 632.
81. Pliny viii. xv (15) § 38.
82. *Enc. Brit.*, "Aurochs."
83. Opp. *Cyn.* ii. 43–158.
84. Harper, *passim.*
85. Harper, *passim.*
86. Harper, p. 544.

METHODS OF HUNTING
    DEER

87. *Red Deer*, p. 198.
88. Hom. *Il.* xv. 271–76.
89. Apollod. ii. v. 3.
90. *Master of Game*, p. 235.
91. Hom. *Il.* xxii. 189–92.
92. Xen. *Cyn.* ix. 5–7.
93. Xen. *Cyn.* ix. 8–9.
94. *Red Deer*, p. 223.
95. Xen. *Cyn.* ix. 18.
96. Babr. 43.
97. Opp. *Cyn.* iv. 385 ff.
98. *Red Deer*, p. 200.

METHODS OF HUNTING
    WILD CATTLE

99. Paus. x. xiii. 1–4.

VI: OTHER GAME

SMALL GAME

1. Opp. *Cyn.* ii. 570.
2. Miller, pp. 15, 895.
3. Miller, p. 115 ff.
4. Miller, *passim.*
5. Babr. 31.
6. Babr. 32.
7. Miller, p. 441.
8. *Enc. Brit.*, "Otter."
9. *Enc. Brit.*, "Primates."
10. *Enc. Brit.*, "Beaver."
11. Miller, p. 898.
12. Miller, p. 577.
13. Miller, p. 865.

BIG GAME

14. Hdt. iii. 97.
15. Arist. 501*b*. 30.
16. Ael. *N.A.* iv. 31; xi. 37.
17. Philostratus, quoted by Mair
    in note to Opp., p. 99.
18. Paus. v. xii. 1–3.
19. Opp. *Cyn.* ii. 493 ff.
20. Plut., 972B.
    Ael. *N.A.* viii. 10.
21. Harper, p. 375.
    Opp. *Cyn.* ii. 551.
22. Ael. *N.A.* vii. 44.
23. Opp. *Cyn.* iii. 461.
24. Liddell-Scott, *passim.*
25. Liddell-Scott, *passim.*
26. Opp. *Cyn.* iv. 354 ff.
    Miller, p. 285.
27. Arist. 600*a*. 27 ff.
28. Arist. 579*a*. 21.
29. Opp. *Cyn.* iii. 159 ff.
30. Opp. *Cyn.* iv. 354 ff.

ASSES AND HORSES

31. Hom. *Il.* xi. 558.
32. Arist. 577*b*. 11 ff.
33. Arr. xxiv. 3.
34. Opp. *Cyn.* i. 317.
35. Haines, *passim*.
36. Opp. *Cyn.* iii. 352.
37. Arist. 498*b*. 32.
38. Arist. 491*a*. 3.
39. Harper, p. 371.

THE FOX, WOLF,
  JACKAL, CIVET CAT,
  AND HYENA

40. Xen. *Cyn.* iii. 1.
   Poll. v. 38.
41. Hom. *Epig*.
42. Arist. 488*a*. 28; 488*b*. 12 ff.
43. Arist. 607*a*. 2.
44. Opp. *Cyn.* iii. 293.
   Miller, p. 315.
45. Liddell-Scott, *passim*.
46. Opp. *Cyn.* iii. 263.
47. Arist. 579*b*. 15 ff.

THE CATS

48. *Enc. Brit.*, "Cat," "Panther,"
   "Puma."

49. Harper, p. 256.
   Miller, p. 457.
50. *Enc. Brit.*, "Cat."
51. Miller, *passim*.
   Harper, *passim*.
52. *Enc. Brit.*, "Cat," "Leopard,"
   "Panther."
53. *Enc. Brit.*, "Cat," "Ounce,"
   "Snow Leopard."
54. *Enc. Brit.*, "Cat," "Cheeta."
55. Opp. *Cyn.* iii. 85 ff.
56. *Enc. Brit.*, "Cat," "Tiger."
57. *Enc. Brit.*, "Cat," "Lion."
58. Xen. *Cyn.* xi. 4.
59. Xen. *Cyn.* xi. 2.
60. Opp. *Cyn.* iv. 124 ff.
61. Arist. 629*b*. 21.
62. Opp. *Cyn.* iv. 147.

THE LION IN EUROPE

63. Meyer, *in toto*.
64. Marinatos-Hirmer, Pl.
   XXXVI.
65. Robertson, p. 169.

THE WILD BOAR

66. Leister, "Pigs."
67. Xen. *Cyn.*, x.

Bibliography and Abbreviations

GREEK AND LATIN AUTHORS

(ET=with English translation on facing pages)

Ael. *N.A.*   Claudius Aelianus, *On the Characteristics of Animals*, ed. A. F. Scholfield. 3 vols. Loeb Classical Library, 1958 (ET).

Ael. *V.H.*   ———, *Varia historia*, ed. Adiamantios Koraes. Paris, 1805.

"Anc. Treat."   "An Ancient Treatise on Military Archery," tr. Wallace McLeod, *Journal of the Society of Archer-Antiquaries*, V, No. 1 (Spring, 1962), 10–11.

Anth. Gr.   *Anthologia Graeca*, ed. W. R. Paton. 5 vols. Loeb Classical Library, 1921 (ET).

Apollod.   Apollodorus, *The Library*, ed. Sir J. G. Frazer. 2 vols. Loeb Classical Library, 1921 (ET).

Ar.   Aristophanes, *Thesmophoriazousae*, ed. Benjamin Bickley Rogers. London: George Bell & Sons, 1904 (ET).

Arist.   Aristotle, *De Animalibus Historia*, ed. Leonardus Dittmayer. Leipzig: Teubner, 1907.

Arr.   Flavius Arrianus, *Cynegeticus*. In *Scripta minora*, ed. A. G. Roos. Leipzig, 1928.

Athen.   Athenaeus, *Deipnosophistae*, ed. C. B. Gulick. 7 vols. Loeb Classical Library, 1927 (ET).

Babr.   Babrius, ed. W. G. Rutherford. London, 1883.

Caes. *B.G.*	Gaius Julius Caesar, *The Gallic War*, ed. H. J. Edwards. Loeb Classical Library, 1919 (ET).
Call.	Callimachus, *Hymns and Epigrams*. In *Callimachus, Lycophron, Aratus*, ed. A. W. Mair. Loeb Classical Library, 1921 (ET).
Cato	Marcus Porcius Cato, *De Agricultura*. In *Cato and Varro*, ed. W. D. Hooper and H. B. Ash. Loeb Classical Library, 1934 (ET).
Claud.	Claudius Claudianus, *Stilicho*, ed. M. Platnauer. 2 vols. Loeb Classical Library, 1922 (ET).
Colum.	Lucius Junius Moderatus Columella, *De re rustica*, ed. H. B. Ash, E. S. Forster, and E. Heffner. 3 vols. Loeb Classical Library, 1941 (ET).
Dio Chrys.	Dio Chrysostomus, *Orationes*, ed. J. W. Cohoon and H. Lamar Crosby. 5 vols. Loeb Classical Library, 1932 (ET).
Diod.	Diodorus Siculus, ed. C. H. Oldfather. Loeb Classical Library, 1933 (ET).
Eur. *Hipp.*	Euripides, *Hippolytus*, ed. W. S. Hadley. Cambridge, 1889.
Geop.	*Geoponica*, ed. H. Beckh. Leipzig, 1895.
Grat.	Grattius, *Cynegeticon*. In *Minor Latin Poets*, ed. J. W. Duff and A. M. Duff. Loeb Classical Library, 1934 (ET).
Hdt.	Herodotus, *History*, ed. A. D. Godby. 4 vols. Loeb Classical Library, 1921 (ET).
Hom. *Epig.* Hom. *Il.* Hom. *Od.*	Homer, *Epigoni*, *Iliad*, and *Odyssey*. In *Homeri opera*, ed. T. W. Allen and D. B. Monro. 5 vols. Oxford, 1908–20.
Hor. *Ep.* Hor. *Sat.*	Quintus Horatius Flaccus, *Epistles* and *Satires*. In *Q. Horatius Flaccus: Erklärt von Adolf Kiessling*, ed. R. Heinze. 3 vols. Berlin, 1955–57.
Luc.	Marcus Annaeus Lucanus, *The Civil War* (*Pharsalia*), ed. J. D. Duff. Loeb Classical Library, 1928 (ET).
Lucr.	Titus Lucretius Carus, *De rerum natura*, ed. W. H. D. Rouse, Loeb Classical Library, 1937 (ET).
Mart.	Marcus Valerius Martialis, *Epigrams*, ed. W. C. A. Ker. 2 vols. Loeb Classical Library, 1920 (ET).

Nemes. *Cyn.*	Marcus Aurelius Olympius Nemesianus, *Cynegetica*. In *Minor Latin Poets*, ed. J. W. Duff and A. M. Duff. Loeb Classical Library, 1934 (ET).
Opp. *Cyn.* ⎱ Opp. *Hal.* ⎰	Oppian, *Cynegetica* and *Halieutica*. In *Oppian, Coluthus*, and *Tryphiodorus*, ed. A. W. Mair. Loeb Classical Library, 1928 (ET).
Ovid *Ars Am.*	Publius Ovidius Naso, *Ars amoris*, ed. J. H. Mozley. Loeb Classical Library, 1929 (ET).
Ovid. *Met.*	——, *Metamorphoses*, ed. F. J. Miller. 2 vols. Loeb Classical Library, 1916 (ET).
Paus.	Pausanias, *Travels in Greece*, ed. W. H. S. Jones. Loeb Classical Library, 1918 (ET).
Pl. *R.*	Plato, *The Republic*, ed. Paul Shorey. Loeb Classical Library, 1930 (ET).
Pl. *Sph.*	——. *The Sophist*, ed. H. N. Fowler. Loeb Classical Library, 1921 (ET).
Pliny	Gaius Plinius Secundus, *Histoire naturelle*, ed. A. Ernout. Vol. VIII. Paris, 1952. (With French translation on facing pages.)
Plut.	Plutarch, *Moralia*, ed. H. Cherniss and W. C. Helmbold. Vol. XII. Loeb Classical Library, 1927 (ET).
Poll.	Julius Pollux (Polydeuces), *Onomasticon*, ed. Ericus Bethe. Leipzig, 1900.
Polyb.	Polybius, *The Histories*, ed. W. R. Paton. 6 vols. Loeb Classical Library, 1922 (ET).
Sen.	Lucius Annaeus Seneca, *Hippolytus* or *Phaedra*. In *Tragedies*, ed. F. J. Miller. 2 vols. Loeb Classical Library, 1917 (ET).
Solin.	Gaius Julius Solinus, *Collectanea rerum memorabilium*, ed. Theodor Mommsen, Berlin, 1895.
Soph. *Aj.*	Sophocles, *Ajax*, ed. Sir Richard Jebb. Cambridge, 1896.
Stat. *Ach.* ⎫ Stat. *Silv.* ⎬ Stat. *Theb.* ⎭	Publius Papinius Statius, *Silvae, Thebaid, Achilleid*, ed. J. H. Mozley. 2 vols. Loeb Classical Library, 1928 (ET).
Strabo	Strabo, *Geography*, ed. H. L. Jones. 8 vols. Loeb Classical Library, 1917 (ET).

Theoc.	Theocritus, ed. A. S. F. Gow. 2 vols., Cambridge, 1950.
Tryph.	Tryphiodorus, *The Taking of Ilios*. In *Oppian, Coluthus, Tryphiodorus*, ed. A. W. Mair. Loeb Classical Library, 1928 (ET).
Varro	Marcus Terentius Varro, *Rerum rusticarum*. In *Cato and Varro*, ed. W. D. Hooper and H. B. Ash. Loeb Classical Library, 1934 (ET).
Verg. *Aen.* Verg. *Geo.*	Publius Vergilius Maro, *Aeneid* and *Georgics*. In *Opera*, ed. F. A. Hirtzel. Oxford, 1900.
Xen. *An.* Xen. *Cyn.* Xen. *Cyr.* Xen. *Eq.* Xen. *Lac. Pol.*	Xenophon, *Anabasis, Cynegeticus, Institutio Cyri* (*Cyropaedia*), *De re equestri*, and *De republica Lacedaemoniorum*. In *Opera omnia*, ed. E. C. Marchant. Oxford, 1904–9.

MODERN AUTHORS

Anderson	J. K. Anderson. *Ancient Greek Horsemanship*. Berkeley: University of California Press, 1961.
Ash, *Dogs*	Edward C. Ash. *Dogs: Their History and Development*. Boston and New York: Houghton Mifflin Co., 1927.
Ash, *New Bk.*	———. *The New Book of the Dog*. New York: Macmillan Co., 1939.
Aymard	Jacques Aymard. *Essai sur les chasses romaines*. Paris, 1951.
Beckford	Peter Beckford. *Thoughts upon Hare and Fox Hunting*. London, 1796.
Blane	William Blane. *Cynegetica*. London, 1788.
Bk. of the Dog	*The Book of the Dog*, ed. Brian Vesey-Fitzgerald. Los Angeles: Borden Publishing Co., 1948.
Bourlière	Françoise Bourlière. *The Natural History of Mammals*. New York: Alfred A. Knopf, 1954.
Brock	D. W. E. Brock. *ABC of Fox-Hunting*. New York: Charles Scribner's Sons, 1936.
Buchanan-Jardine	Sir John Buchanan-Jardine. *Hounds of the World*. London: Methuen & Co., 1937.

Butler   A. J. Butler. *Sport in Classic Times*. London, 1930.

Cox   Harding Cox and Gerald Lascelles. *Coursing and Falconry*. ("Badminton Library.") London: Longmans, Green & Co., 1892.

Darling   F. Fraser Darling. *A Herd of Red Deer*. Oxford, 1937.

Fox   The Fox. (*Fur, Feather and Fin Series*, ed. A. E. T. Watson.) London: Longmans, Green & Co., 1912.

Garbutt   Raymond J. Garbutt. *Diseases and Surgery of the Dog*. New York: Orange Judd Publishing Co., 1938.

Gardiner   E. Norman Gardiner. *Greek Athletic Sports and Festivals*. London: Macmillan Co. 1910.

Haines   Francis Haines. *Appaloosa: The Spotted Horse in Art and History*. Austin, Tex.: University of Texas Press, 1963.

Hare   The Hare. (*Fur and Feather Series*, ed. A. E. T. Watson.) London: Longmans, Green & Co., 1896.

Harper   Francis Harper, *Extinct and Vanishing Mammals of the Old World*. (Special Publication No. 12, American Committee for International Wild Life Protection: 1–849.) Baltimore: Lord Baltimore Press, 1945.

Houston   Mary Houston. *Ancient Greek, Roman, and Byzantine Costume and Decoration*. London: A. and C. Black, 1931.

Hull   Denison B. Hull. *Thoughts on American Fox-Hunting*. New York: David McKay Co., 1958.

Keller   O. Keller. *Die antike Tierwelt*. Leipzig, 1909.

Leister, "Antelopes"   Claude W. Leister, "Wild Antelopes in Retrospect," *Bulletin of the New York Zoological Society*, XLI, No. 3 (1938), 75–93.

Leister, "Pigs"   ———, "The Wild Pigs of the World," *Bulletin of the New York Zoological Society*, XLII, No. 5 (September–October, 1939).

Littauer   V. S. Littauer. *Jumping the Horse*. New York: Derrydale Press, 1931.

McLeod, "Egpt. Bows, N.Y."   Wallace McLeod, "Egyptian Composite Bows in New York," *American Journal of Archaeology*, LXVI, No. 1 (January, 1962), 13–19.

McLeod, "Trig."   ———, "Τριγλώχις," *American Journal of Archaeology*, LXIV, No. 4 (October, 1960), 370–71.

McLeod, "Unpub. Bow, Brkln."   ———, "An Unpublished Egyptian Bow in the Brooklyn Museum," *American Journal of Archaeology*, LXII, No. 4 (October, 1958), 397–401.

Magna Graecia   Leonard von Matt and Umberto Zannoti-Bianco. *Magna Graecia*. New York: Universe Books, 1962.

Manns   Otto Manns. *Über die Jagd bei den Griechen*. London: Cassell & Co., 1888.

Marinatos-Hirmer   Spyridon Marinatos and Max Hirmer. *Crete and Mycenae*. New York: Harry Abrams, 1960.

Master of Game   *The Master of Game*, ed. Wm. A. and F. Baillie-Grohman. London: Chatto & Windus, 1909.

Merrick   A. C. Merrick, *How To Own a Dog and Like It!* Garden City, N.Y.: Country Life Press, 1940.

Meyer   A. B. Meyer, "The Antiquity of the Lion in Greece," tr. from *Zoologischer Garten*, in *Annual Report of the Board of Regents, Smithsonian Institution, for* 1903. Washington D.C., 1904.

Miller   Gerrit S. Miller. *Catalogue of the Mammals of Western Europe*. London: Longmans, Green & Co., 1912.

Mireaux   Emile Mireaux. *Daily Life in the Time of Homer*. London: George Allen & Unwin, 1959.

Nat. Geog.   *The National Geographic Book of Dogs*. Washington: National Geographic Society, 1958.

Paget   J. Otho Paget. *The Art of Beagling*. London: H. F. and G. Witherby, 1931.

Petrie   W. M. Flinders Petrie. *The Arts and Crafts of Ancient Egypt*. Chicago: A. C. McClurg & Co., 1910.

Pollard   Hugh B. C. Pollard. *The Mystery of Scent*. London: Eyre & Spottiswoode, 1937.

Rabbit   *The Rabbit.* (*Fur, Feather and Fin Series*, ed. A. E.
                        T. Watson.) London: Longmans, Green & Co.,
                        1898.

Red Deer   *The Red Deer.* (*Fur and Feather Series*, ed. A. E. T.
                        Watson.) London: Longmans, Green & Co.,
                        1896.

Robert   Louis Robert. *Hellenica.* XI–XII, 271–76. Paris,
                        1960.

Robertson   Martin Robertson. *Greek Painting.* Geneva: Alfred
                        Skira, 1959.

Robinson   C. H. Robinson. *Everyday Life in Ancient Greece.*
                        Oxford, 1933.

Rose   H. J. Rose. *A Handbook of Greek Mythology.*
                        London: Methuen & Co., 1928.

Shakesp.   William Shakespeare. *Midsummer Night's Dream*,
                        ed. A. Quiller-Couch and J. D. Wilson. Cam-
                        bridge, 1958.

Shaw   George Russell Shaw. *Knots Useful and Ornamen-
                        tal.* Boston and New York: Houghton Mifflin
                        Co. 1924.

Simpson   George Gaylord Simpson, "The Principles of Clas-
                        sification and a Classification of Mammals,"
                        *Bulletin of the American Museum of Natural
                        History*, LXXXV, No. 16 (1945).

Traité   *Traité de zoologie*, ed. Pierre P. Grassé. Vol. 17,
                        2d fasc. Paris, 1955.

Twici   William Twici, *The Art of Hunting, or Three Hunt-
                        ing Mss.*, ed. Alice Dryden. Northampton, 1908.

Verrill   A. Hyatt Verrill. *Knots, Splices and Rope Work.*
                        New York: Norman W. Henley, 1919.

Whitney   Leon F. Whitney. *How To Breed Dogs.* New York:
                        Orange Judd Publishing Co., 1937.

Winge   Öjvind Winge. *Inheritance in Dogs.* Ithaca, N.Y.:
                        Comstock Publishing Co., 1950.

                        REFERENCE BOOKS

D.C.A.   *Dictionary of Classical Antiquities*, ed. Nettleship
                        and Sandys. New York and London, 1908.

Enc. Brit.	*Encyclopaedia Brittanica*, 1943 ed.
Godefroy	*Lexique de l'ancien français*, ed. Godefroy. Paris, 1901.
Holder	*Altceltischer Sprachschatz*, ed. Alfred Holder.
Liddell-Scott	Liddell and Scott, *Greek-English Lexicon*. 9th ed., Oxford, 1940.
Meyer-Lübke	*Romanisches etymologisches Wörterbuch*, ed. Meyer-Lübke. 3d ed.
O.C.D.	*Oxford Classical Dictionary*. Oxford: 1949.
Pauly	Pauly-Wissowa, *Realenkyklopädie*.

Greek Technical Words
and Their Modern Equivalents

WORDS RELATING TO NETS

ἀκρωλένιον	end-mesh
ἄρκυς	{ purse-net (specifically) net (generically, in late Greek)
δίκτυον	{ long-net (specifically) net (generically)
ἐνόδιον	road-net
ἐπίδρομος	head-line
κορυφαῖον κορυφίστερα	} cod-end
μαστός	clinch
περίδρομος	{ foot-line (specifically) skirting-line (generically)
σαρδόνιον σαρδῶν	} margin
στάλιξ	stake
στροφεῖον στρόφιον	} band
σχαλίς	prop
σχαλίδομα	stay
ὑποσχαλίδομα	support

OTHER WORDS

ἀρκυωρός	net-watcher. *See also* λινόπτης
δικτυαγωγός	net-carrier
ἕλμινθες	worms; intestinal parasites
ἱπποκόμος	groom
κυνάγχη	distemper; canine hepatitis
κυναγωγός	huntsman (applied to servant only)
κυνηγέτης	{ huntsman (applied to amateur only) master of hounds hunting man; hunter (one who hunts)

λινόπτης	net-watcher. *See also* ἀρκυωρός
λύσσα	rabies
ποδάγρα	{ arthritis of feet or legs (in dogs) { gout (in human beings)
ψῶρα	mange

In Arrian's *Cynegeticus* the following special usages also occur:

ἀγαθαὶ κύνες	greyhounds (literally "good hounds")
ὠκεῖαι κύνες	gazehounds (literally "fast hounds")

Catalogue of Animals

*A partial list compiled from Aelian, Aristotle, Oppian,
Pollux, and Xenophon's* Cynegeticus

αἴγαγρος	wild goat, *Capra aegagrus* (Aegean)
αἴλουρος	{ domestic cat, *Felis domesticus* (world-wide) { wild cat, *Felis silvestris* (Europe, Asia, Africa) { Peloponnesian wild cat, *Felis silvestris morea* (Peloponnesus)
αἴξ	goat (generically)
ἀλωπεκιδεύς ἀλωπέκιον	} fox cub
ἀλωπεκίς	supposed hybrid of fox and dog

ἀλώπηξ	fox, *Vulpes vulpes* (Europe, Asia, North Africa, North America)
ἀρήν	lamb
ἄρκηλος	panther cub
ἄρκιλος	*see* ἀρκτύλος
ἄρκτος	brown bear, *Ursus arctos* (Europe, Asia, North America)
ἀρκτύλος	bear cub
ἅρπαξ	"robber" wolf
ἀσπάλαξ	{ mole, *Talpa caeca* (Europe [except Cyclades], Asia, North America) "mole rat," *Spalax typhlus* (Europe, Western Asia, Africa) "mole rat," *Spalax graecus* (near Athens)
ἀχαΐνης	a young red deer, older than a calf, but not full-grown; a brocket; a spay; a staggard
βίσων	European bison, or *Wisent*, *Bison bonasus* (Europe, Asia)
βληχητά	"bleaters," i.e., sheep
βούβαλις	hartebeest, *Alcelaphus buselaphus* (North Africa)
βούβαλος	*see* βούβαλις
βοῦς	{ domestic ox, bull or cow, *Bos taurus* (world-wide) aurochs, *Bos primigenius* (Europe, Asia) buffalo, *Bubalus bubalis* (India)
γαλέη	{ weasel, ferret, polecat, etc., *Mustela* (Europe, Asia, North Africa, America) marten, sable, fisher, *Martes* (Europe, Asia, North America)
δορκαλίς	*see* δορκάς
δορκάς	{ roe deer, *Capreolus capreolus* (Europe) gazelle, *Gazella dorcas* (Asia, Arabia, Africa)
δόρκος δόρκων	} *see* δορκάς
ἔλαφος	red deer, *Cervus elaphus* (Europe)
ἐλέφας	{ African elephant, *Loxodonta* (Africa) Indian elephant, *Elephas* (India)
ἐνυδρίς	otter, *Lutra* (Europe, Asia, Africa, America)
ἔριφος	kid
εὐρυκέρως	fallow deer, *Dama dama* (Europe, Asia)

ἐχῖνος χερσαῖος	{ hedgehog, *Erinaceus europaeus* (Europe) spiny mouse, *Acomys* (Mediterranean, Asia, Africa)
ζορκάς ζόρξ	} *see* δορκάς
ἡμίονος	mule
θώς	{ civet cat, *Viverra* (Asia) civet cat, *Civettictis* (Africa) jackal, *Canis aureus* (world-wide) Cape hunting dog, *Lycaon pictus* (Africa)
ἰκτῖνος	"kite," a wolf
ἴορκος	*see* δορκάς
ἵππαγρος	"wild horse," perhaps gnu, *Connochaetes gnu*, or nilgai. *See* ἱππέλαφος and κατώβλεπον
ἱππέλαφος	nilgai, *Boselaphus tragocamelus* (India)
ἵππος	horse, *Equus caballus*
ἰχνεύμων	ichneumon, *Mungos ichneumon* (Egypt)
καμηλοπάρδαλις	giraffe, *Giraffa* (Africa)
κάμηλος	{ Arabian camel or dromedary, *Camelus dromedarius* (North Africa, Arabia) Bactrian camel, *Camelus bactrianus* (Asia)
κάπρος	wild pig, *Sus scrofa* (Europe, Asia)
καρτάζωνος	*see* ῥινοκέρως
καστορίς κάστωρ	} European beaver, *Castor fiber* (Europe)
κατώβλεπον	gnu, *Connochaetes gnu* (Africa)
κεμάς	a young deer, older than a calf, but not full grown; a brocket; a spay; a staggard
κίρκος	"hawk," a wolf
κόνικλος	European rabbit, *Oryctolagus cuniculus* (Europe, North Africa)
κυνοκέφαλος	{ Hamadryas baboon, *Papio hamadryas* (Southwest Asia, Egypt) "Dog-head," name of a tribe of people.
κύων	dog, *Canis familiaris* (world-wide)
λαγιδεύς λαγίδιον λάγιον	} leveret
λαγώς	European hare, *Lepus europaeus* (Europe, parts of Canada)

206

λέων	lion, *Felis leo* (Europe, Western Asia, Africa)
λύγξ	{ lynx, *Lynx lynx* (Greece, Spain) { caracal, *Caracal caracal* (North Africa)
λυκιδεύς	wolf cub
λύκος	wolf, *Canis lupus* (world-wide)
μολοβρίτης	young of the wild pig
μονόκερως	unicorn
μόνωψ	Paeonian name for bison
μοσχίον	young calf
μόσχος	calf
μυοξός	{ European dormouse, *Glis glis* (Europe) { garden dormouse, *Eliomys* (Europe, North Africa, Asia) { Asiatic dormouse, *Dryomys* (Asia)
μῦς	mouse, *Mus musculus*. See σμίνθος
νεβρός	{ calf of the red deer { fawn of the fallow deer { kid or fawn of the roe deer
ὄϊς	sheep (generically)
ὄναγρος	{ wild ass, *Asinus hemionus* (Persia, Syria, Palestine, Arabia, Iraq) { Persian onager, *Asinus hemionus onagrus*
ὄνος	ass, *Asinus asinus* (Europe, Asia, North Africa)
ὀρεύς	*see* ἡμίονος
ὄρυγξ	{ zebra, *Equus zebra* { spotted horse similar to the Appaloosa
ὄρυξ	{ Arabian or Beatrix oryx, *Oryx leucoryx* (Northern Arabia, head of Persian Gulf) { beisa oryx, *Oryx beisa beisa* { white oryx, *Oryx algazel* (North Africa)
πάνθηρ	{ leopard, *Felis pardus* (Asia, Africa) { wild cat, *Felis silvestris* (Europe, Asia, Africa)
πάρδαλις	leopard, *Felis pardus* (Asia, Africa)
πάρδιον	unknown
πίθηκος	{ Barbary ape, *Inuus ecaudatus* (North Africa) { common rhesus monkey, *Macacus rhesus* (Africa) { Hamadryas baboon, *Papio hamadryas* (Arabia, Ethiopia, Egypt)

πόρδαλις	*see* πάρδαλις
πρόξ	roe deer, *Capreolus capreolus* (Europe)
πτώξ	"cowerer," i.e., European hare
πύγαργος	"white rump," an antelope
ῥινοκέρως	{ Indian rhinoceros, *Rhinoceros* (India, Java) white rhinoceros, *Ceratotherium* (Africa) black rhinoceros, *Diceros* (Africa)
σκιοῦρος	squirrel, *Sciurus vulgaris* (world-wide)
σκυλακεύς	}
σκυλάκιον	puppy
σκύλαξ	
σκυμνίον	cub
σκύμνος	lion cub
σμίνθος	mouse, *Mus musculus.* See μῦς (world-wide)
σοῦβος	possibly a sheep, *Ovis ophion anatolica*, or a goat, *Capra nubiana*
σπαθίνης	a young deer
σῦς	wild pig, *Sus scrofa* (Europe, Asia)
ταῦρος	bull, *Bos taurus* (world-wide)
τετράκερως ὄϊς	four-horned antelope, *Tetracerus quadricornis* (Asia)
τίγρις	tiger, *Felis tigris* (Asia)
τοξευτήρ	"archer," a wolf
ὕαινα	{ spotted hyena, *Crocuta* (Africa) striped hyena, *Hyaena* (Africa)
ὗς	*see* σῦς
ὕστριξ	porcupine, *Hystrix cristata* (Europe, Asia, Africa)
χρύσεος	"golden" wolf

Plates and Figures

Opposite

PLATE I   YOUNG HUNTING MAN
Lekythos by the Pan Painter
Courtesy of the Museum of Fine Arts, Boston

211

Opposite

PLATE II HOPLITES HUNTING   *Sarcophagus with cover. Cypriote sculpture, ca. 500 B.C.*
Courtesy of the Metropolitan Museum of Art, New York, The Cesnola Collection

PLATE III A HARE HUNT;   a) *following with haresticks*, b) *chasing the hare into the net. Oinochoe attributed to the Paris Painter.*
Etruscan, ca. 520 B.C. Courtesy of the Seattle Art Museum, Norman Davis Collection

IIIa

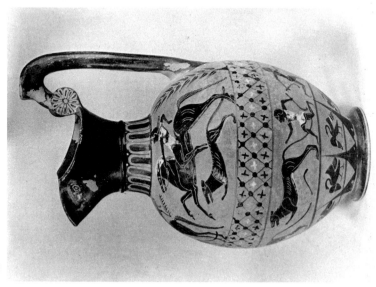

IIIb

PLATE IV
DEATH OF ACTAEON   *Laconian hounds*
Bell Crater by the Pan Painter
Courtesy of the Museum of Fine Arts, Boston

PLATE V
DEATH OF ACTAEON   *Laconian hounds*
Bell Crater by the Lykaon Painter. Attic
Courtesy of the Museum of Fine Arts, Boston

215

PLATE VI
ATHLETE WITH LACONIAN HOUND
Kylix, int., by Brygos Painter
Courtesy of the Museum of Fine Arts, Boston

216

PLATE VII

SEATED FIGURE WITH DOG, *possibly a Molossian*
Kantharos, south Italian, Apulian
Courtesy of the Museum of Fine Arts, Boston

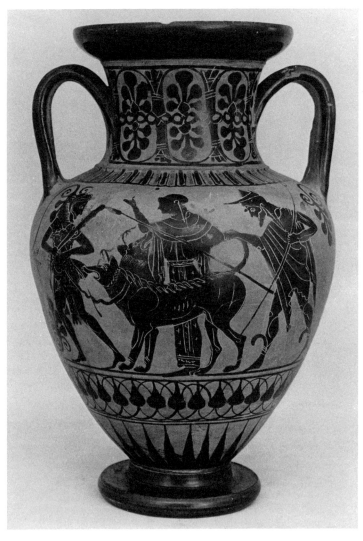

PLATE VIII
HERAKLES AND KERBEROS, *a two-headed Molossian*
Neck amphora, end of sixth century B.C.
Courtesy of the Metropolitan Museum of Art, New York, Rogers Fund, 1906

218

PLATE IX
QUADRIGA AND WARRIORS,   *with Molossian hound*
Amphora, ca. 530 B.C., *attributed to the Swing Painter*
Courtesy of the Metropolitan Museum of Art, New York, Rogers Fund, 1917

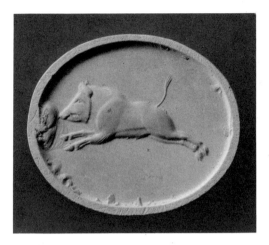

PLATE X   WILD BOAR
Chalcedony scaraboid, Graeco-Persian, fifth–fourth centuries B.C.
Courtesy of the Metropolitan Museum of Art, New York, Bequest of
W. Gedney Beatty, 1941

PLATE XI   LION HUNT,   *mounted, with bow*
Chalcedony scaraboid, Graeco-Roman, fifth–fourth centuries B.C.
Courtesy of the Metropolitan Museum of Art, New York, Bequest of
W. Gedney Beatty, 1941

Opposite
PLATE XIII   HOUND SEIZING HARE
Votive statuette, limestone, Cypriote, seventh–fifth centuries B.C.
Courtesy of the Metropolitan Museum of Art, New York, The Cesnola Collection

PLATE XII   ARCHER WITH SCYTHIAN BOW
Plate by Epiktetos, ca. 520–510 B.C.
Courtesy of the British Museum, London. Photograph by Max Hirmer

PLATE XIV   BULL CAUGHT IN NET   *Gold Cup 1 from Vaphio, Laconia,* ca. 1500 B.C.
Courtesy of the National Museum, Athens. Photograph by Max Hirmer

PLATE XV   LION HUNTING DEER   *Gold plaque on six-sided wooden box,*
from Grave V, Citadel of Mycenae
Courtesy of the National Museum, Athens. Photograph by Max Hirmer

PLATE XVI   LIONS   *Bronze dagger inlaid in gold, silver, and niello,*
from Grave IV, Citadel of Mycenae, ca. 1570–1550 B.C.
Courtesy of the National Museum, Athens. Photograph by Max Hirmer

PLATE XVII   HOUND'S HEAD,   *a Laconian*
Rhyton by the Brygos Painter, ca. 500–490 B.C.
Courtesy of the Museo Nazionale di Villa Giulia, Rome. Photograph by Max Hirmer

223

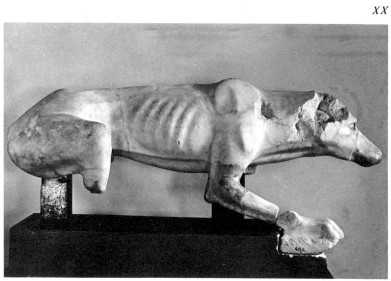

XXI

PLATE XXI
ARABIAN OR BEATRIX ORYX
Courtesy of the New York Zoological Park

PLATE XXII
FOUR-HORNED ANTELOPE
Courtesy of the Chicago Natural History Museum

PLATE XXIII
DORCAS GAZELLE
Courtesy of the Chicago Natural History Museum

PLATE XXIV
A RED DEER STAG
Courtesy of the New York Zoological Park

XXII

XXIII

XXIV

226

Figures by the Author

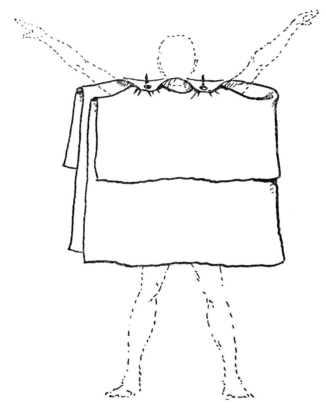

FIG. 1. PRINCIPLE OF THE CHITON

FIG. 2. HEAD OF BOAR SPEAR

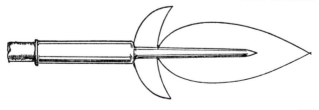

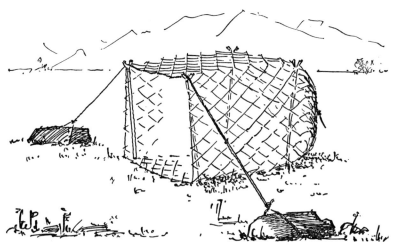

FIG. 3. PURSE-NET FOR HARE

FIG. 4. DETAIL OF NET

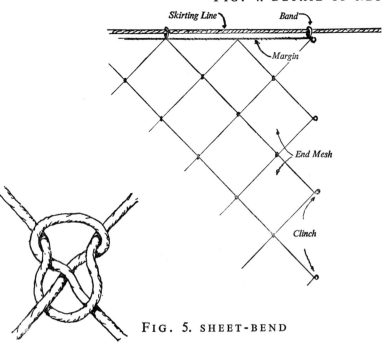

Skirting Line   *Band*

Margin

End Mesh

Clinch

FIG. 5. SHEET-BEND

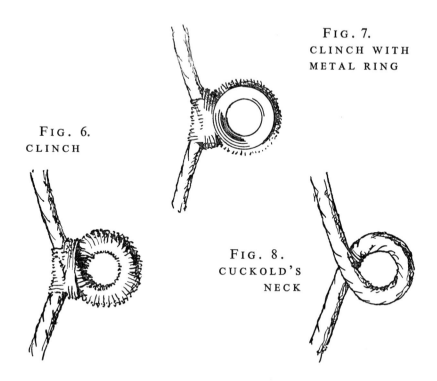

FIG. 7.
CLINCH WITH
METAL RING

FIG. 6.
CLINCH

FIG. 8.
CUCKOLD'S
NECK

FIG. 9. THE LONG NET

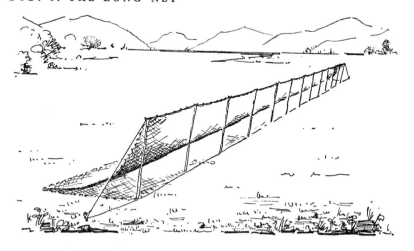

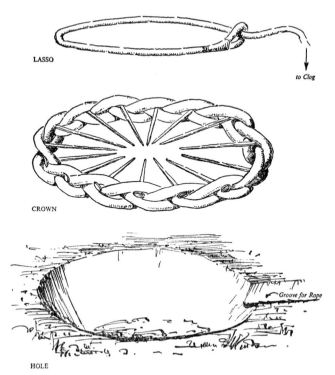

LASSO

to Clog

CROWN

Groove for Rope

HOLE

FIG. 10. PARTS OF THE FOOTSNARE
(clog not shown)

FIG. 11. LACONIAN HOUND

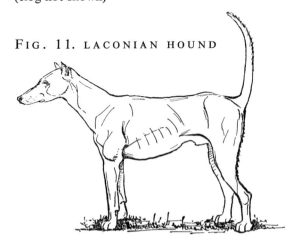

Index

This book,
designed by Suzette Morton Zurcher,
was composed and printed at
The University of Chicago Press.
Plates are by The Meriden Gravure Company.
mcmlxiv

Date Due